Medical Law in Spain

Published by:
Kluwer Law International B.V.
PO Box 316
2400 AH Alphen aan den Rijn
The Netherlands
Website: www.wklawbusiness.com

Sold and distributed in North, Central and South America by:
Wolters Kluwer Legal & Regulatory U.S.
7201 McKinney Circle
Frederick, MD 21704
United States of America
Email: customer.service@wolterskluwer.com

Sold and distributed in all other countries by:
Turpin Distribution Services Ltd.
Stratton Business Park
Pegasus Drive, Biggleswade
Bedfordshire SG18 8TQ
United Kingdom
Email: kluwerlaw@turpin-distribution.com

ISBN 978-90-411-6929-7

This title is available on www.kluwerlawonline.com

Medical Law in Spain

Carlos M. Romeo-Casabona
Asier Urruela Mora

Co-authors:

Iñigo de Miguel Beriain
Emilio José Armaza Armaza
Sergio Romeo-Malanda

This book was originally published as a monograph in the International Encyclopaedia of Laws/Medical Law.

General Editors: Roger Blanpain, Frank Hendrickx
Volume Editor: Herman Nys

Wolters Kluwer

The Authors

Carlos M. Romeo-Casabona is a graduate in Law and in Criminology. He holds doctorates in Law (Extraordinary Prize of the Law School) and in Medicine. He is full Professor of Criminal Law at the University of the Basque Country and Director of the Inter-University Chair in Law and the Human Genome at the University of Deusto and the University of the Basque Country. He has been Dean of the Faculty of Law and Director of the Centre for Studies in Criminology at the University of La Laguna. He has also served as associate judge in Saragossa's High Court. Expert advisor of the Spanish Ministries of Health, Science and Innovation and of Justice, the UNESCO, UNODC, Council of Europe, the WHO and the EC.

He is a single author of more than 20 books on Medical Law, Criminal Law, Genetics and Biotechnology Law and the Law of Information Technologies (cybercrimes). He has co-authored (50) and edited or coordinated several books (30) and numerous articles (more than 220; in other six languages: 60 works).

He has received several awards from many Spanish national and international institutions. He is a member of the Saragossa Royal Academy of Medicine and of the National Academy for Law and Jurisprudence. He has received Doctor *honoris causa* from six universities.

He has collaborated with the Spanish Government in several laws related to biomedicine (such as the Law on Organ Transplantation, the Patient's Autonomy Law, the Law on Biomedical Research and some provisions of the Penal Code).

He is a member of the following bodies: National Commission on Assisted Human Reproduction; Ethics Advisory Committee on Science and Technology to the Government; Committee on Bioethics of the Council of Europe; HUGO Ethics Advisory Committee; Bioethics Committee of Spain; European Research Area Board to the European Commission; Commission on Use of Human Cells and Tissues; Chair of the Clinical Research Ethics Committee of the Basque Country.

Director of the journals 'Derecho y Genoma Humano/Law and the Human Genome', 'Estudios de Derecho Penal y Criminología', 'Biblioteca de Derecho y Ciencias de la Vida', and of the Encyclopaedia 'Bioderecho y Bioética'.

The Authors

Asier Urruela Mora was graduated in Law and in Economics from the University of Deusto (1997), Doctor (PhD) in Law which was awarded by the University of the Basque Country (2002, Extraordinary Prize of the Law School), Doctor (PhD) in Medicine awarded by the University of Zaragoza (2014), and Expert in Criminology by the Universidad Nacional de Educación a Distancia (UNED – 2005). Since 2006 he is Professor of Criminal Law at the University of Zaragoza. At present, he is also Advisor of the Inter-University. Chair, Provincial Government of Biscay in Law and the Human Genome, University of Deusto – University of the Basque Country.

Iñigo de Miguel Beriain holds a European Doctorate in Law and a Doctorate in Philosophy. He is the author of several books related to bioethics and biolaw. He has published more than fifty book chapters and twenty-five papers in JCR indexed journals. He has participated in ten EU funded projects on these topics. He has been awarded with several prizes related to bioethics and biolaws. He has been appointed as a member of the Experts Group on Ethics and Scientific Integrity (Swafs-Ethics) for the Science with and for Society Programme at Horinzon 2020.

Emilio José Armaza Armaza (Doctor in Law, University of the Basque Country) is Professor of Criminal Law at the University of Deusto, Post-doctoral researcher at the Inter-University Chair, Provincial Government of Biscay in Law and the Human Genome, University of Deusto – University of the Basque Country and Professor at the Inter-University Master Program in Bioethics and Biolaw of the Universities of La Laguna, Las Palmas de Gran Canaria, Zaragoza and Rovira i Virgili.

The Authors

Sergio Romeo-Malanda (Doctor in Law) is Senior Lecturer in Criminal Law at the Faculty of Legal Sciences of the University of Las Palmas de Gran Canaria (Spain), where he also teaches Biolaw at the Faculty of Health Sciences in the Master of Bioethics and Biolaw programme. He is a Visiting Professor in International and Comparative Biolaw at the Faculty of Medicine and Health Sciences of the American University of Sovereign Nations (U.S.A.), and a Visiting Senior Lecturer at the Faculty of Law of the University of Tasmania (Australia).

The Authors

Table of Contents

Table of Contents

List of Abbreviations

ADS	Actualidad del Derecho Sanitario (Journal)
Art.	Article
CC	Código Civil (Civil Code)
DS	Derecho y Salud (Journal)
ECTS	European Credit Transfer System
EU	European Union
GP	General Practitioner
INE	Instituto Nacional de Estadística (National Statistic Institute)
INSALUD	National Institute of Health
LAP	Ley básica sobre autonomía del paciente (Patient's Autonomy Law of 2002)
LEC	Ley de Enjuiciamiento Civil (Civil Procedure Act)
LGS	Ley General de Sanidad (General Health Law of 1986)
LIB	Ley de Investigación Biomédica (Biomedical Research Law of 2007)
LL	La Ley (Journal)
LO	Ley Orgánica (Organic Law: Law affecting Fundamental rights which needs to be approved a qualified majority in the Parliament)
LRJPAC	Ley 30/1992, of 26 November, Ley de Régimen Jurídico de las Administraciones Públicas y del Procedimiento Administrativo Común (Law of 1992 on the Legal System of Public Administrations and on the Common Administrative Procedure)
LTRA	Ley 14/2006, of 26 May, Ley sobre Técnicas de Reproducción Humana Asistida (Medically Assisted Human Reproduction Law of 2006)
MO	Ministerial Order

List of Abbreviations

OMC	Organisation of Colleges of Physicians
PC	Penal Code (Código Penal: as in latest reform of 2015)
RD	Royal Decree
RDS	Revista de Derecho Sanitario (Journal)
RevDerGenH	Revista de Derecho y Genoma Humano / Law and the Human Genome Review
SNS	Sistema Nacional de Salud (Spanish National Health System)
WHO	World Health Organization

Acknowledgement

This present work is a partial result of a Research Project supported by the Government of the Basque Country (Research Groups, 2016–).

Acknowledgement

General Introduction

Chapter 1. The General Background of the Country

§1. Geography and Climate

1. Lying at the southwestern end of the European continent, and with a total area of 504,782 km^2, which includes the Balearic and Canarian archipelagos, Spain occupies the bulk of the Iberian Peninsula. Of its 5,849 km of peninsular perimeter, 3,904 correspond to the Cantabrian Sea, the Atlantic and the Mediterranean, with the remainder taken up by the country's borders with Portugal (to the East) and France and the principality of Andorra (to the North). Spain is the second most mountainous country in Europe after Switzerland and is characterized by a combination of mountain ranges and river basins. The country enjoys one of the most benign climates in Europe, with a marked contrast between the predominantly mild climate and even temperatures of the coastal areas and archipelagos and the more continental climate inland, although even here temperatures rarely fall to very low levels.

§2. Cultural Make-Up

2. Although the country's national language is Spanish, the official status granted to the Catalan, Basque, Galician and Valencian languages in their respective Autonomous Communities has led to a strengthening of the corresponding regional cultures.

3. Spain has no established church of the state, as the Constitution of 1978 abolished the Roman Catholic Church as the official state religion. However, it plays a significant role in Spanish society. According to a Survey of 2015, 69.03% of the population define themselves as Catholic, 26.3% as non-believers or atheists and 1.9% other religions. Among believers, 60.8% assert they almost never go to any religious service, by contrast, 13.7% attend one or more masses almost every week.

§3. Political and Judicial System

4. The Spanish Constitution of 1978 is the body of legislation which underpins the country's political system. Article 1 stipulates that Spain is a social and democratic state based on the rule of law and also describes the political system as a parliamentary monarchy.

5. The King (or Queen) is the head of state, without legislative powers, and is also commander in chief of the armed forces. Currently the King of Spain is Felipe VI.

6. The government, or executive branch, is responsible for the country's international and national policies, as well as the state administration. It consists of the president, vice-presidents, ministers and other members stipulated by law. The King proposes a candidate for the presidency of the government after consultation with the leaders of the political groups which gain parliamentary representation in a general election. The candidate put forward must obtain the approval of the Congress of Deputies.

7. Legislative power lies with the Cortes Generates, which comprise two Chambers: the 350-member Congress of Deputies, which represents the Spanish people as a whole, and the 225-member Senate, which represents territories and provinces. Both chambers are elected by universal suffrage in elections at which all Spaniards over the age of 18 are entitled to vote. Voters choose between candidates in each of the country's fifty-two Constituencies (fifty provinces, together with the Autonomous Cities Ceuta and Melilla, located at northern of Africa's coast). Exceptionally, however, some senators are appointed directly by the Autonomous Communities.

The seventeen Autonomous Communities (Andalucía, Aragon, Asturias, Balearic Islands, Basque Country, Canary Islands, Cantabria, Castilla-La Mancha, Castilla-Leon, Catalonia, Extremadura, Galicia, La Rioja, Madrid, Murcia, Navarra and Valencia) have their own governments and regional parliaments. The extent to which each Community is competent to handle its own affairs depends on the processes provided for in the Constitution and the corresponding Statutes of Autonomy. State and Autonomous Community elections are held every four years.

8. The judicial power is tailored to the State's political structure, in accordance with the provisions of the Constitution of 1978 and the subsequent Organic Law on Judicial Power of 1985. The system consists of a Supreme Court, National High Court, Central Magistrates' Courts and Central Criminal Courts, which have jurisdiction over the entire nation; High Courts of the Autonomous Communities; Provincial High Courts, Petty Courts with criminal jurisdiction, as well as courts for administrative litigation, labour disputes, prison matters and juvenile courts, all of which have provincial jurisdiction; courts of first instance and penal magistrates' courts, corresponding to juridical districts and justices' courts in municipalities where none of the above exist.

9. The Constitutional Court is supreme in matters relating to the interpretation of the country's Constitution. Its competences and workings are laid down in the Constitution itself and in the Constitutional Court Law of 1979. A single body integrated of twelve judges, whose jurisdiction extends over the entire country, the

Court deals with appeals and questions of constitutionality concerning laws, normative provisions or enactments which have the force of law. It also handles appeals for constitutional protection in cases involving the violation of fundamental rights and public freedoms ('amparo' or protection complaints) and conflicts of competence which arise between the State and Autonomous Communities or between the Autonomous Communities themselves. On this later matter the European Court on Human Rights has also jurisdiction after having exhausted Spanish internal process.

10. Spain's Constitution of 1978 was drawn up with Europe in mind. Title III of Chapter III concerning international treaties provides for a flexible system for the conclusion of treaties under which competences derived from the Constitution may be transferred to international organizations or institutions (Article 93). It also provides for the incorporation of such treaties into national legislation (Article 96). Spain joined the European Communities in 1986, although it was not until 1992, following the Maastricht agreements which marked a substantial step forward in the process of European integration, that modifications have been made to the Constitution to adapt it to EU legislation. On the one hand, Article 13 was amended to extend voting rights in local elections to foreign EU residents. On the other hand, on September 2011, Article 135 of the Spanish Constitution on public debt was amended, setting in the text the concept of 'budget stability' while introducing the absolute priority of debt and interest repayment.

§4. Population and Vital Statistics

11. Spain's population as of 1 January 2015 was 46.439.864, from which 22.820.775 were male and 23.619.089 female (51%). Its population density, at 91.4/km^2 (229/sq. mile), is lower than that of most Western European countries. With the exception of the capital, Madrid, the most densely populated areas lie around the coast.

According to data released by INE, a total of 426,303 babies were born in Spain in 2014, 588 more than in 2013. The figure marks a rise of 0.1% year-on-year, and is the first increase recorded in the country in five years. In terms of births, the report shows that the number of babies born in Spain has fallen 18% since 2008. Meanwhile, the number of fertile women (those aged between 15 and 49, according to the statistical series) fell from 11.6 million in 2009 to 10.98 million in 2014, as a result of a decrease in the number of immigrants living in Spain, and the high emigration rate among Spaniards – both factors attributable to the lingering effects of the economic crisis. In terms of deaths, the report reveals that 395,045 people died in Spain in 2014, a 1.2% rise compared to the previous year. That's 8.5 deaths per 1,000 inhabitants. Infant mortality was 2.9 deaths per 1,000 live births. Life expectancy also rose in 2014 compared to the previous year, going up 0.2 years to 83, the highest on record. Average life expectancy for men in Spain is 80.2 (0.2 years higher than in 2013), and 85.7 (0.1 higher) for women. Spain's fertility rate (the number of children the average woman will have during her lifetime) is one of the lowest in the world. It was last measured at 1.32 in 2013, according to the World Bank.

Concerning voluntary interruption of pregnancy, the latest official statistics confirm what can be considered a growing trend in Spain: the number of abortions being carried out in the country is steadily falling. The latest figures, for 2013, show that the number of women who terminated a pregnancy fell in that year by 3.2% compared to the year before. At total of 108,690 women opted for the procedure during 2013 – 3,700 fewer than the previous year – under legislation that has been in place in Spain since 2010, and allows access to abortion on demand until the fourteenth week of pregnancy. The majority of the women who decided to have an abortion in 2013 (19.43%) were aged between 20 and 24. The minority (3.92%) were over 40. There are no specific figures for minors, although the data supplied by the Health Ministry reveals that of the total number of terminations, 12.23% were performed on women aged '19 and under'.

§5. Social and Cultural Values regarding Health

12. According to the Annual Report on the National Health System of Spain 2013, as of 1 July 2013 the most frequent chronic health problems in Spain were pain in the lumbar spine, high blood pressure, osteoarthritis, arthritis or rheumatism, high cholesterol and pain in the cervical spine. For children, the most prevalent chronic conditions are allergy (10.0%) and asthma (5.2%).

There were 5.0 reported cases of pertussis for every 100,000 inhabitants, 30.0 cases of parotitis, 0.3 cases of measles and 0.01 case of rubella. All of these transmissible diseases are included in the vaccination calendar and have exhibited a downward trend since the 1990s, although the parotitis has appeared in epidemic waves. Hepatitis A, with 1.3 cases per 100,000 inhabitants, has fallen significantly in the last five years. In the case of hepatitis B, the decline was from 1.9 to 1.5 and prevalence remained steady in other types of viral hepatitis, with 1.6 cases per 100,000 inhabitants. Since 2005 an upward trend has been observed in the estimated incidence per 100,000 inhabitants of gonococcal infection (7.1) and syphilis (8.0). The number of new HIV infections has been stable for some years, while acquired immune deficiency syndrome (AIDS) cases are declining.

The leading causes of mortality were ischaemic heart diseases in men and cerebrovascular diseases in women. With regard to tumours, the type responsible for the highest mortality were bronchial/lung cancer and colon cancer. The cancer that caused the most deaths among men was bronchial/lung cancer, while among women it was breast cancer. The adjusted suicide rate was 6.4 out of every 100,000 persons, with a slight increase over preceding years and returning to values similar to those of 2008.

As for tobacco use, 24% of the population aged 15 and older smoked on a daily basis, 3.1% described themselves as occasional smokers and 19.6% said they were ex-smokers. With respect to alcohol, 65.6% of the population aged 15 and older had consumed alcohol at some time in the past year (77.5% men and 54.3% women). 4.5% had drunk heavily within the past month.

With regard to body weight, 53.7% of the population aged 18 and over showed obesity or overweight. The percentage is 27.8% in the case of children aged 2 to 17.

Spain continues to hold its place as the global leader in the number of organ transplants conducted. The National Transplants Organization (ONT) has reported that in 2014 Spain once again broke its own record after carrying out a total 4,360 transplants. Figures show that there was a donation rate of 36 donors per one million inhabitants last year. Spain has been the world leader in organ transplants since 1992. Spain also broke records last year in relation to the number of kidney and heart transplants. A total of 2,678 kidney transplants were carried out in 2014, up 5% from the previous year, and 265 patients received new hearts, up by 6% from 2013. One striking figure was the number of kidney transplants made from living donors – 423 – which accounts for 15.8% of all kidney transplants that took place in 2014. In 2004, there were just 61 transplants from living donors. The majority of organs (65.6%) come from people who died from strokes. Half of all donors were over the age of 60. Approximately one-third of liver transplants were carried out on hepatitis C sufferers.

Chapter 2. General Description of the Health Care System

§1. General Review of the Spanish Health Care System

13. The precursors of the National Health System put in place by the General Health Law (Ley General de Sanidad – LGS – of 1986) were the Institution of Public Welfare, the National Health Institute and the Social Security National Institute.[1] Up to the early years of the last century, the Public Welfare was a state scheme which catered for the needs of the destitute and the poor. In addition to providing health cover, the scheme also covered other areas of need such as food, education and employment;[2] the advent of epidemiological diseases led to a strengthening of action in the field of public health.[3]

There was, however, a large sector of society which, although not destitute, did not have sufficient means to meet its health needs. Demands were growing for a type of protection to ensure that such people would not be forced into poverty, which was a requirement for Public Welfare eligibility. Particularly vulnerable were workers who although they found it difficult to make ends meet, were not entitled to Public Welfare given that they were not 'poor'. Others, meanwhile, were better off and could afford to take out private social insurance cover. In this way independent social insurance gradually became established as a means of providing cover for old age, subsistence, accidents at work, family responsibilities, common illnesses, invalidity, illnesses derived from the exercise of one's profession, etc. Eventually, the State responded to working class demands and created a Compulsory Insurance Scheme under a Law passed on 14 December 1942. The scheme provided protection for the least well-off sectors of the population and afforded health assistance for general medical care as well as a variety of outpatient surgery specialities and medicines. National health care centres[4] were set up to deal with certain illnesses, whereas other levels of (hospital) health care were provided by local corporations and non-profitmaking institutions such as the Catholic Church and the Red Cross. Subsequent endeavours were made to develop a Social Security system. A first step was the promulgation of Law 193/1963 of 28 December which established the bases

---

1. *See* M. Beato Espejo, 'El sistema sanitario español: su configuración en la Ley General de Sanidad', in *Revista de Administración Pública*, n. 119, May–August 1989, p. 385.
2. The first law on Health was passed in 1855. On the basis of physicians' freedom to practice their profession, the law aimed to provide assistance for the poor; the health care it included covered collective – as opposed to individual – health only. 1925 saw the passing of Municipal and Provincial Regulations which once again focused on collective health and assistance for the poor. *See* P.P. Mansilla Izquierdo, *Reforma Sanitaria. Fundamentos para un análisis* (Ministerio de Sanidad y Consumo, Madrid 1986), pp. 5–7.
3. The General Public Health Instructions issued in 1904 created a system for the control of epidemiological diseases; similarly, the Regulations of 26 Jul. 1945 governing the fight against infectious diseases, disinfection and protection against insect pests, and the Regulations of 4 Feb. 1958 on the fight against trachoma, venereal diseases and dermatosis. *See* J. Pemán Gavín, *Derecho a la salud y Administración sanitaria* (Publicaciones del Real Colegio de España, Bologna 1989), p. 119.
4. The 1944 law which established the foundations of the National Health System marked the first attempt to coordinate existing health care networks (those of municipalities and provincial governments organised under the welfare system) and to cater for individual and not just collective health. *See* Mansilla Izquierdo, *Reforma Sanitaria*, p. 9.

of the Social Security system. This law attempted to bring together all existing forms of social insurance and was followed by the Social Security Law of 21 April 1966, which aimed to provide health assistance for a specific sector of society, i.e., workers. Workers were brought under the system because as paid employees they (together with their employers) helped finance the cost of Social Security services (Revised Text approved by Decree 2065/1974 of 30 May). The scheme forms part of the current National Health System, which covers a wide range of beneficiaries.[5]

The health care system underwent gradual transformation until the State decided to include the Social Security system as yet another of its functions. The system was granted its own normative provisions and it began to move away from the 'labour' criterion on which entitlement to health assistance was previously founded.[6]

14. A new stage was reached with the passing of the Spanish Constitution of 1978, which recognizes the right to health protection in Article 43.1. Entitlement covers all Spaniards as well as foreigners resident in Spain;[7] however, Article 41 of the Constitution stipulates also that 'the public authorities shall maintain a public Social Security system for all citizens, to guarantee sufficient social assistance and services ... '. One can deduce from this that the Social Security system has become totally 'decoupled' from worker status, given that it has to cater for all Spaniards, which has obvious repercussions on the manner in which the system is financed. Under this constitutional principle, the authorities are obliged to implement and safeguard health protection; health thus is given the status of a *public service* in accordance with the provisions of Article 43.2 of the Constitution.[8] A reflection of

5. The extension of Social Security cover since 1983 has been based on the labour status of the beneficiary. Cover was thus extended to the unemployed and unemployed members of their families (Law 31/1984 of 2 August), self-employed persons and their families (Royal Decree 43/1984 of 4 January), dependants under the age of 26 (Royal Decree 1377/1977 of 4 July), emigrants and their children (Royal Decree 916/1986) and persons over 26 who are unemployed and live with the direct beneficiary (Royal Decree 1682/1987 of 30 December). At 31 Dec. 1989 38,433,425 people – 96.14% of the total population of Spain – were entitled to health care cover, according to a report on health care institutions by the Ministry of Health and Consumer Affairs. Cover was further extended under Royal Decree 1088/1989 of 8 September to those with insufficient incomes, which brought many elderly persons and those on the edges of society into the system. The 'health cover for all' process was completed by Social Security Law 26/1990 of 20 December, which partly reformed the Revised Text and created non-contributory pensions for retired people and invalids. Under this system pension entitlement is extended to persons over 65 resident in Spain, who have not paid social security contributions and do not have sufficient income.
6. *See* A. Palomar Olmeda, 'Las normas jurídicas de Seguridad Social y las normas jurídicoadministrativas', in *Revista de Administración Pública*, No. 126, September–December 1991, p. 412.
7. For an analysis of proposals for the reform of the health care system made during the period 1977–1982, *see* F.J. Elola Somoza, *Crisis y reforma de la asistencia sanitaria pública en España (1983–1990)* (Fondo de Investigaciones Sanitarias de la Seguridad Social, Madrid 1991), pp. 71 ff.
8. Article 43.2 of the Constitution states that 'the authorities shall organise and safeguard public health through the taking of preventive measures and the provision of the necessary facilities and services. In this respect, the law shall determine the rights and duties of all concerned'. In the opinion of J.M. Rodriguez Pastrana, *El servicio público de la Sanidad: el marco constitutional* (Civitas, Madrid 1984), pp. 31 ff., 'what is inferred from the Constitution is, therefore, a *Public Health Service*, which should not be confused with a monopolised National Health Service ... . The basic idea of the National Health Service is, to a certain extent, the socialisation of health management, which is placed in public hands ... However, in a Public Health Service, although the State is certainly ultimately

this can be seen in the universalization of Social Security assistance which resulted from the creation of a system of non-contributory pensions.

The basic principles on which the National Health System is founded are those set out in the LGS, which was drawn up to enforce the mandate of Article 43.2 of the Constitution.[9] The public bodies responsible for health protection are the State Administration, Autonomous Communities and local corporations. The National Health System comprises all the Health Services of the State Administration and those of the Autonomous Communities. Decentralization, which is a requirement set out in the Constitution and in the respective Statutes of the Autonomous Communities, is a fundamental principle which determines to a large degree the way in which health services are provided. These services are brought under the wing of the Autonomous Communities, while the State is essentially charged with powers of management and co-ordination. The State is competent as regards basic concepts of care, general co-ordination and top-level inspection, aspects which aim to maintain unity in the field of health and to achieve basic equality among citizens as regards their health. Executive-type services are the responsibility of the Autonomous Communities, which also exercise normative powers where the State has not reserved these for itself in relation to health. Local corporations participate in the management and control of Health Areas.

§2. Regulation of the Health Care System

15. A new legal framework to govern health was needed in view of the fact that the 1944 Law which established the bases of the National Health Service had become obsolete and out of touch with society's needs and health requirements. The LGS under which the current National Health System was created, gave specific form to the health care principles and objectives which had been mapped out previously in the Constitution. In doing so, it did away with the models of public health care action which had prevailed in the nineteenth and early twentieth centuries and which concentrated on collective as opposed to individual assistance. Today's priorities include health promotion, prevention of illnesses and diseases and health education. The system, which covers mental health also, caters for the entire population, including those not covered by Social Security and persons without means of subsistence (Article 3 of the LGS).

Management of the health services has been progressively transferred to all Autonomous Communities, while some continue to be operated by the National Institute of Health Management (Instituto Nacional de Gestión Sanitaria, INGESA), part of the Ministry of Health and Social Policy. The activity of these services is harmonized by the Interterritorial Council of the Spanish National Health Service

responsible for all public and private health care activities, it does not reserve for itself the exclusive management of said activities … ' Elsewhere, Art. 3.2 of the General Health Law states that public health care assistance shall extend to the entire population.

9. Article 7 of the General Health Law states that health care services shall be organised and shall function in accordance with the principles of efficiency, promptness, economy and flexibility.

(Consejo Interterritorial del Servicio Nacional de Salud de España, CISNS) in order to give cohesion to the system and to guarantee the rights of citizens throughout Spain.

Article 46 of the *Ley General de Sanidad* establishes the fundamental characteristics of the SNS:

(i) Extension of services to the entire population.
(ii) Adequate organization to provide comprehensive health care, including promotion of health, prevention of disease, treatment and rehabilitation.
(iii) Coordination and, as needed, integration of all public health resources into a single system.
(iv) Financing of the obligations derived from this law will be met by resources of public administration, contributions and fees for the provision of certain services.
(v) The provision of a comprehensive health care, seeking high standards, properly evaluated and controlled.

16. The protection of *public health*, particularly aspects of prevention, is a primary concern of the Spanish State, as reflected in the passing of Organic Law 3/1986 of 14 April on Special Public Health Measures, which empowers the health authorities to adopt certain measures in cases or situations of emergency or need. The measures cover examinations, treatment, hospitalization or control when there exists reasonable grounds to assume that the health of the population may be at risk (Article 2). It also enables the Administration to temporarily centralize supplies of medicines or health products where problems of supply exist, in order to ensure efficient distribution. Furthermore, in addition to authorising preventive action – with the corresponding curtailment of citizens' freedoms –, the law also empowers the Administration to control the sick or persons who have been in contact with them and their environment in cases where public health has already been affected, especially in the case of an epidemic (Article 3). The legal system for the protection of collective is present also in the Criminal Law, which penalizes a series of conducts deemed to be dangerous to the health of the public;[10] in addition to all the above, there exists a wide range of administrative regulations governing aspects relating to health protection.

17. The *individual health* of citizens is a public health priority of the State, both in terms of prevention and assistance. State care is a constitutional obligation and an area in which significant progress has been achieved, particularly as regards the care provided by the Social Security system. The universalization of individual protection, which has entailed partial abandonment of the former mode of financing the

10. See Articles 359–378 of the Spanish Criminal Code. Among conducts deemed to constitute an offence are the unauthorised manufacture and selling of substances which are dangerous to health, breaches of regulations governing trade in such substances, the illegal dispensing of drugs and medicines, the alteration of medicinal substances, or fraud concerning food products and illegal drug trafficking, among other.

system through contributions, means that public health care is now available to all citizens.

The LGS allows citizens to choose their primary care GP in their Health Area; it provides for the creation of an integrated network of public hospitals and the association of private general hospitals to the National Health System when required. It also provides for the right to freely practice a health care profession and for freedom of enterprise in the health sector, in accordance with the provisions laid down in the Constitution.

18. The structure of the model of assistance is thus conceived as a whole, which comprises activities to enhance and promote health, prevention, curative assistance and rehabilitation. Health services are *structured* in such a way as to facilitate user proximity and a form of decentralized management which allows for public participation. Each Autonomous Community has its own Health Service, which includes all the centres, services and establishments in the Community in question. The cornerstones of these Services are the Health Areas, which are generally designed to cater for populations of between 200,000 and 250,000 and which provide all the services available under the health system. For smoother running, Health Areas are divided into Basic Health Zones for primary health care. The Zones' Health Centres and General Hospitals, in addition to providing assistance, also play a role in promoting health, preventing illness and disease and in teaching and research, all in accordance with the programmes which each Health Area draws up as complementary activities to those undertaken by the primary care network. To this end, the basic organization of the system centres on the National Institute of Health (which is managed by the Social Security system), with health services reorganized as follows:

(1) On the territorial level, the health system comprises essentially Health Areas, divided in turn into Basic Health Zones, as the unit for a primary health care team.
(2) As regards assistance, the following levels exist:
    (a) *Primary Care*. It is a basic level of patient care that guarantees the comprehensiveness and continuity of care throughout the patient's life, acting as manager and coordinator of cases and regulator of issues.[11] Primary care includes health promotion, health education, prevention of illness, health care, maintenance and recuperation of health, as well as physical rehabilitation and social work. Primary health care includes service provided either on-demand, scheduled, or urgently, both in the clinic as well as in the patient's home. The Health Centres are staffed by general practitioners, paediatricians, nursing staff, social workers and administrative personnel. The staff carry out their work in the Centre itself and in the patient's home, and may be called to deal with emergencies. Health education is also undertaken by Centres.

11. Article 12 of Law 16/2003 of 28 May, on Cohesion and Quality of the National Health System.

(b) *Specialist Care.*[12] Hospitals, which are better equipped both in terms of staff and facilities, are the cornerstones of specialist care. They also act as centres for teaching and research and carry out their own health promotion and prevention activities, in accordance with Health Area programs.

Medical assistance comprises General Medicine, as well as Specialist and Emergency Medicine services which are provided in health centres, on an inpatient basis or in the patient's home. Users covered by Social Security receive such services free of charge, and do not have to pay anything in addition to their normal contributions.

Pharmaceutical assistance covers pharmaceutical specialities, items and accessories as well as prescriptions issued by doctors under the Social Security system. These are completely free of charge in certain cases (OAPs and their dependants, the handicapped, persons who have sustained accidents at work, etc.). In other cases, users pay 40% of the retail price of the drug or medicine, except for some of a special nature. The fee is paid directly to the dispensing chemist.[13]

In addition, promotion and prevention work is carried out in the field of primary health care via the Health Centres. In some cases such action is targeted specifically on, for example, family planning, mental health and maternity care (Family Planning Units and Centres, Mental Health and Psychoprophylaxis Units).

19. General Health Care Co-ordination is the means by which minimum common goals for prevention, protection, perception and assistance are determined. To this end, a number of competences are granted for co-ordination purposes and support is available from the Inter-Territorial Council of the National Health System, a body chaired by the Minister for Health and Consumer Affairs and consisting of a representative appointed by each Autonomous Community and an equal number of State Administration representatives. Co-ordination is also achieved by means of the Integrated Health Programme which is of paramount importance in ensuring that health services function efficiently. This integrated programme brings together State and Autonomous Community programmes as well as any joint plans drawn up to enable both sides to carry out their respective health care functions. Co-ordination at State level is also achieved through agreements concluded by the State and the Autonomous Communities, and any joint action which they may agree to undertake.

20. In general, health services are organized on the basis of direct public management, that is, through publicly owned centres staffed by personnel who are subject to Public Law statutes.[14] However, provision is also made for the use of private forms of management of health services; this means that privately owned centres

12. *See* Royal Decree 521/1987 of 15 April on the structure, organisation and functioning of hospitals managed by the National Institute of Health.
13. Users may also be entitled to other services, such as payment for drugs or medicines not available in Spain, for fixed and orthopedic surgical appliances of a permanent or temporary nature, invalid vehicles, use of ordinary means of transportation (ambulances) for patients who require them frequently to follow treatment such as dialysis, radiotherapy, rehabilitation, etc.
14. Prior to 1978, the Social Security system was managed by the National Providence Institute (Instituto Nacional de Previsión), which was dissolved under Royal Decree 36/1978 of 16 November. Its

may provide assistance on behalf of the health care system. The public network is thus complemented through association agreements reached with private centres or through the linking up of private hospitals to the public system.

In order to exercise its functions,[15] the State relies on the administrative machinery of the Ministry of Health. All health care centres and services come under the Autonomous Communities,[16] with the exception of the Instituto de Salud Carlos III, an independent institution belonging to the State Administration, set up to provide technical and scientific support to State and Autonomous Communities Health Services.

The State health administration is charged with assessing the suitability of medicines and other health products and articles and is also responsible for authorising their use and controlling the quality of such products.

The LGS lays down certain minimum principles to be followed by the Autonomous Communities in the organization of their Health Services, although it does not interfere with their competences granted to them under their respective statutes. Each Community delimits its Health Areas, which, in addition to an Area Board and Manager, must also include an Area Health Council, a collegiate body for consultation and monitoring of public health management in which the public participates (citizens, trade unions). In exercising their competences the Autonomous Communities must allow for democratic participation by all interested parties, including representatives of unions and employers' organizations. Each Community draws up its own Health Plan which contains all the actions necessary to help accomplish the goals set for its health care centres. The plan also regulates the organization, functions and allocation of material and staff.

§3. Financing of the Health Care

21. The Law of Cohesion and Quality of 2003 establishes that the financing of the Spanish health system is the responsibility of the autonomous communities in conformity with the accords of transfer and the current system of autonomic financing, notwithstanding the existence of a third party liable to pay.[17] Sufficient financing of services is determined by the resources assigned to the autonomous

---

functions were taken over by, among other bodies, the management institutions of the Social Security system: the National Institute of the Social Security (INSS), which handles payments of benefits under the system; the National Social Services Institute (INSERSO today IMSERSO – Instituto de Mayores y Servicios Sociales –) which manages complementary social services (for the elderly and handicapped), and the National Institute of Health (INSALUD), which managed and administered the system's health care services.

15. Under Art. 149.1.17 of the Constitution, the State is exclusively competent to draw up 'the basic legislation and establish the economic regime of the Social Security system, although services may be provided by the Autonomous Communities'. Under Art. 149.1.16 it is solely responsible for 'external health. The bases and overall coordination of health. Legislation governing pharmaceutical products'.
16. Under numbers 20 and 21 of Art. 148.1 of the Spanish Constitution, and in accordance with the terms laid down in their respective Statutes, Autonomous Communities may take on competences in relation to social assistance and health and hygiene.
17. Article 10.

communities in conformity to what is established in the laws of autonomic financing. Inclusion of a new service in the catalogue of services of the National Health System is accompanied by an economic memo that contains the positive or negative financial impact it is expected to imply. This memo is brought up to the Council of Fiscal Policy and Finance for analysis and approval as to whether to proceed.

The LGS advocates a tightened belt approach to solve the problem of the large health service deficit caused by increased expenditure and squandering of resources.[18] Obviously, if the goals of the new health system were to be attained, an increase in spending was necessary to enable care to be extended to the entire population. The planning and fixing of the major principles of the system was crucially important, as were the search for sources of financing and the distribution and management of financial resources.[19] Prior to 1986, restrictive health budgets were the order of the day; however, the gradual widening of the system of social security assistance to cover the entire population required more spending on public health and, therefore, increased funding for the sector.[20]

The system is financed by social security contributions paid by employees and employers, transfers of State funds, fees charged for certain services and contributions made by the Autonomous Communities and local corporations.

Financial functions in the field of health care are exercised by the State. The funds which it transfers to the Autonomous Communities depend on the size of the population to be covered. In addition, the Communities receive financing for their health care centres from the Social Security budget, although they also contribute their own funds and raise money by charging for health services provided to third parties.

Apart from this basic funding mechanism, the State may at its discretion use other complementary forms to correct imbalances between regions. It may draw up its own action plans, including those for investment, and may provide partial or total financing of Autonomous Communities health programmes, or contribute to the financing of joint programmes drawn up between the State and one or all of the Communities.

22. *Reducing financial costs*. The costs of health care supported by the Public Health System have increased constantly, and today is one of the highest economic

---

18. *See* Elola Somoza, *Crisis y reforma de asistencia sanitaria pública en España*, p. 109.
19. Article 81 of the General Health Law (LGS) states that 'the generalisation of the right to health protection and assistance, which entails bringing public health assistance and services into line, shall be accomplished by allocating financial resources which take into account both the size of the population in need of assistance in each Autonomous Community and also investments in health which need to be undertaken to correct health care inequalities between territories, in accordance with Article 12'.
20. Increased expenditure was caused not merely by the extension of health care to the entire population, but also by the need to cater for mental health, the organisation and structure of the National Health system, research and the Instituto de Salud Carlos III. *See* Elola Somoza, *Crisis y reforma de la asistencia sanitaria pública en España*, p. 113. Somoza argues that '*the increase in health expenditure produced by the LGS was clearly underestimated*. This, combined with the aforementioned ambiguity and the absence of specific commitments in the Law, lends support to the theory that *the LGS lacked sufficient policy backing to enable it to carry out its proposals. To a certain extent, it served rather to lay out a final scenario which successive reforms should aim towards*, insofar as sufficient resources could be allocated in future to implement them'.

burdens to which public finances is faced with. Some measures have been taken to reduce these costs to keep the system sustainable while preventing any inequality based on economic or territorial situation of citizens.[21] We will mention the most important measures taken for medicines and for other diagnostic or therapeutic treatments.

1. *Medicines*. The *encouragement in the market of generic drugs*, as they are cheaper, since they become free of patent rights; and the copayment of the prescribed medicine by patients themselves.[22] The emergence in recent years of generic drugs, clinically proven products and cheaper to have the exclusivity period expired original drug data, ensures identical terms of quality, safety and efficacy to low price. Therefore, in this goal of sustainability, the measures incorporated in the Act on medicines are intended to eliminate obstacles to greater presence of these drugs on the market. According to Article 87 of Royal Legislative Decree 1/2015, health authorities will encourage the prescription of medicines identified in the medical receipt by their active principle. In cases where the professional prescriber indicated in the receipt simply an active principle, the pharmacist will dispense the medicine with the lowest price.

The *copayment of the prescribed medicines* by patients themselves is a legally established general practice.[23] The question is whether still a surplus (co)payment as it was decided by some Autonomous Communities (one euro extra for each medicine) is lawful or not. The authorities of the State (Central Government) claimed to the Constitutional Court against these decisions as exceeding the constitutional competences accorded to the Regional Governments (Comunidades Autónomas). In its Judgment 85/2014, of 29 May 2014, the Spanish Constitutional Court upheld the appeal lodged by the Government against the implementation in Catalonia of the 'Euro per prescription' system. The Constitutional Court pointed out that on the matter of public health, as opposed to other shared competences between the State and Autonomous Communities, 'the economic sustainability structure is part of basic State competences'. The LOFCA (Public General Act on Economical Sustainability of Autonomous Communities) states, furthermore, that 'the State will guarantee throughout Spanish territory a minimum level of the fundamental public services under its competence', to include public health. The Constitutional Court recalls that the National Health System is but one and that its financing depends on the Public Service Guarantee Fund, specific social funds used to 'ensure that each Autonomous Community receives the same resources per inhabitant necessary to finance fundamental public services essential to the Welfare State'. Therefore, the judgment states, given that public health is a basic competence of the State, there can be no 'imposition of a rate as the one being reviewed, which alters, at an extra cost for the beneficiaries, the cost participation system established' in the Act.

---

21. Article 91 of Royal Legislative Decree 1/2015, of 24 July, which approves the refunded text of the Law on guarantees and rational use of medicines and health products (*Real Decreto Legislativo por el que se aprueba el texto refundido de la Ley de garantías y uso racional de los medicamentos y productos sanitarios*).
22. N. Laguna-Goya et al., 'Legislación sobre autorización de genéricos', in *Farmacia Hospitalaria*, Nr. 30, 2006, pp. 379–384.
23. *See* Art. 101 of Royal Legislative Decree 1/2015.

2. *Reviewing the common services portfolio* of the National Health System. In order to prevent arbitrariness and unequal provisions of medical care services for all citizens (including lawful foreign residents) the Spanish National Health System (NHS, Sistema Nacional de Salud) has regulated which of these provisions should be included. More specifically the aim of establishing this common portfolio is to ensure the protection of health, equity and accessibility to adequate health care, which have right all citizens regardless of their residence, making effective provisions to through the portfolio of common services of the National Health System, which sets out the techniques, technologies or procedures that currently covers that system. This regulation is intended to define, ensure and establish the procedure of updating the provisions that currently are being offered by the Public Health System to citizens.[24]

Health authorities have perceived that it is necessary to control the very high costs of health care provisions today and that for this aim a clarification and reduction of the common services portfolio is needed. This is the reason why one of the first measures taken by the current Government have been to reorganize the sector, and to enhance sustainability, improve management efficiency, achieve greater territorial coordination, reduce spending and defaulting for providers of the public health system among others.[25]

24. See Royal Decree 1030/2006, of 15 September, for establishing the common services portfolio of the National Health Service and the procedure for updating.
25. Royal Decree-Law 16/2012, of 20 April, on urgent measures to ensure the sustainability of the National Health System and improve the quality and safety of their services.

Chapter 3. Medical Law

§1. Definitions and Functions of Medical Law

23. Medical Law is not clearly circumscribed in the Spanish legal system and is often confused with Health Law, Legal Medicine and – in the past – Medical Deontology; currently there is also some overlapping with Bioethics.[26] Strictly speaking, Health Law embraces the legal system of health in its entirety, particularly the public health system, public health actions and citizens' relations with the health care system ('Derecho Sanitario'). Legal Medicine is the part of medicine which is kept as an auxiliary instrument in the administration of justice. Bioethics (as well as Biolaw) is an interdisciplinary approach to life and health related conflicts.

Medical Law can thus be defined initially as *the parts of the law which concern with Medicine, that is, the medical profession and, by extension, other health or health-related professions*. Medical law refers to the professional relations of physicians (and other similar professionals) with the system of health care, with (public and private) health care users and patients, and other health professionals. However, in view of the constant widening of the scope of actions affecting health, nowadays Medical Law includes also *the legal implications of the application to human beings of the so-called Biomedical Sciences*, that is, not just medicine but also biology (e.g., genetics), biochemistry, biophysics, biotechnology, etc. To a certain degree also it takes in the specific legal aspects of the use by health professionals of certain technologies, such as computers (bioinformatics). A problem currently exists with regard to the delimitation of Bioethics, due in particular to the influence exerted on the concept by the Americans, who understand Bioethics as comprising not just the ethical aspects (applied ethics) of the biomedical sciences but also philosophical, sociological and legal considerations as well. Both Bioethics and (Bio)Medical Law study the biomedical sciences and how they affect human beings, although they do so from different perspectives: the former from the ethical viewpoint and the latter from the legal standpoint. However, it is now accepted that Bioethics, in the broad sense of the term, may constitute a focal point for the multidisciplinary study of the implications of the biomedical sciences for human beings. It should be stressed nonetheless that these sciences are independent and autonomous disciplines.

Medical Law as such is not taught officially in Spanish universities, although it does figure occasionally in postgraduate courses (i.e., Masters in Biolaw, Medical Law or Bioethics) or as a short matter in graduate studies in Medical and Law Schools. In the case of Schools of Medicine most curricula have tended to include Bioethics, due partly to the confusion referred to just now and partly because it is probably considered that teachers of Bioethics will not necessarily require previous

26. See CM Romeo-Casabona, *El médico y el Derecho Penal, vol. II, 1* (Rubinzal Culzoni, Santa Fe 2011), p. 17.

training in the subject (an opinion which, if that is indeed the case, would be misguided).[27]

In any case, it has to be accepted that (Bio-)Medical Law today is an autonomous discipline which is of crucial theoretical and practical importance given its potential effects on society.

§2. Sources of Medical Law

24. Specific medical law sources in Spain have developed considerably over the years, especially along the last two decades. As will become clear in the following pages, a number of Laws in Spain address medical issues: the 30/1979 Law on the Removal and Transplantation of Organs, the LGS 14/1986, as examples of the oldest and Law 14/2007 on Biomedical Research as the youngest most relevant.

Other Laws have been updated or are completely new: the 41/2002 Law on patient's autonomy and on rights and duties related to information and clinical records, the 14/2006 Law on Techniques of Human Assisted Reproduction, the 2006 Law on guarantees and the rational use of medicines, the 2/2010 Organic Law on reproductive health (voluntary interruption of pregnancy), partially modified by Organic Law 11/2015, and others.

These issues are taken up further in Royal Decrees, which cover other aspects also such as blood donation, organs and tissues for therapeutic purposes, biobanks and human samples for research purposes, clinical trials; and in Ministerial Orders. Although still rather scarce in this field, court rulings have implemented its quantity and quality (arguments) also can constitute substantive sources of Medical Law and provide important (although not legally binding for third parties) points of reference.

25. As regards non-specific sources, mention should be made first and foremost of the Spanish Constitution of 1978, which sets out fundamental rights which may be affected by medical practice: the right to life and to physical and moral integrity (Article 15), the right to ideological freedom (Article 16), the right to freedom (Article 17), the right to privacy (Article 18), the right to the scientific creation and production (Article 20), etc. The Constitution also enshrines the principle of non-discrimination (Article 14) and refers to the dignity of the human person and the free development of personhood (Article 10.1). In addition to the above, there are numerous provisions in both criminal and civil law which are applicable to the practice of medicine, particularly as regards liability in respect of malpractice and personal data protection.

On the international level, special reference should be made to the human rights Conventions subscribed and ratified by Spain and which, as result, now form part of domestic law (Article 96 of the Constitution) and are of help in the interpretation of the fundamental rights laid down in the Constitution. Of particular interest in this

27. See CM Romeo-Casabona, Bioderecho y Bioética *in CM Romeo-Casabona (Dir.) 'Enciclopedia de Bioderecho y Bioética'* (Cátedra Interuniversitaria de Derecho y Genoma Humano – Ed. Comares, Bilbao – Granada, 2011), p. 189 ff.

regard is the Universal Declaration of Human Rights, which is mentioned expressly in the Constitution (Article 10.2). Other examples include the European Convention for the Protection of Human Rights and Fundamental Freedoms (1950) and the International Covenant on Civil and Political Rights (1966).

Along last decades International Law has developed specific legal instruments, binding or not binding, in matters directly related with biomedical activities on which Spain is a part: Council of Europe Convention on Human Rights and Biomedicine (Oviedo Convention, 1997) and its Additional Protocols,[28] UNESCO's Declarations on the Human Genome and Human Rights (1997), on Human Genetic Data (2003), on Bioethics and Human Rights (2005).[29]

28. The Oviedo Convention was signed by the Kingdom of Spain on 4 Apr. 1997 and ratified on 23 Jul. 1999 (in power since 1st Jan. 2000). Concerning Additional Protocols Spain has signed and ratified this referred to the Prohibition of Cloning Human Beings (Paris, 12 Jan. 1998; in power since 1st Mar. 2001).
29. Concerning the UN Declaration on Human Cloning (8 Mar. 2005) Spain abstained from voting.

Part I. The Medical Profession

Chapter 1. Access to the Medical Profession

§1. Health Care Education

26. From a general viewpoint, Spanish law incorporates the freedom of professional practice in the Article 35.1 and Article 36 of the Constitution. The first of these articles includes, in general, the right of every citizen 'to the free choice of profession', right which not has to be confused with the right to engage in any professional activity. Meanwhile, Article 36 of the Constitution states that the peculiarities of the exercise of each profession must be regulated by specific laws. In this sense, it is up to the lawmaker to decide when a profession requires an Official Degree to be exercised, if there is other kind of requirements for such purpose, as well as the definition of the minimum content of the activities included in said profession.

27. Spanish legal literature maintains that until 2003 there was an unsatisfactory regime of the peculiarities and requirements for the exercise of the health professions. Until then, it had been only regulated the legal system of professions related to dentistry and of other oral health related professionals.[30] Finally, such deficiency would be corrected with the entry into force of the Law 44/2003 of 21 November, on the Regulation of Health Professions. Said norm states that the exercise of a health profession (both in private and in public sector[31]) requires the possession of the pertinent Official Degree that expressly authorizes the holder to exercise his profession.

28. Our legal system states that 'Graduated Health Professions' are those whose undergraduate or specialized training is specifically and primarily aimed to provide applicants with the knowledge, skills and attitudes for health care, and are organized in Professional Associations officially recognized by the Public Authorities. Taking into account the type of the University Degree, Spanish law classifies such professions into two groups:

30. Aspects developed, in a generic way, in the Law 10/1986 of 17 March, governing dentists and other oral health professionals.
31. Are similar the regulations governing the legal relationship that links health professionals with the public administration. Consult the Art. 30.5.b) of the Law 55/2003 of 16 December, on the Framework Statute for Health Services Staff.

(1) Health Professions of Bachelor level: Are those professions whose practice is authorized by the degrees of Bachelor of Medicine, Pharmacy, Dentistry and Veterinary Medicine, and the Official Degrees of Specialist in Health Sciences (these latter could be obtained by the Bachelors in Psychology, Chemistry, Biology, Biochemistry and other University Bachelors).[32] However, the Law 44/2003 also states that, when necessary[33] and by a regulation having the force of Law, it would be possible to formally declare the character of 'Graduated Health Professions' of an activity not included in the previous list.
(2) Health Professions of Diploma level: Are those professions whose practice is authorized by the Degrees of Diploma in Nursing, Physiotherapy, Occupational Therapy, Podiatry, Optics and Optometry, Speech Therapy and Human Nutrition and Dietetics, as well as the Official Degrees of Specialist in Health Sciences for those Diplomas specified in the Title II of the Law 44/2003.

29. It is important to remark that in Spain they are not considered 'Health Professions' the Vocational Education and Training (VET) Qualifications (or equivalent Qualifications) linked to the family of health professions, even if they are of Medium[34] or Superior[35] Level. This type of VET Qualifications confers to its holder the consideration of 'Technician' or 'Superior Technician', respectively, and do not authorize him to exercise a health profession, but to perform their duties under the supervision and with respect for the competence of Health Professionals.

§2. Education of Health Professionals

30. In general terms, we can affirm that regulation of the health professions in Spain is currently in line with the guidelines laid down by European Community Law, particularly the Directives designed to harmonize conditions and requirements for entry to and specialization in medical studies throughout a Community which is highly sensitive to the importance that the professions holds for society.

31. Would-be students of the different kind of health sciences at university must pass compulsory aptitude tests designed to examine whether they are properly prepared for such studies. The tests, which are taken after the two-years pre-university course (Baccalaureate in Sciences[36]), focus on the mainstream and optional subjects of the degree syllabus and are similar for all Spanish universities. Said access

32. See Arts 6.3 and 19.1 of the Law 44/2003 of 21 November, on the Regulation of Health Professions.
33. Due to the characteristics of the activity, to improve the efficiency of health services or to adapt the health care structure to the scientific and technological progress.
34. Some of these VET Qualifications are: Technician in Auxiliary Nursing Care and Pharmacy.
35. Some of these VET Qualifications are: Superior Technician in Pathologic Anatomy and Cytology, in Dietetics, in Health Documentation, in Oral Hygiene, in Imaging for Diagnostic, in Clinic Diagnostic Laboratory, in Ortho Prosthetic, in Dental Prosthesis, in Radiotherapy, in Environmental Health and in Audio Prosthesis.
36. See Art. 34.1 of the Organic Law 2/2006 of 3 May, of Education (recently modified by the Organic Law 8/2013 of 9 December, for the improvement of Educational Quality). Art. 42.1 of the Organic Law 6/2001 of 21 December, of Universities, establishes that 'to access to the University, applicants must hold a Baccalaureate degree or equivalent'.

tests consist of two stages: the first one aims to assess the maturity and basic skills of the applicant after his/her Baccalaureate education in order to follow the official studies at the University, and the second one is a non-compulsory and specific stage that aims to evaluate the knowledge and the reasoning skills in some specific disciplinary fields, linked, all of them, with the studies that the applicant pretend to develop in the University and that may permit to improve the qualification obtained in the previous stage. In any case, the aforementioned tests are held annually in universities and may be taken by Spaniards resident abroad and foreigners who attest to having followed a suitable course of study abroad. Once they have successfully taken these tests, candidates cannot then be asked to take further entrance exams, although faculties may limit the number of places on offer, in which case those who obtain the highest marks in the university entrance exam will be admitted.[37]

32. In Spain, the basic medical training leads to obtain the Official University 'Qualification of Bachelor' of Medicine, established by Royal Decree 1417/1990 of 26 October, or to obtain the 'Qualification of Graduate' established in accordance with the provisions contained in the Order ECI/332/2008 of 13 February, under the terms of the Agreement of Council of Ministers of 14 December 2007. Persons who have either of these two Qualifications can be considered as 'Graduated Health Professionals'. The degrees itself are valid throughout the country, although each faculty is at liberty to organize and plan its own syllabus leading to the award. Syllabuses are designed primarily to ensure that doctors trained in faculties of medicine gradually acquire sufficient clinical experience and expertise. The aforementioned Royal Decree[38] stipulates that training must provide students with:

(1) an adequate knowledge of the sciences which form the basis of medicine and a sound understanding of scientific principles, including the measurement of biological functions, evaluation of scientifically proven facts and data analysis;
(2) an adequate knowledge of the structure, functions and behaviour of human beings, healthy and otherwise, as well as of the relationships between states of health and man's physical and social environment;
(3) an adequate knowledge of clinical subjects and practice, in order to provide students with a coherent view of mental and physical illnesses, of the preventive aspects of medicine, of diagnosis and therapeutics, and of human reproduction;
(4) adequate and appropriately supervised clinical experience in hospitals.

Training focuses on the preventive, diagnostic and therapeutic aspects of medicine, with the help of clinical experience acquired in hospitals. Agreements reached between the public administrations and universities and health institutions in which

37. Article 42.3 of the Organic Law 6/2001 of 21 December, of Universities, establishes that 'in accordance with the basic regulations established by the Government with the prior report of the University Coordination Council and taking into account the programming of the number of places available, Universities will establish the procedures for the admission of the applicants' students, always with respect for the principles of equality, merit and ability'.
38. *See also* Art. 23.1 of the Council Directive 93/16/EEC of 5 Apr. 1993.

university training is provided guarantee the practical teaching of medicine (universities have at least one teaching and research hospital).[39]

The Royal Decree guidelines state that medical studies shall be split into two cycles, each one lasting three years.[40] Each cycle must offer a minimum of 250 course credits (a credit is the equivalent of ten hours of theory or practical instruction), with a weekly teaching load of between twenty and thirty hours, including practicals. The amount of theoretical content shall not exceed fifteen hours per week.

Although each faculty can plan its own courses leading to the degree in medicine, there are certain compulsory core subjects which must be included in medical studies in all Spanish universities to ensure that the qualifications awarded are consistent and uniform.[41]

RD 1393/2007 of 29 October, organizes and classifies the official university education into three cycles (Bachelor, Master and Doctorate). Postgraduate students wishing to obtain the Master or PhD degrees must follow and pass, respectively, the master and doctorate programmes, courses and seminars offered by the relevant department and successfully submit a master and doctoral thesis giving evidence of original research work.

33. Dentistry has been part and parcel of medical studies since the beginning of the century. It was made a specialist subject (Stomatology) by a Decree of 7 July 1944. However, the scarcity of dental health specialists, the criteria in force in neighbouring countries and in particular Community directives,[42] and also the need to avoid possible discrimination between specialists trained in Spain and the rest of the EC, made it necessary to create the specific profession of Dentistry. This came about through Law 10/1986 of 17 March, governing dentists and other dental health professionals, and Royal Decree 970/1986 of 11 April (subsequently modified by RD 1418/1990 of 26 October, RD 1267/1994 of 10 July, RD 1561/1997 of 10 October, RD 371/2001 of 6 April) which develops this law and creates the official qualification of Degree in Dentistry, which entitles the holder to practise the profession and thus firmly establishes dentistry as a separate academic discipline.

Thus, dentistry is granted its own syllabus, which is broken down into theoretical, practical and clinical teaching provided in two cycles of two and three years respectively. Training aims to provide dentists with the necessary competence to prevent, diagnose and treat abnormalities and diseases of the teeth, mouth, jaws and

---

39. Article 104.1 of the General Health Law (Law 14/1986 of 25 April) states that all care structures of the health system must be made available for the undergraduate, postgraduate and continuous teaching of professionals. RD 1558/1986 of 28 June sets out the general bases of the system of agreements between universities and health care institutions. Among other things, such agreements aim to assure clinical training for undergraduate and postgraduate medical students. *See also* Art. 12 paragraphs a), b) and c) of the Law 44/2003 of 21 November.
40. *See also* Art. 23.2 of the Council Directive 93/16/EEC, which envisages that such studies shall comprise at least a six-year course or 5500 hours of theoretical and practical instruction given in a university or under supervision of a university.
41. *See* Annex to RD 1417/1990 of 26 October. The Annex was subsequently amended by RD 1267/1994 of 10 June, RD 1561/1997 of 10 October, 1332/1999 of 31 July and RD 371/2001 of 6 April.
42. *See* Directives 78/686/EEC, 78/687/EEC and 78/688/EEC of 25 Jul. 1978 and 81/1057/EEC of 14 Dec. 1981.

tissues. However, in this field of health the highest level of specialization continues to be stomatology and maxillo-facial surgery.

34. Finally, it is important to remark that the regulation of the training and educational action in the field of health professions is based on the following guiding principles:[43]

(1) The permanent collaboration between the agencies of the competent public Administrations in matters of education and health.
(2) The agreement between universities and teaching centres of vocational training and the institutions and health centres, to ensure the practical teaching of lessons that require it.
(3) The disposition of the whole structure of the health system to be used in undergraduate, specialized and continuous teaching of professionals.
(4) The consideration of the health centres and services, also, as centres of scientific research and training of professionals, as long as the conditions suitable for those purposes are fulfilled.
(5) The permanent review of teaching methodology and lessons in the health field in order to achieve a better adaptation of the professional knowledge to the scientific and technical evolution and to the health needs of the population.
(6) The permanent updating of knowledge, through continuous education, of health professionals, as a right and a duty for them. For this aim, health institutions and centres will facilitate the realization of continuous training activities.
(7) The establishment, development and updating of methodologies for the evaluation of knowledge acquired by professionals and of the functioning of the own training system.

§3. Licensing of Physicians

I. General Practitioners

35. GPs perform their duties in the field of primary health care and diagnose and treat their patients' illnesses. In order to practise as a GP, it is sufficient to hold a degree in medicine, although registration with the provincial College of Physicians is compulsory.[44]

The rights and duties of GPs who work for the National Health System are regulated by the General Statute of Statutory Personnel of the Health Services.[45] GPs' general duties consist of a series of obligations related with the respect of the Constitution; the practice of the profession with loyalty, effectiveness and in compliance

43. All af them are included into the Art. 12 of the Law 44/2003 of 21 November.
44. *See* Art. 35 of the General Statutes of the Spanish Medical Colleges Organization (OMC) and the RD 1018/1980 of 19 May, governing the Statutes of the Organisation of Colleges of Physicians and the General Council of Colleges of Physicians. Professional practice by a physician who has not registered beforehand with the College of Physicians may constitute illegal practice and be punishable via RD 1018/1980 of 19 May (*see* next chapter on the illegal practice of medicine).
45. Law 55/2003 of 16 December, of General Statute of Statutory Personnel of the Health Services.

with the technical, scientific, ethical principles; the respect of human dignity and privacy of patients, etc.[46] The specific duties are described in the Circular 1/1982 of 9 December, some of them are: to provide medical assistance in health care centres or in the patient's home to persons aged over seven who are covered by social security; physicians are obliged to remain in the centre during their surgery hours, and to attend emergency calls and take samples in patient's homes for clinical analysis where no local analyst is available or where this task cannot be performed by a nurse (requests for home visits may be made by telephone and must be met the same day); as regards surgery commitments, GPs must set aside two and a half hours every day, except holidays, to attend patients; surgery times are designed in such a way as to take account of co-ordination between medical teams, local employment factors and public transport.[47]

Although GPs are not specialists, they play such an important role in the community that they are forced to constantly up-date their scientific knowledge and therapeutic techniques. RD 3303/1978 of 29 December regulates Family and Community Medicine as a specialist form of medicine. This specialist branch was available in hospitals only and outside the hospital context it had failed to match the advances made by General Medicine and by primary care in general, in spite of the fact that continuous training of this type was crucial in terms of helping meet the health care needs of individuals in their family and community environment.[48]

36. Moreover, concern for the continuous training of physicians was evident at EC level, as reflected in the adoption of Council Directive 85/547/EEC of 15 September 1986, which provided for specific and essentially practical training in general medicine lasting two years on a full or part-time basis. GP continuous training has not been overlooked in Spain, and at the present day the Law 44/2003 of 21 November, on the Regulation of Health Professions establishes a set of detailed provisions on this matter. Article 33.1 of the aforementioned Law establishes that Continuing Training is the active and permanent teaching and learning process, to which the health professionals are entitled and obliged, which starts at the end of undergraduate or specialized studies, and that is intended to update and improve the knowledge, skills and attitudes of health professionals taking into account the scientific and technological development, as well as the social and health system demands and needs. In any case, we should note that the Continuing Training has been presented, in the aforementioned Article 12 f) of Law 44/2003, as one of the guiding principles of the training and teaching action on the field of health professions and that has been configured from two dimensions: as a right and as an obligation. This implies that, on the one hand, the employer must provide such training and, on the other, the health professional must attend and participate in such training. In addition, we must remark that, in order to ensure the achievement of the objectives of Continuous Training, the Law 44/2003 has created the Commission on

46. *See* Article 19 of the Law 55/2003 of 16 December.
47. *See* Circular 1/1982 of 9 December issued by the Under-Secretary of State for Health and Consumer Affairs, on compliance with current regulations regarding duties and functions of the physicians who provide services in open and closed Health Institutions of Social Security.
48. Ministerial Order of 19 Dec. 1983 sets out provisions for the postgraduate training in Family and Community Medicine.

Continuing Training of Health Professions. Such a commission is a body composed of representatives of Interterritorial Council of the National Health System, Professional Organizations, Universities, National Council of Specialties in Health Sciences and of Scientific Societies. Some of the functions of this Commission are:[49]

(1) The detection, analysis, study and assessment of the needs of professionals and the health system in the field of continuous training, according to the proposals of the competent bodies of the autonomous communities, scientific societies and, where appropriate, of professional organizations represented in the Professional Advisory Commission.
(2) The proposal for the adoption of programs or for the development of activities and actions of continuous training of priority and common character for the entire health system.
(3) The proposal for the adoption of appropriate measures to plan, coordinate and harmonize the activities of the various actors in the field of continuous training of health professionals.
(4) The study, report and proposal for the establishment of procedures, criteria and requirements for accreditation of centres and activities of continuous training.
(5) The study, report and proposal for the establishment of procedures, criteria and requirements for the accreditation and the advanced accreditation of professionals in a specific functional area of a profession or specialty, following the development of the accredited continuous training activities.

II. Medical Specialists

37. Specialist medical training was not regulated in Spain initially. Previously, the degree in medicine and surgery authorized the holder to engage in any medical activity, specialist or otherwise, and status as a specialist was obtained through constant practice by qualified physicians who performed specialist activities in health institutions, or physicians who had followed a specialist training course at post-graduate level and also those who were actually practising as specialists.[50] This rather chaotic situation came to an end with the promulgation on 20 July 1955 of a Law governing the teaching and practice of, and qualifications needed for, specialist branches of medicine (the law was developed further by the Decree of 23 December 1957). This law created the official degree of Specialist Physician, awarded by the State to graduates in medicine on completion of the appropriate specialist studies and prescribed periods of practical work. These courses were offered in university departments with chairs in the relevant subject or in Ministry of Education-approved specialist institutes or schools and clinics managed by university professors. In all cases, an examination had to be taken at the end of the specialist training.

49. *See* Art. 34.4 Law 44/2003.
50. *See* Rodriguez Pastrana, 'Régimen Jurídico de las especialidades médicas', in *Revista de Administración Pública*, n. 116, 1988, pp. 158 f.

At the same time, alongside the system created by the 1955 law, and in response to the over-growing need for specialist doctors, a special system was being put in place in Social Security institutions.[51] This training system was no longer tied directly to universities, and candidates (interns and resident doctors) were linked to the Social Security by virtue of an employer-employee relationship, as opposed to the teacher-student relationship which operated in universities. Access to this type of training was limited by a *numerus clausus* mechanism and candidates were chosen on the basis of merit and their performance in an examination. On completion of the training, successful candidates were not awarded a degree (Specialist Physician) but rather a certificate attesting the type of specialist training received.

Subsequently, it was decided to adopt a single specialist training system, which was taken out of university hands. The first step in this direction was the passing of Royal Decree 2015/1978 of 15 July, which regulated the awarding of qualifications in specialist branches of medicine,[52] although this was later derogated by RD 127/1984 of 11 January,[53] which regulated specialist training and the awarding of the degree of Specialist Physician. Here again access is limited by a *numerus clausus* mechanism. A maximum quota of candidates for each speciality is established by the MIR system (the Spanish acronym for interns and resident physicians), although exceptional forms of access are permitted for academic staff of Faculties of Medicine.[54]

The medical training system established by RD 127/1984 was considered unsatisfactory by most in medical circles, on the grounds that it prevented free access to the study of specialist subjects, which are limited in number and nature to those offered each year by the State in approved centres. For the access to specialist training, applicants had to pass a nationwide test, which was used to select the candidates who will follow specialist programmes in the various Teaching Centres.[55] The number of places available was made public every year by the Ministry of Education and the Ministry of Health and Consumer Affairs, after consultation with the competent authorities in the Autonomous Communities and with the National Committees of each specialist field.

38. At present, Law 44/2003 recognizes the specialized training in Health Sciences as a regulated and official training that has as a goal to 'provide to the professionals of the knowledge, skills, abilities and attitudes of the corresponding specialization, simultaneously with the gradual assumption by the applicant of the

51. *See* Ministerial Order of 28 Jul. 1971 on Internists and Resident Physicians and Ministerial Order of 9 Dec. 1977, which regulates postgraduate training in Social Security institutions.
52. The Ministerial Order of 11 Feb. 1981 establishes equivalences for specialist branches already in existence prior to the passing of RD 2015/1978 of 15 July and, in order to respect acquired rights, sets up a transitory system for the awarding of specialist qualifications to cater for those who had commenced their training before 1 Jan. 1980.
53. Derogatory Provision Number 1 also derogates the Law of 20 Jul. 1955.
54. The Ministerial Order of 4 Jun. 1987, which develops Art. 18 of RD 127/84, regulates access to the Specialist Physician qualification by physicians who are teaching assistants and tenured medical faculty staff.
55. The Ministerial Order of 30 Nov. 1984 (subsequently extended by the Order of 2 Nov. 1987) established the rules governing selective tests for residents.

inherent responsibility to the autonomous exercise of said specialization'.[56] This new regulation represents the structural reform of the specialized training. Some of the more important news of the current system includes:

(1) The 'system of residence' is conceived as the appropriate procedure for the training in all specialties in health sciences of the bachelor or other university degrees that allow the access to them. In this sense, even those specialties that until now did not have the residence system, must to be removed or modified within five years. This system consists of a programmed and remunerated clinical practice that progressively allows the professional to assume responsibilities while the supervision of his/her activities is reduced.[57] It is important to note that in order to participate in the system of residence (specialized training), the applicant must successfully pass an annual and national selection process. In this respect, the new regulation represents a significant change concerning this selection process, given that the test that applicants must pass is not a simple knowledge test anymore. Such process is composed by a test or a group of tests that aims to evaluate the theoretical and practical knowledge, the clinical and communication skills, as well as, the academic and professional merits of the applicants. The number of vacancies available for this training system is set by the so-called Commission on Human Resources of the National Health System, with the previous reports of the National Council of Specialties in Health Sciences and of the Ministry of Education, Culture and Sport, taking into account the proposals made by the Autonomous Communities, the needs of specialists of health system and the available budget.
(2) It is possible to group the specialties in Health Sciences with core training criteria, with a minimum common training of two years. The 'core', 'trunk' or 'backbone' training could be defined as the common formative period of a group of specialties in Health Sciences, that is based on the acquisition of clinical competences shared by all the specialties that make up the 'trunk' (formed by two or more specialties), and with a minimum duration of two years. With this new system, specialized training comprises two periods: The backbone formative period, in which common competences to all trunk specialties are acquired; and the specific training period, in which the resident will be trained in each specialized skills. It is important to remark that Government must establish which degree/qualification is required in order to access to each speciality.
(3) The 'Areas of Specific Training' are created, as an upper cycle after specialization, within one or more specialties in Health Sciences and based on specific programs and in competence assessment tests.[58] The Certificate of Specific Area of Training (issued by the Ministry of Health, Social Services and Equality) has official character and national validity. This Certificate entitles to its holder to

56. *See* Art. 15 Law 44/2003.
57. Article 20.3 of the Law 44/2003 establishes the criteria governing the training through the system of residence.
58. This definition must be explained in the context of the RD-Law 16/2012 of 20 April, concerning urgent measures to ensure the sustainability of the National Health System and to improve the quality and safety of its services.

use the title of 'specialist in a particular area of specific training', but it is not a requirement to obtain a job (as it is the official qualification of specialist). However, can be valued as a merit to access to a highly specialized work in public or private centres or establishments.

(4) Under the new system were created the 'Diploma of Accreditation' and the 'Diploma of Advanced Accreditation'. Such certifications will allow accreditation training, knowledge or skills to those professionals that, without having obtained the qualification of specialist, direct their GP activity to areas such as aesthetic or acupuncture.

§4. Manpower Planning Freedom of Establishment

39. As was stated earlier, the National Health System devised by the Spanish Constitution is based on the setting up of a public health service. In the words of Rodríguez Pastrana,[59] this merely means that:

> thenceforth the State possesses a legal instrument which allows it to intervene to regulate and control activities. However, in no way is it prejudged that management of the system will be the exclusive prerogative of the State or will be achieved through a state monopoly, directly or indirectly, or that it will coexist alongside private initiative, albeit one which would come under the system's specific regime.

Article 36 of the Constitution provides that 'the law shall regulate specific aspects of the legal regime of Professional Associations and the exercise of professions requiring qualifications … ', although it also acknowledges the freedom to choose one's profession (Article 35.1) and freedom of enterprise in the health sector (Article 38). Moreover, Article 88 and Article 89 and ff. of the LGS recognize both the right to freely practise a health profession and freedom of enterprise, in accordance with constitutional provisions. In short, freedom to engage in professional practice must be guaranteed, although room is made for limitations imposed by constitutional requirements, which aim to protect users of medical services by ensuring that the providers of such services are properly trained. Furthermore, Law 2/1974 of 13 February (subsequently modified by Law 74/1978 of 26 December) which deals with the rules governing professional associations, whose chief task is to regulate the exercise of the professions and defend the professional interests of members (Article 1.3), states that the State shall guarantee the exercise of professions requiring qualifications, in accordance with statutory provisions (Article 2.1).

40. It was stated above that the medical profession is one which requires a professional qualification and is regulated by law. A person may call himself a physician only if he has obtained a Degree in Medicine, on completion of a university course. However, the holding of the degree in itself is not enough to commence practice. Article 35 of the Statutes of the OMC makes registration a compulsory

59. J.M. Rodriguez Pastrana, *El servicio público de la sanidad: el marco constitucional*, p. 31.

requirement for anyone wishing to practise medicine of any form, in both public and private centres. The OMC, which comprises all physicians in professional practice of any kind, either as independent doctors or in the employment of central or local administration, in Autonomous Communities, all public or private entities,[60] requires members to comply with a series of obligations (membership fees, national health insurance, etc.) and to adhere to certain rules of discipline.[61] Specialists must hold the appropriate specialist qualification, regardless of whether they work in the public or private sector.[62]

41. Freedom of enterprise must also be assured in the health sector, and this enables public and private health care to coexist in the sector. The acceptance of the premise that health, under the Spanish Constitution, is a public service necessarily implies that the public administrations are empowered to regulate and control private health sector activities also. However, this cannot be taken to mean that the Administration is the sole body entrusted with health care management. The LGS – which provides for private health services also – presupposes direct management of public health services, although at the same time it contemplates two basic avenues of indirect management, namely, agreements concluded with approved hospitals and other forms of association.

Agreements of this type enable the public administrations to harness outside resources to provide health services. In doing so, they can guarantee assistance and at the same time ensure that the approved centres do not themselves put in place complementary services which would undermine the optimal use of public resources. In concluding agreements with private centres, public administrations must give priority to non-profit making entities, as long as they are competitive with other centres in terms of efficiency, quality and cost (Article 90.2 of the LGS). In all cases, the Administration will carry out the role of inspectorate with regard to

60. Constitutional Court doctrine (particularly ruling 89/1989) endorses the view that compulsory registration with the College is constitutional, even for physicians employed by the Administration. It is not incompatible with freedom of association since, according to ruling 131/1989 of 19 July, which deals specifically with the issue, 'although the professional services are provided under the public service regime or are dependent on a public organisation, the profession of physician is still being exercised, albeit with a compulsory registration requirement imposed by the legislature and the corresponding statutory provisions ... at the end of the day, this circumstance does not modify in any way whatsoever the nature of the activity, which continues to serve the same users. Although it is true that the requirement does involve a restriction on freedom of association, in that a physician is not free *not* to register, it is justified in the light of the general interest at stake in the professional practice of medicine: professional discipline, ethical rules, the good faith of third persons, all of which must be protected in conjunction with the constitutional values and rights of health, health care and the lives and physical integrity of the population'.
61. The General Statutes of the Spanish Medical Colleges Organization (OMC) and of the General Council of Colleagues were passed by RD 1018/1980 of 19 May. Professional practice denotes the provision of medical services of all types, even where the physician does not practise privately or where he does not have his own facilities (Article 35.2 of the Statutes).
62. Article 13 of the General Health Law empowers the government to adopt regulations to prevent illegal practice and malpractice, even though both are covered by Penal Code provision (Art. 403) and administrative sanctions govern professional practice by unregistered physicians and aiding and abetting malpractice (Art. 40.1 and Art. 44 sections b) and m) respectively of the OMC General Statutes).

health, administrative and economic aspects in relation to each patient (Article 94.2 of the LGS).

Private hospitals which are linked to the public sector are virtually placed on an equal footing with their publicly owned counterparts. As Pemán Gavín[63] has pointed out, linking 'brings them under the wing of the public system and helps make their activities better known'. The centres and establishments in question, as well as their services, remain in private hands, although the public administration is responsible for inspections and for all health, administrative and financial controls, just as for any public hospital (Article 66.3 and Article 94.1 of the LGS).

42. The exercise of non-nationals' freedom of establishment and freedom to provide services in Spain is regulated by Royal Decree 1837/2008 of 8 November, which regulates the recognition of diplomas, certificates and other medical and specialist qualifications issued in the States members of the European Union. The provisions were drawn up in response to the need to incorporate various EC directives on the subject into Spanish legislation.[64] Also, we must remark that the RD 459/2010 of 16 April, regulates the conditions for recognizing professional effects to the foreign qualifications of Specialist in Health Sciences obtained in a country which is not a member of the European Union.

63. *See* Pemán Gavín, *Derecho a la salud y Administratión Sanitaria*, p. 213.

64. *See* Directive 2005/36/EC of the European Parliament and of the Council, of 7 Sep. 2005, and Directive 2006/100/EC of the Council, of 20 Nov. 2006, concerning the recognition of professional qualifications, as well as certain aspects of the exercise of the legal profession.

Chapter 2. Illegal Practice of Medicine

43. In the previous chapter we described the procedure for access to the medical profession. To recap briefly, it is necessary first to have completed university studies leading to obtain the Qualification of 'Bachelor' or the Qualification of 'Graduate' in Medicine which is awarded by Faculties of Medicine; it is also compulsory to register with the College of Physicians (Colegio Oficial de Médicos) in the intended area of practice:[65] furthermore, specialists must hold the appropriate diplomas accrediting that they have completed the relevant studies and practical work enabling them to call themselves specialists and seek employment as such in all private or public centres;[66] this means that although all graduates in medicine may practice any branch of medicine, no one may use the title of specialist (or take up such a position) unless he holds that appropriate qualification. The profession may be practised only when the above-mentioned legal requirements have been met. All the above make up the exclusive rights of professional practice which is conferred on physicians in view of the high degree of qualification required and the subsequent penal protection afforded to the profession to prevent practice by non-members or non-qualified practitioners.

Illegal practice can indeed constitute an offence of encroachment and is punished by Spain's Penal Code (Article 403, governing the offence of usurpation of functions):

> 1. Any person who practices a profession without holding the corresponding academic qualification, issued or recognised in Spain according to the current law, shall be liable to a fine between twelve and twenty four months. If the professional activity requires an official qualification that certifies the necessary training and that legally authorize to its bearer for its exercise, a fine between six and twelve months will be imposed to any person who practices such activity without holding the aforementioned qualification. 2. A prison sentence of six months to two years shall be imposed if concurs any of the following circumstances: a) When the offender, in addition, publicly confers himself the quality of professional certified by the alluded qualification. b) When the offender executes the acts described in the preceding paragraph in a local or establishment open to the public in which the provision of services of that profession is announced.

It is generally held[67] that persons who commit such an offence harm various interests which have repercussions on society as a whole. The most important of these

---

65. RD 1018/1980 of 19 May, governing the Statutes of the Organisation of Colleges of Physicians and the General Council of Colleges of Physicians, stipulates in Art. 35 that it is compulsory for physicians to register with the College in order to practice any form of medicine, including where the physician does not practise privately or does not have his own surgery.
66. *See* Arts 1 and 3 of the RD 183/2008 of 8 February, which determine and classify the specialties in Health Sciences and certain aspects of specialized health training system are developed.
67. J. Montero García-Andrade, 'Comentario al Artículo 403', in *Código penal comentado. Comentarios tras las Leyes Orgánicas 1/2015 y 2/2015, de 30 de marzo*, A. Roma Valdés (Director), Bosch, Barcelona, 2015, pp. 653 ff.; P. Lloria García, 'Intrusismo', in *Enciclopedia de Bioderecho y*

is the requirement concerning academic qualifications as a means of ensuring correct professional practice; the State endorses the validity of these qualifications in that it, and it alone, is empowered to award them. On a second level lies the collective interest of the profession concerned, which must ensure that professional practice is limited exclusively to those who can provide the necessary guarantees in the form of the recognized qualification. This exclusive right of practice means also that users (in this case, patients) will receive the services of a qualified professional, although it should be said that an unauthorized person who has provided satisfactory services and has cured the patient's illness will still nevertheless have committed an offence.

44. For an offence to exist the following requirements must be fulfilled:

(1) An offence is committed only where the profession – such as medicine – which is practiced illegally requires an academic qualification (notwithstanding the fact that the Penal Code refers to an 'official' qualification, which is a much broader term).[68] Alternatively, the qualification may be one which is recognized in Spain according to the current law, which affects in particular physicians or specialists (both Spanish and non-Spanish) who have obtained their professional qualification abroad.

(2) The offender must perform actions proper to the profession of physician as stipulated in the regulations governing medical practice (see Chapter 1 of this Part). No encroachment takes place where a patient treats himself or is aided by a relative, under the guidance of a physician. This is an important point given the increasing frequency with which patients, particularly the chronically ill, treat themselves at home (diabetics who administer their own insulin injections, patients with terminal renal insufficiency who receive dialysis in their own home, patients with respiratory problems who give themselves oxygen, etc.). The offence does not exist either in the case of charlatans (quacks) as long as they do not undertake operations or administer products (e.g., prescribe drugs) which may only be given by physicians.[69] This does not mean, however, that such persons are exonerated from liability in respect of possible injuries they might cause to their patients or where the latter's condition seriously worsens as a result of being prevented from seeking the assistance of a qualified practitioner. The charging of a fee is not an indispensable requirement of illegal

---

Bioética, Tomo II, C.M. Romeo-Casabona (Director) (Comares, Granada 2011), pp. 1018–1020; G. Rodriguez Mourullo, 'El delito de intrusismo', in *Revista General de Legislación y Jurisprudencia*, 1969, pp. 235 ff.; D.M. Luzon Peña, 'Problemas del intrusismo en el Derecho penal', in *La Ley*, 1985, pp. 1257 ff.; A. Serrano Gómez, 'El intrusismo en la Odontología, in *Actualidad Penal*, 1988, p. 1067.

68. P. Lloria García, "Intrusismo", p. 1020; D.M. Luzon Peña, 'El título académico oficial en el delito de intrusismo', in *La Ley*, 1989, pp. 497 ff. Ruling of Supreme Court (2nd Chamber), 6 Jun. 1989 (for a ruling in the opposite sense, i.e., not putting official qualification on an equal footing with an academic one, *see* Ruling of Supreme Court (2nd Chamber), 13 May 1989).

69. The Supreme Court has on occasions punished such acts (where medicines have been prescribed: Ruling (2nd Chamber) of 18 Oct. 1978; and also in the case of a person who ran a Natural Medicine Surgery using the professional title of Dr in Naturopathy and Diet Counsellor: Ruling (2nd Chamber) of 23 Jan. 1984).

practice,[70] although exceptionally any such charge may mean that the impersonator is guilty of fraud (e.g., if he deceives the patient by leading him to believe in the treatment, when in fact it will not cure him at all or has little bearing on the nature of the problem being treated).

(3) There is debate as to whether one single action of the type mentioned above is in itself sufficient to constitute an offence or whether several are required. Although it is widely held that one single action suffices (except where the very nature of the profession or its regulations requires something more habitual),[71] we are of the opinion that professional practice in general is characterized by repetition with various persons, and thus the activity deemed to constitute illegal practice must comprise several acts, at least in the case of medicine. Habitualness or repeated actions of the type mentioned above shall give rise to one offence only.

(4) Encroachment may only be committed intentionally and thus it cannot stem from negligence, although this does not rule out a legal appraisal of the conduct of someone who mistakenly believes that he can carry out professional acts without the appropriate qualifications.

45. Any person who practices illegally in this way and, in addition, publicly confers himself the quality of professional certified by the alluded qualification shall be guilty of a more serious offence (Article 403, paragraph 2.a) of the Penal Code). For this aggravated offence to exist it is not sufficient for the offender to pass himself off as a qualified practitioner in the presence of one or more patients, but rather – and in addition to actions of encroachment – he must also make others believe that he holds the status in question. It is important to note that same punishment will be imposed when the offender executes the acts in a local or establishment open to the public in which the provision of services of that profession is announced (Art. 403, paragraph 2.c) of the Penal Code).

46. The offence of encroachment may be concurrent with other offences: if, during the course of unlawful practice, harm is caused to a patient's health or life, because the treatment is inadequate due to the offender's lack of professional training, the person may be liable also for an offence of recklessness leading to homicide or bodily injury;[72] or of forgery of documents (academic or degree certificates);[73] and also, as has been mentioned above, in exceptional circumstances fraud.

47. A physician who fails to register with the College of Physicians, that is, a qualified practitioner who practises without first having registered with the appropriate association or body, where such a requirement is mandatory, shall be guilty of an administrative misconduct (minor administrative offence) and liable to a fine

70. *See* Ruling of Supreme Court (2nd Chamber) of 1 Dec. 1970.
71. P. Lloria García, 'Intrusismo', p. 1023; Rodriguez Mourullo, 'El delito de intrusismo', pp. 259 ff.; Supreme Court Rulings (2nd Chamber) of 1 Dec. 1970 and 19 Jun. 1990.
72. Ruling of the Barcelona Provincial Court of 6 Feb. 1990, by which a nurse was found guilty of professional recklessness, although she was cleared of charges of illegal practice.
73. Supreme Court Ruling of 2 Oct. 1990 (forgery of official document, Art. 303 of former Penal Code).

according to the RD 1018/1980 of 19 May, governing the Statutes of the Organisation of Colleges of Physicians and the General Council of Colleges of Physicians.[74]

48. Spanish courts have had to deal frequently with cases of illegal medical practice and have used the full weight of this criminal offence to punish such acts, whether by professionals of lower rank (nurses, for example)[75] who have impersonated physicians, or by persons who have no connections whatsoever with the health care professions.[76] Dentistry has traditionally been the field to suffer most from encroachment. Although case law includes clear examples which constitute illegal practice of dentistry, such as when a dental technician undertakes implants or other activities proper to a qualified dentist,[77] or where such practices are undertaken by members of the nursing profession,[78] we would question the conviction of a graduate in medicine who does not hold the appropriate qualification required for dental practice, merely because he has habitually practised the speciality although without passing himself off as, or attributing to himself the status of, a qualified dentist, which is the only offence that is expressly prohibited, as was stated above.[79] The Supreme Court (2nd Chamber) ruled that an offence is committed by a medical graduate who, although not holding a qualification in dentistry, engages in habitual practice, but *not* when he does so occasionally and in special circumstances which justify his action, depending on the specific case.[80]

Other health care professions, such as nursing,[81] have fallen foul of illegal practice by persons who do not have the necessary training or qualifications.

To sum up, illegal practice (called literally impersonation or encroachment in Spanish) is an offence which may be committed by laypersons, by persons with no connections whatsoever with the profession, but also by health professionals whose qualifications are insufficient to entitle them to perform such activities. It may even be committed by physicians who do not hold the relevant specialist qualification.[82]

---

74. *See* Art. 40.
75. Ruling of Supreme Court (2nd Chamber) of 8 Mar. 1968.
76. The aforementioned rulings of the Supreme Court of 18 Oct. 1978 and 23 Jan. 1984.
77. Rulings of Supreme Court (2nd Chamber) of 26 Feb. 1981, 25 Sep. 1987, 11 Apr. 1989, 29 Jun. 1991; Lérida Provincial Court Ruling of 3 Feb. 1990. Law of 17 Mar. 1986, which regulates dental health professions, list the competences of dental technicians as the design, elaboration, making and repair of dental apparatus using products, materials and techniques as indicated and prescribed by dentists. (Art. 1.2).
78. Rulings of Supreme Court (2nd Chamber) of 8 Mar. 1968, 18 Oct. 1969; (3rd Chamber) 11 Oct. 1991 (competence to hire a nurse to take blood and carry out analytical tests on council premises).
79. The view is shared by Serrano Gómez, 'El intrusismo en la Odontología', p. 1068.
80. Ruling of Supreme Court (2nd Chamber) of 13 Jun. 1990 (although the verdict was that an offence had been committed, the accused was cleared because in the court's opinion he had unwittingly committed an unavoidable error due to the incorrect legal guidance given by the College of Physicians on a somewhat 'grey' issue (to use the Court's expression); Ruling of 12 Mar. 1990 (dismissing possible error on the part of the physician), 21 Jun. 1991. A previous ruling, using different arguments, had been given by the Supreme Court (2nd Chamber) on 18 Oct. 1969.
81. For example, in Ruling of Supreme Court (2nd Chamber) of 28 Mar. 1980.
82. C.M. Romeo-Casabona, *El Médico ante el Derecho* (Serv. Public. del Ministerio de Sanidad y Consumo, Madrid 1985, 3d. repr. 1990), p. 5.

Chapter 3. Control over the Practice of Medicine

§1. The Order of Physicians

I. Legal Framework and General Competences

49. In view of the importance of medicine in the community and the complex nature of medical services, the Administration has sought to reserve medical professional activity for those who are highly qualified both technically and scientifically.[83] Elsewhere we have discussed the fact that the position of physician or specialist can only be attained on completion of the relevant degree course in General Medicine or in the specialist field. The State has the exclusive right to issue such degree certificates, thus providing a guarantee that holders are qualified to provide medical services. However, the medical profession makes a further demand: it is not enough to simply guarantee that those who are admitted to the profession are properly qualified, it is also essential to ensure that medical practitioners perform their duties in accordance with the shared interests of the profession, thus establishing a kind of self-imposed control of the medical profession. The Spanish Constitution reflects this in its recognition of the value of professional associations for such purposes, stating in Art. 36 that 'the law shall regulate the specific legal attributes of Professional Colleges. The internal structure and procedures of the Colleges must be democratic'.[84] The Professional Colleges Law of 1974 ('Ley General de Colegios Profesionales'), which is the basic corpus of regulations in this respect, had to be revised to bring it into line with constitutional provisions, particularly with regard to the democratic processes required of Colleges.[85] Legal exercise of the medical profession is subject to prior membership of a College.[86] Membership is compulsory,[87] as it is in other professional fields, and although this is the subject of

83. *See* Romeo-Casabona, *El médico ante el Derecho*, p. 5: 'Medicine has extended its scope considerably and at the same time has at its disposal a wide range of increasingly efficient and sophisticated procedures and techniques. This situation in turn makes it essential that doctors possess a body of knowledge and technical skill that is also constantly expanding. As a result, a greater degree of specialization, with the accompanying depth of knowledge of this narrower field, is demanded … Trough this radical process Medicine has become a complex and interdependent activity.'
84. This is perhaps the constitutional provision of greatest relevance to professional colleges, although reference to them is also made in Arts 52 and 26. Art. 52 sets out that 'the law shall regulate professional organisations that defend their own economic interests. Their internal structure and procedures must be democratic'. And in Art. 26: 'Honorary tribunals are prohibited in the area of civil administration and professional organisations'.
85. This was accomplished through Law 74/1978 of 26 December.
86. Following a certain amount of doubt in the past as to whether membership of a college should be compulsory or not, clause 34 of the Law which established the bases of the National Health Service (1944) stated that it was indeed compulsory for physicians. *See* Art. 35. 1 of the RD 1018/1980 of 19 May, which passed the General Statutes of the OMC, in relation to Art. 3.2 of Law 2/1974 of 13 February, on Professional Colleges. Failure to comply with this obligation may be viewed as constituting illegal practice and give rise to criminal liability.
87. Aside from the obligation to register with a College, and with the appropriate social security scheme, there is also a right to join a College if one holds the necessary degree and meets all the other conditions are satisfied (Art. 3.1 of the Professional Colleges Law). The right to join a medical college

no small amount of controversy in a wide range of professions, it provides a guarantee for the public and relieves them of the responsibility of establishing whether or not the person performing a medical act does indeed hold the appropriate qualifications for professional practice. Furthermore, it provides an efficient means for members to defend their professional interests against inappropriate, unethical and illegal practice.

50. From the organizational point of view, aside from the above-mentioned law on professional bodies, medical practice is regulated by the Statutes governing the Organisation of Colleges of Physician and the General Council of Colleges of Physicians, as passed by Royal Decree 1018/1980 of 19 March, which repealed the previous Regulations dating back to 1 April 1967. Nowadays, the in force regulation of the Statutes Governing the General Council of Colleges of Physicians is the one set up by Royal Decree 757/2006, of 16 June (which repealed in this specific point the RD 1018/1980 of 19 March). The system is made up of the provincial Colleges of Physicians, Associations of Colleges of Physicians and the General Council of Colleges of Physicians, which constitute the organs of representation and the governing body of the Organisation of Colleges of Physicians (known by its acronym in Spanish, OMC). With the exception of the Associations of Colleges of Physicians, these bodies are corporations which are governed by public law and endowed with their own legal personality and full capacity to achieve their aims.[88]

51. The *Organization of Colleges of Physicians* brings together all physicians who carry out professional activity of any type, whether independently or in the service of the Public Administration or private institutions. It is the sole representative body of the medical profession, with exclusive responsibility for the regulation of medical practice within its area of jurisdiction and the defence of professional interests (Article 1.4 of the General Statutes of the OMC). The fundamental aims of the OMC, according to Article 3 General Statutes of the OMC, are as follows:

(1) The regulation, within its jurisdiction, of medical practice; exclusive representation of physicians and the defence of the professional interests of its members, without prejudice to the powers and responsibilities of the Public Administration in respect of physicians who are public servants.
(2) The safeguarding and observance of the deontological and ethical principles of the medical profession, as well as its dignity and prestige, through the drawing up and application of the relevant codes of practice.
(3) The promotion, by all available means, of the continuing scientific, educational, economic and social development of members through the organization and maintenance of all kinds of educational institutions and the taking of all appropriate measures to ensure adequate social protection for members.

---

cannot be denied – except in those cases established by the General Statutes of the OMC (Art. 38) – which means that the right to practise a profession is guaranteed (Art. 35 of the Constitution).

88. *See* Art. 1 of the General Statutes of the OMC and Art. 1 of the Professional Colleges Law.

(4) Co-operation with the public authorities in the provision of health care services, to which all Spanish citizens are entitled, and of the most efficient, just and equitable regulation of health care services and medical practice, as stipulated by the Professional Colleges Law.

52. The provincial *Colleges of Physicians* are the key element in the organization of medical practice.[89] Article 4.3 of the Professional Colleges Law prohibits the creation of any other college for the same profession within the limits of the territory concerned. Even so, each College may divide its provincial territories into districts, headed by a district council elected by the members in the area to perform the executive functions delegated by the College Board (Article 29 of the General Statutes of the OMC). Among the powers and duties of the Colleges of Physicians, apart from those specifically stipulated in their individual statutes, are the following (Article 34 of the General Statutes of the OMC):

(1) Responsibility for the representation of physicians before provincial authorities and institutions.
(2) The defence of the rights and prestige of the members they represent, or any other member, if they are subjected to harassment, injury, lack of consideration or disregard in professional matters, so long as any such situation occurs within the province. The College is also responsible for reporting instances of illegal practice piracy.
(3) The keeping of a list of members, a register of professional qualifications and a list of medical districts in the province. They are also responsible for the gathering of statistics necessary for the carrying out of studies, projects and proposals concerning medical practice.
(4) The application of the rules of ethics governing medical practice.
(5) The taking of disciplinary action in cases of unfair competition, breaches of ethics and abuse of professional status as a physician. Colleges are also responsible for the implementation of disciplinary measures.
(6) The study of the financial relationship between physicians and their clients and, where appropriate, the power to discipline members whose actions might undermine the dignity of the profession in this respect.
(7) Regulation of the minimum fees for private practice. Colleges shall also express an opinion in fee-setting procedures and shall defend the interests of the medical profession before the Administration, Institutions Courts, Organizations and private individuals in accordance with the current provisions.
(8) Responsibility for the collection of professional fees and charges.
(9) Co-operation with the public authorities in the formulation of health care policy and planning and implementation thereof, as well as participation in all matters relating to health promotion and health care.
(10) The development and implementation of general and scientific educational programmes to complement those envisaged under the Plan drawn up by the General Council.

89. There are also Colleges in Ceuta and Melilla, to which the Statutes of the OMC apply. Their jurisdiction is limited to the respective municipal areas.

(11) The development and administration of services and institutions to ensure adequate social security cover and other forms of professional cover for members.
(12) Raise the revenues needed to fund these institutions.
(13) Encourage public or private bodies to provide to the collegiate (medical practitioners) for their professional practice a minimum of material and personnel necessary to perform quality medicine.[90]

Each College must have an Ethics, Medical Law and Authorisations Committee. Furthermore, professional interests are most efficiently served by the setting up within the Colleges of specific Sections that bring together members working in the same professional area and with the same professional concerns. These Sections are responsible for matters relating to the specialist field concerned and for presenting studies and proposals to the college bodies. A certain number of sections are obligatory,[91] although others may be created in the interests of the college concerned and in accordance with its statutes.

The governing bodies of the Colleges are the Board and the General Assembly of Members. The Board consists of a Plenary and a Standing Committee. Among other powers and responsibilities, it can take disciplinary action within its area of jurisdiction. For its part, the General Assembly is the College's highest representative body at provincial level[92] and comprises the total membership of the college. The Board is accountable to the General Assembly.

The financial running of the Colleges is independent of the General Council. They are autonomous in terms of the management and administration of their financial affairs. Each provincial college draws up an annual budget that has to be approved by the Assembly. College funds come from initial registration fees, the ordinary and extraordinary membership fees paid by members,[93] and a percentage of fees charged for the issuing of certificates, official stamps, official forms, medical assessments, etc.

53. Associations of Colleges of Physicians, which occupy a middle ground between the Colleges themselves and the General Council, are designed to coordinate and represent the Provincial Colleges and are governed by their own statutes.

---

90. *See* Arts 33 and 34 of the General Statutes of the OMC.
91. Article 27 of the General Statutes of the OMC stipulates that the following sections are obligatory: Head Physicians, Rural Medicine, Hospital Physicians, Social Security Outpatients' Physicians, Physicians in group practices, Physicians in private practice, Recent graduates (those who have graduated in the last five years and/or are still following a course of training) and Retired Physicians.
92. Agreements adopted by the General Assembly are binding on all college members. Nevertheless, in Colleges with more than 500 members, or where specific provision has been made in the statutes of the College concerned, and in all cases where there are more than 2000 members, the Assembly may delegate its functions to an Assembly of Delegates elected by personal vote in a secret ballot of all members.
93. In addition to the registration fee payable on joining, members must pay monthly subscriptions, the minimum level of which is set by the General Council. These amounts may be increased by the individual Colleges subject to approval by the General Assembly (Arts 50, 51 and 52 of the General Statutes of the OMC).

Responsibility for representation falls obligatorily on one of the presidents of the Colleges making up the Association. The Associations carry out whatever functions the General Council delegates to them.[94]

54. The General Council of Colleges of Physicians is the body that brings together, co-ordinates and represents all the provincial Colleges of Physicians in Spain. It is composed of the General Assembly,[95] a Plenary and a Standing Committee, as well as an advisory body (Deontology, Medical Law and Authorisation Committee).[96] The Council is charged with the representation and defence of the legitimate aspirations of the medical profession, ethical guidance and control of professional practice, social, cultural and professional development and the promotion of the right to health. Among its most important functions are the drafting of the General Statutes of the Colleges, the passing of internal college regulations, the taking of disciplinary action against members of College Boards and of the Council itself, the drawing up of binding ethical rules to govern the medical profession and the application and interpretation of such rules with a view to full and consistent compliance. The Council also handles and resolves appeals against Colleges presented by members, and sets minimum charges for private practice, etc.[97]

55. The democratic structure and workings of professional bodies imposed by the Constitution is reflected in the extensive regulations governing voting procedures for the election of office bearers, length of period of office and the causes of dismissal, conditions of eligibility and candidacies. The OMC also has disciplinary regulations applicable to members who commit any of the offences set out in the Statutes, be they minor, serious or highly serious, as well as the corresponding penalties, which may take the form of a private reprimand, an official warning, temporary suspension from practice or expulsion from the College (Articles 63–68 of the General Statutes of the OMC). Notwithstanding Article 63.2 of the General Statutes of the OMC, which states that disciplinary responsibility is not to be understood as exempting members from liability of any other type that they might incur, the doctrine of the Constitutional Court with regard to breaches of the *non bis in idem* principle should be taken into account.

56. The fact that all practising physicians must register with a College does not preclude freedom of association in the context of a trade union organization. Although the trade union movement is not normally associated with this kind of profession (or rather it has not been associated with it historically), recently doctors

94. The Associations' jurisdiction must correspond to the territorial organisation of the Spanish State (Art. 4 of the General Statutes of the OMC). If the Colleges of Physicians are provincial and the General Council's powers cover the entire country, it follows that the Associations should have as their jurisdiction the Autonomous Communities, although it might be argued that they have an area of jurisdiction smaller than the Autonomous Community, but larger than the province.
95. The General Assembly is the highest organ of government of the Council and is made up of the presidents of all the official Colleges of Physicians, as well as national representatives of the obligatory Sections and other persons (president of the Council, Vice-president, general secretary, etc.).
96. Article 26 of the RD 757/2006, of 16 June.
97. *See* the more extensive provisions of Art. 9 of RD 757/2006, of 16 June (Art. 2).

have become extremely active in trade union relations as a result, chiefly because they more and more are gradually moving from what was traditionally independent practice towards salaried or civil service positions. Physicians' demands are therefore falling more within the realm of labour relations than the general framework of medical practice. We will not go into a detailed discussion of the ideological principles of each association, but will merely make passing reference to the trade unions which currently cater for physicians: CESM (Confederación Estatal Sindicatos Médicos), CCOO (Comisiones Obreras), UGT (Unión General de Trabajadores) and CSIF-Sanidad (Central Sindical Independiente y de Funcionarios-Sector Sanidad).

II. Professional Duties Towards Colleagues

57. The notions of 'fraternity' and 'loyalty' describe well the way in which members should conduct themselves towards colleagues, both in the exercise of the profession and in other areas. This involves not only the expectation that they will bring prestige and dignity to the profession, but that they will treat with respect those who receive medical treatment, i.e., patients. Patients should not be subjected to doctors casting aspersions on the morals or scientific abilities of a colleague in order to (for example) attract the latter's clients. A special ethical principle prevents a doctor from suffering moral, professional or economic harm as a result of the activities of a colleague. Legal and ethical endorsement for the manner in which physicians should behave towards one another can be found in the Professional Colleges Law, the OMC Statutes and also in the Code of Medical Deontology (2011).[98]

58. Among the functions attributed to them under the Professional Colleges Law, colleges must 'achieve harmony and cooperation among members and prevent unfair competition' (Article 5 k). This is undoubtedly the physician's chief duty towards colleagues, since unfair competition, for example, does not only imply unfairly taking a patient from a colleague or depriving him of the resultant earnings or prestige, but also poses a threat to the patients' dignity and health. The General Statutes of the OMC (RD 1018/1980) oblige members to 'maintain the utmost *loyalty* in relations with the College and fellow members by notifying the College of knowledge of any ill-treatment or abuse suffered by a colleague in the exercise of his/her profession'.[99] What underlies this precept is the notion of *solidarity* and

98. In this way, apart from the relevant legal regulations, traditionally physicians have drawn up their own codes and regulations for ethical professional practice. In the Code of Medical Ethics the issue of professional conduct towards colleagues has not been overlooked. Chapter eight of the Code of 2011 devotes five lengthy articles (Arts 37–42) to relationships between physicians.

99. This meaning is conveyed in Art. 37 of the Code of Medical Deontology (2011), which reads as follows: '1. Co*fraternity* among physicians is a primordial duty and only the rights of the patient have priority over this duty. 2. Physicians must treat one another with due deference, respect and loyalty, whatever the hierarchical relationship between them (…)'. Art. 38.4 also states that 'a doctor who informs his/her college with due discretion of breaches of the rules of medical ethics or professional competence committed by a colleague shall not be deemed to have failed to comply with the duty of cofraternity.'

mutual support that must govern the actions of physicians with regard to their peers.[100]

Duties are also laid down in connection with self-protection of the profession and of medical ethics in relation to activities of members that might encourage illegal practice by third parties. Therefore, one of the functions of professional colleges is to 'adopt whatever measures are necessary to prevent illegal practice' (Article 5.l of the Professional Colleges Law). Similarly, the General Statutes of the OMC, for the same reasons, prohibit members from 'tolerating or abetting a person who does not hold a degree in medicine and who attempts to practice the profession' (Article 44 b), and also 'allowing their surgeries to be used by persons who, while they may be graduates in medicine, have not registered with the appropriate College of Physicians' (Article 44 m).

Other ethical duties apply to medical care and scientific matters. The Code of Medical Deontology (2011) restrains a physician from interfering in the treatment of another physician's patient, except in emergencies or at the specific request of the patient (Article 39.1). It also states that scientific, professional or deontological disputes between doctors should be resolved through the appropriate channels and should not become a focus of public controversy (Article 38.3 Code of Medical Deontology). In this regard, Colleges of Physicians may also 'intervene to achieve agreement or arbitration on questions of a professional nature that may arise between members'.[101]

III. Disciplinary Competences

59. Once again we must begin by turning to the Constitution and in particular Article 36 which states that 'The Law shall regulate specific aspects of the legal regime of professional bodies and the practice of professions for which a qualification is required. The internal structure and the functioning of such bodies must be democratic.'

60. This constitutional formula led to the drafting of the Code of Medical Ethics, endorsed by the Ministry of Health and Social Security on 23 April 1979, which put an end to the vacuum created by the reorganization of professional bodies in 1967, when the ethical rules governing the medical profession in Spain contained in the annex to the 1945 Statute were derogated.[102]

In 1990, a new Code of Medical Ethics and Deontology was unveiled. This Code, tailored to take account of the reports submitted by the Ethics Committee of the Organisation of Colleges of Physicians and the European Medical Guide, consisted of forty-four articles and one further concluding article.

Finally, in 2011 the presently in force Code of Medical Deontology was unveiled. Divided into twenty-one Chapters and sixty-six articles one additional disposition

100. The Code of Medical Deontology expresses it thus in Art. 37.2: 'they have the duty to defend a colleague who is the victim of unjust attack or accusations'.
101. Article 5 m) of the Professional Colleges Law.
102. C. Segura & L. Martínez Calcerrada, *Derecho Médico 1* (Tecnos, Madrid 1986), p. 59.

and a final disposition, it laid down, among other aspects, the general principles which should guide professional practice (Chapter II), physician-patient relations (Chapter III), health care quality (Chapter IV), professional secrecy (Chapter V), conscientious objection (Chapter VI), medical care at the end of life (Chapter VII), relations between physicians and with other health professionals (Chapter VIII), relations with the College of Physicians (Chapter IX), work in health institutions (Chapter X), organ transplants (Chapter XI), human reproduction (Chapter XII), genetic tests (Chapter XIII), biomedical research on human beings (Chapter XIV), torture and abuse of the person (Chapter XV), sports doping (Chapter XVI), medical expertise's (Chapter XVII), teaching in medicine (Chapter XVIII), professional publications (Chapter XIX), medical advertising (Chapter XX), economy and fees (Chapter XXI). Among the main contributions of the code of deontology the following ones should be emphasized: safety, respect, humanism, responsible and ethical behaviour by the professional on the basis of a changing social reality. It stands, therefore, as the main guarantor on the hand of the Colleges of Physicians, of increased competition and better performance by the medical professionals.

61. Mention should also be made of the General Statutes of the Organisation of Colleges of Physicians (Organización Médica Colegial – OMC) were approved by Royal Decree 1018/80 of 19 May 1980. The General Statutes of the General Council of Colleges of Physicians were set up by Royal Decree 757/2006, of 16 June.
Article 3 of the General Statutes of the former (RD 1018/1980) states that the Organization's fundamental goals are to:

(2) Safeguard and observe the ethical and social principles of the medical profession, as well as its dignity and prestige. To that end it shall draw up and apply the appropriate Codes.
(4) Collaborate with the authorities in giving effect to the right of all Spaniards to protection of their health and to the most efficient, just and fair regulation possible of health care and the practice of medicine, as well as to all the rights contained in the Law governing Professional Associations.

Article 31 RD 1018/1980 lists among the General Council's general powers the exercise of the functions set out in the Council's own rules and regulations in relation to the aims attributed to it under Article 3 of the Statutes and the Professional Colleges Law. Specific competences are outlined in Article 32:

(1) Ethics: supervision of professional practice. Control over professional publicity of media information with reference to the profession, which might prove harmful to public health or to the legitimate interests, traditional prestige and dignity of the medical profession.

The General Statutes also provide for the setting up within the General Council of a Central Committee on Ethics, Medical Law and Authorisations to advise the Council on all matters relating to its sphere of competence, to report on appeals lodged with the Council against decisions of Colleges on such matters and to handle all correspondence with the Administration on the above issues.

Article 33 and Article 34 RD 1018/1980 set out the competences of the provincial Colleges, which are charged with the application of ethical rules governing medical practice (Article 34 d); it is their job also to ensure that registered member comply with their professional ethical and legal obligations (Article 34 e); to take disciplinary action against members who engage in unfair competition, or who breach ethical rules or abuse their position as practitioners (Article 34 f); to study the financial relationship between physicians and their clients and, where appropriate, take disciplinary action against members whose actions may undermine the prestige of the profession in this respect (Article 34 h).

Title VIII of the General Statutes of the OMC deals specifically with Rules of Discipline, the general principles of which are given in Article 63:

(1) Members shall be liable to disciplinary action in the cases and circumstances set forth in the present Statutes.
(2) The rules of discipline contained in the present Statutes do not exempt members from liability of any other type in which they may incur.
(3) Disciplinary measures may only be taken after the setting up of an enquiry to examine the case in question and in accordance with the procedure laid down in the present chapter. However, in cases involving minor infringements and following a hearing of the member concerned, action may be taken without a specific enquiry.
(4) The power to impose disciplinary measures lies with the Boards of the Colleges of Physicians. However, the appraisal and punishment of breaches of discipline committed by Board members shall be entrusted to the Assembly of College Presidents.
(5) Any disciplinary action agreed upon shall be enforced with immediate effect, although decisions may be appealed. However, where enforcement might lead to irreparable or virtually irreparable harm, the body concerned may of its own initiative or at the request of the party concerned suspend the action against which the appeal has been lodged.
(6) Colleges shall notify immediately the General Council of all disciplinary action taken in respect of serious or highly serious offences, and shall forward an extract of the file of enquiry. The General Council shall keep a register of action taken.

Breaches of discipline are described in Article 64 RD 1018/1980 and are classified as minor, less serious, serious and highly serious:

(1) Minor misdemeanours:
    (a) Non-compliance with regulations governing College documentation or documents which must be processed by the College.
    (b) Failure to inform the College of changes affecting professional status, etc., which must be recorded in the member's personal record.
    (c) Failure to heed College requirements or to submit reports when so requested by the College.

(2) Less serious offences:
   (a) Failure to provide a certificate or information where provision does not entail risk to the patient.
   (b) Passing oneself off as having a qualification or competence when this is not the case.
   (c) Failure to submit contracts for College approval.
   (d) Manifest abuse in billing for services or charging a fee below the minimum stipulated fee.
   (e) Persisting in the commission of minor misdemeanours during a period of one year after being disciplined for such offences.

(3) Serious offences:
   (a) Deliberate and rebellious lack of discipline towards College governing bodies and, in general, serious disrespect towards the latter.
   (b) Acts and omissions which undermine the morals, decorum, dignity, prestige and honour of the profession or which entail disrespect towards members.
   (c) Serious intentional or negligent breaches of professional secrecy resulting in harm to third persons.
   (d) Non-compliance with rules governing the restricted use of drugs and the exploitation of drug addiction for personal gain.
   (e) The issuing of reports or certificates known to be false.
   (f) Persisting in the commission of less serious offences during a period of one year after being disciplined for such offences.

(4) Highly serious offences:
   (a) All conducts constituting offences of intent, within the field of the profession.
   (b) Intentional violation of professional secrecy.
   (c) Attacks on the dignity of persons in the course of professional practice.
   (d) Malicious or intentional neglect of patients.
   (e) Persisting in the commission of serious offences during a period of one year after being disciplined for such offences.

The article adds also that:

> failure to comply with the duties set out in Article 43 of the present Statutes, violation of any of the prohibitions laid down in Article 44 or non-compliance with the rules contained in the Code of Ethics, which are not covered by numbers (1), (2), (3) and (4) above, shall be adjudged in the light of the similarity of the offence with those listed above. In all cases, the Ethics Committee shall be heard before any disciplinary action is taken.

Still on matters of discipline, Article 65 RD 1018/1980 states as follows:

(1) The following measures may be taken in respect of disciplinary offences covered by the previous article:
   (a) Private caution.
   (b) Official caution.
   (c) Temporary suspension from professional practice.

(d) Expulsion from the College of Physicians.

(2) Minor misdemeanours shall give rise to a private caution by agreement of the Board.

(3) Official warnings shall be given in respect of less serious offences.

(4) Serious offences shall be punishable by temporary suspension from practice for a period not exceeding one year.

(5) Highly serious offences shall be punishable by temporary suspension from practice for a period of between one and two years.

(6) Any member who is expelled from a College shall be barred from registering with another unless expressly authorized by the General Council. This punishment is applicable only where a member persists in the commission of highly serious offences. The decision to expel a member shall be taken by the Plenary Meeting of the Board, at which at least two thirds of Board members must be in attendance. At least half of those in attendance must vote in favour of expulsion.

(7) In taking disciplinary action Colleges shall assess the responsibility of the accused in relation to the nature of the offence committed, as well as the importance of the offence committed and any other factors which might alter said responsibility. Where more than one punishment is laid down for each offence, the College is empowered to take the action it feels to be most appropriate.

(8) Highly serious offences which affect the general interest may be reported in College publications.

Article 66 RD 1018/1980 governing the expiry of disciplinary liability reads as follows:

(1) Disciplinary liability shall expire:
  (a) On the death of the accused.
  (b) When the member complies with the disciplinary action taken.
  (c) On prescription of the offence(s).
  (d) On prescription of the disciplinary action, or by agreement of the College concerned, which shall be ratified by the General Council.

(2) Details of disciplinary action which are placed on the member's record shall be deleted provided that, once the member has complied with the action taken, he conducts himself properly for a period of three months (minor misdemeanours), six months (less serious offences), two years (serious offences) or five years (highly serious offences).

(3) Offences shall prescribe one year after they are committed if no enquiry has been opened, except for offences which constitute a felony, in which case prescription shall be the same as that laid down for the felony, if greater than one year.

Authority to handle matters of discipline is regulated by Article 67 RD 1018/1980, which states that 'minor misdemeanours shall be dealt with by the President of the College of Physicians, by agreement of the Board and in accordance with the provisions of Article 63.3'.

Other offences shall be dealt with by the Board, following the holding of a disciplinary enquiry and in accordance with the procedure described in the next article.

Where the disciplinary matter relates to an offence committed by a member of another Provincial College, the enquiry shall be undertaken in full by the College in whose territory the alleged offence took place. Any action taken shall be notified to the member's College through the General Council.

Disciplinary matters involving Board and General Council members shall be handled by the latter.

Lastly, Article 68 RD 1018/1980 regulates disciplinary procedure as follows:

(1) The procedure shall be initiated automatically or at the request of a party, by agreement of the competent body, either of its own initiative or following denunciation.
(2) On learning of an alleged offence, the Board of the College is empowered to conduct a confidential investigation prior to taking the decision to undertake an official enquiry. Alternatively, on the basis of the information available to it, it may choose to take no further action and order that no disciplinary measures be taken or impose one of the punishments applicable to minor misdemeanours.
(3) Once it has chosen to proceed, the body may take any interim measures it deems appropriate to assure the proper implementation of its eventual decision. No interim measures may be taken which might cause irreparable harm to those concerned or which involve a violation of rights protected by law.
(4) On ordering an enquiry, the Board shall appoint a person to act as the 'instructing judge' from among its members or from among the College's ordinary members. The person appointed must have more years of service than the person facing the disciplinary action or, alternatively, must have at least ten years professional practice. Acceptance of the appointment is compulsory, unless the appointee has good reason not to do so or his/her appointment is challenged before the Board by the member facing the action. The Board may appoint a Secretary or authorize the instructing judge to designate one from among the members of the College.
(5) The only reasons which may justify non-acceptance of or challenge to an appointment are consanguinity up to the fourth degree or affinity to the second, close friendship, clear enmity or personal interest in the matter.
(6) In order that they may be challenged, the appointments of the instructing judge and secretary shall be notified to the person against whom the proceedings have been instigated. The latter may exercise his/her right to contest the appointments within a period of eight days following receipt of notification.
(7) The person against whom proceedings have been instigated may appoint a member to defend him or to serve as arbiter. He shall be notified of this possibility and shall be given ten days in which to notify the Board of the name of the person he chooses to appoint and also that said person is willing to act in such a capacity. The appointee shall be present in all the enquiries undertaken by the instructing judge and may propose that other lines of investigation be explored on behalf of the defendant.

The person facing the disciplinary action may also have his/her counsel accompany him during all proceedings.

(8) The instructing judge is empowered to request any background information deemed necessary and to order any enquiries and other actions which might help clarify the circumstances under examination or which might help determine whether or not these merit disciplinary measures.

(9) In addition to taking the appropriate statements, the instructing judge shall provide the accused with a written list of accusations, indicating clearly the alleged offences with which he is being charged. The accused shall be given a non-extendable period of eight days following receipt of the notification in which to answer the charges and furnish any proof he may wish. On receipt of this answer, or on expiry of the eight-day limit, the instructing judge shall admit or reject the proof offered and order any action which he considers to be of help in clarifying the circumstances.

(10) On completion of his/her enquiries, and no later than four months after the opening of proceedings, the instructing judge shall propose a solution to the case. A copy of this proposal shall be provided to the accused, who shall have eight days following the date of receipt in which to study the contents and adduce further arguments in writing.

(11) All the above proceedings shall be notified to the College Board, which, on receipt of the arguments presented by the accused or once the time-limit for the presentation of any such arguments has lapsed, shall take a decision on the case during the first session held thereafter. The Board shall hear the opinion of the College's legal adviser (if one exists) or the Ethics, Medical Law and Authorisations Committee and shall notify the accused of the full text of its final decision.

(12) The Board may choose to send the file back to the instructing judge and request further enquiries not pursued at the time but which are crucial to the final decision. In such cases, prior to sending the file back for further enquiries, the Board shall inform the accused of its decision so that he may, within eight days, present any arguments he considers appropriate. This period is not to be counted as the period for the presentation of further arguments referred to above.

(13) Any decision marking the end of the disciplinary enquiry shall be grounded on specific motives. No circumstances other than those which served to draw up the list of accusations or the proposed solution shall be admitted, although said circumstances may well be appraised differently.

(14) The accused may lodge an appeal to the General Council against the final decision within fifteen days. All appeals shall be submitted to the College, which shall forward the disciplinary file and its own report within three days to the Council.

(15) The defendant may appeal against the decision of the General Council to the Court for Administrative Disputes.[103]

103. Through assimilation to the Administration's powers in matters of discipline. With regard to the appropriateness of this avenue in terms of the Administration's disciplinary powers, which we shall

62. As was seen in Chapter 3 §1 I, the problem may arise that more than one disciplinary body becomes involved. A case of this nature was dealt with by the Supreme Court (4th Chamber) with its ruling of 24 January 1989 (rapporteur magistrate Bruguera Manté). On 27 January 1983, following a disciplinary case concerning a physician charged with a serious offence, the Standing Committee of the General Council of Physicians suspended the accused from practice for a period of nine months. The decision was confirmed by the (as it was then) Territorial Court on 14 May, following an appeal by the accused. However, the Supreme Court allowed the appeal on the following grounds:

> It is inadmissible that, while a criminal procedure is being followed with regard to the very same events which gave rise to the disciplinary action, the case should have been proceeded with and resolved without first waiting for the ruling of the Criminal Court (. . .) However, it is true that in cases such as this, which involve a relationship of subjection or a special kind of supremacy between the physician and his/her professional association, the power to handle disciplinary matters may be different to and independent of criminal responsibility (. . .), although this does not mean that the principle of *non bis in idem* or no two punishments for the same offence should be violated.

However, the ruling also states that 'the necessary subordination of disciplinary powers to the jurisdiction of the criminal courts when a criminal procedure is being followed with regard to the same event means that the disciplinary proceedings may not be proceeded with, opened or concluded while the criminal enquiry continues'.

63. Separate mention should be made of the disciplinary powers of the Administration with regard to staff of the Social Security system. The Framework Statute provided for in Article 84 of the LGS (Law 14/1986) came into existence with Law 55/2003, of 16 December.

It goes without saying that these rules and regulations apply only to employees of the Social Security system, in accordance with statutory provisions.

Disciplinary offences and actions are dealt with in Chapter XII Law 55/2003. Article 71 sets out the basic principles of the Administration's disciplinary authority: principles of tipicity, efficacy and proportionality in the whole public health system and the proceeding is subjected to the principles of immediacy, procedural economy and full respect of the corresponding rights and guarantees. In any case, and on the basis of the administrative decentralization existing in Spain (where each Autonomous Community has its own regional health service), the disciplinary authority corresponds to the health service in which the person concerned is serving at the time of commission of the misdemeanour or offence.

Offences are classified in Article 72:

(1) Highly serious offences. Article 72.2 establishes a set of twenty-two highly serious offences (letters 72.2.a to 72.2.u), including among others:

---

examine further on in relation to medical employees of the Social Security system, *see* Supreme Court Rulings of 11 Feb. 1985, 16 June and 21 Oct. 1986 and 4 Apr. 1988.

- Failure to comply with the due respect to the Spanish Constitution or with the respective Statute of Autonomy when exerting his/her functions (Article 72.2.a).
- The breach of the due reservation with respect to data relating to the Centre or institution or to the personal privacy of users and to information related to their processes and stays in institutions or health care facilities (Article 72.2.c).
- Abandoning one's place of work (Article 72.2.d).
- The notorious breach of duties or of the rules governing the functioning of the services (Article 72.2.f).
- Failure to comply with the essential services established in case of strike (Article 72.2.j).
- The requirement of any type of compensation for services provided to the users of public health services (Article 72.2.q).

(2) Serious offences. Article 72.3 establishes a set of fourteen highly serious offences (letters 72.3.a to 72.3.n), including among others:
- The lack of obedience due to the superiors (Article 72.3.a).
- Abuse of authority in the exercise of their functions (Article 72.3.b).
- Breach of duties or the rules governing the functioning of the services when not integrating a highly serious offence (Article 72.3.c).
- The serious disregard with superiors, peers, subordinates, or users (Article 72.3.d).
- Sexual harassment, when the active subject of harassment with his conduct create an intimidating, hostile or humiliating work environment for the person who is the subject of the same (Article 72.3.e).
- Any damage or deterioration in facilities, equipment, instruments or documents, when they occur by an inexcusable reckless act (Article 72.3.f).
- The lack of professional performance that affects the normal functioning of the services when not integrating a highly serious offence (Article 72.3.g)

(3) Minor misdemeanours. Article 72.4 establishes a set of seven highly serious offences (letters 72.4.a to 72.4.g), including among others:
- Unjustified non-compliance with working hours, when not integrating a serious offence (Article 72.4.a).
- Unjustified absence when not integrating a serious offence (Article 72.4.b).
- The incorrectness with superiors, peers, subordinates, or users (Article 72.4.c).
- Neglect or dereliction of their duties when not affecting users, Administration, or health services (Article 72.4.d).
- Neglect in the fulfilment of the express provisions on safety and health (Article 72.4.e).
- Breach of its duties or obligations, when not integrating a serious or highly serious offence (Article 72.4.f).
- The cover-up, consent or aiding with any act to the commission of serious offences (Article 72.4.g).

According to Article 72.5 the Autonomous Communities may, by norms with the status of law, establish other offences in addition to the established in the previous sections.

The next article (73) sets out the punishments applicable to the above offences:

(a) Separation from service. This sanction shall entail the loss of the status of statutory staff and only be imposed for the commission of highly serious offences.
(b) Forced relocation with change of locality, without right to compensation and with temporary prohibition of participating in mobility procedures for returning to the locality for a maximum of four years. This punishment may be imposed only as a result of highly serious offences.
(c) Suspension of functions. When this sanction is imposed for highly serious offences, it may not exceed six years or be less than two years. If it is imposed for serious offences, it shall not exceed two years. If suspension does not exceed six months, the person concerned will not lose his/her professional destination.
(d) Forced relocation in another institution or centre without change of locality, with temporary ban, up to a maximum of two years for participating in mobility procedures for returning to the centre of origin. This punishment may be imposed only as a result of serious offences.
(e) Warning that will always be in writing, and shall only be imposed for minor misdemeanours.

§2. Professional Liability

I. General Aspects

64. The medical profession has become increasingly regulated in recent years;[104] as was seen in Chapters 1 and 2 above, this process of regulation stemmed from the need to define the scope of medical activity in the light of legal provisions governing professions which require academic qualifications, as stipulated in Article 36 of the Spanish Constitution. It can be explained also by the importance which medical activity holds for society, which demands thorough regulation not merely to ensure that users may be defended against malpractice and physicians held liable for their actions, but also as a way of providing points of reference for professionals in situations in which they may have doubts as to their role,[105] and to help them take decisions when faced with difficult situations (organ transplants, euthanasia, abortion, etc.)[106] Regulation must keep in mind at all times the ultimate objective of the process, which is to confer on what is rapidly becoming increasingly complex medical activity a clear legal framework to enable the physician to perform his duties in a context of security.

---

104. *See* Segura Fuente & Martínez-Calcerrada, *Derecho Médico, I.*, p. 58 on the need for regulation; Romeo-Casabona, *El médico ante el Derecho*, pp. 6 ff.
105. *See* Segura Fuente & Martínez Calcerrada, *Derecho Médico I*, p. 56, in line with the views of Rico Pérez.
106. Romeo-Casabona, *El médico ante el Derecho*, pp. 5–10.

Some have viewed this increased regulation of medical practice as being tantamount to a recourse on the part of the patient or his next-of-kin against the provider of treatment should conflict arise if the treatment does not achieve the expected curative results; conversely, it has also been seen as affording legal backing to physicians in such circumstances, protecting their diligent and responsible actions even though the patient's state of health has not been restored as well as could have been hoped.

There is certainly an element of truth to the above, which is why it would be rather one-sided to consider that regulating medical practice aimed essentially to persecute physicians; fears of this type gave rise to the threat of *defensive medicine*, that is, the physician would endeavour to confirm his diagnosis through numerous repetitive examinations which would serve to delay commencement of treatment, push costs up and undermine efficiency.[107] Practitioners themselves have long advocated that the conditions governing physicians' liability should be spelled out as clearly as possible, and their demands in this respect have been met by Spain's legal order in a way which shall be examined later.

65. The manifestations of professional medical practice, the professional activities, and consequently any liability derived therefrom, may be studied from the standpoint of the legal nature of the provisions which regulate all such manifestations. A distinction is drawn between criminal and civil liability.

II. Criminal Liability

66. The body of legislation governing the matter is the Spanish Criminal Code, which distinguishes between liability stemming from conducts involving intent and those of a negligent nature.

A. Liability in Respect of Intentional Conduct

67. Intentional conducts covered in the Penal Code presuppose that a conscious and wilful attack has been made on the legally protected interest. The author of such conducts shall be liable for them if, in addition, another series of requirements are fulfilled, although he will be exonerated from liability in certain cases if, for example, a justifying cause is involved, such as circumstances which render lawful the conduct that represents an attack on the legally protected interest, given that the harm caused is permissible by law (for instance, a person who acts in legitimate self-defence or out of necessity).

68. Clearly, this type of criminal liability covers physicians in the same way and under the same conditions as any other citizen. It would be extremely difficult –

107. On this point *see* Romeo-Casabona, *El médico ante el Derecho*, pp. 8–10; J. Santos Briz, 'La responsabilidad civil de los médicos en el Derecho español', in *Revista de Derecho Privado* (julio-agosto) 1984, p. 644.

although not impossible – to imagine that a physician, in the course of professional practice and when performing a curative action, would intentionally commit homicide (Article 138 and ff) or cause injury (Arts. 147 and ff.). In such cases, there are no criteria which might differentiate the physician's scope of liability or different rules of incrimination based exclusively on his status as a professional. Given that there is nothing to distinguish the intentional conduct of a physician from that of any ordinary person, and also that such offences are not commonplace in medical practice, the argument advanced by some that physicians should be held criminally liable only for any intentional offences they commit should be rejected. A different situation occurs when a physician uses his special knowledge to facilitate or secure the commission of an offence or to ensure that it goes unpunished. However, here again this situation is by no means limited to physicians but rather is equally applicable to health care workers, pharmacists, chemists, biologists, gunsmiths, police officers, etc.

69. It is worth highlighting that the Spanish Criminal Code included an article directly devoted to punishing the conduct of health care workers who deliberately omitted their duty to treat:

> a medical practitioner who, while under obligation to do so, were to refuse health assistance or abandon the provision of health services, when refusal or abandonment were to cause serious risk to personal health, shall be punished with the penalties of the preceding Article, in the upper half and with that of special barring from public employment and office, profession or trade, for a term of six months to three years.

Case law[108] and doctrine determined the concrete circumstances in which this article would be applicable. These were:

(a) When the perpetrator refused the provision of necessary health care, being aware of its need.
(b) When health care assistance was required. This requisite would fail if another form of performance were at least as effective as the one required. For example, if urgent medical professional home care (the most frequent course of action foreseen by Article 196 CP) was requested, and it was evident that the movement of the patient to the health centre would be equally effective, this requisite would not be applicable.
(c) When there was a serious risk to the health of the patient due to the previously mentioned actions.[109]

108. See Supreme Court Rulings on 29 Nov. 2001 and 28 Jan. 2008.
109. See A. Urruela Mora & S. Romeo Malanda, 'Tendencias actuales de la jurisprudencia española en materia de responsabilidad penal médica', in *Revista de Derecho Penal*, 34, 2011, pp. 35–74; G. Portilla Contreras, 'La omisión del deber de socorro', in Gonzalo Quintero Olivares y Fermín Morales Prats (coords.), *El Nuevo Derecho Penal Español. Estudios Penales en Memoria del Profesor José Manuel Valle Muñiz* (Aranzadi, Pamplona 2001), pp. 1665–1696; Carlos María Romeo-Casabona, 'Artículo 196', in José Luis Díez Ripollés/Carlos María Romeo-Casabona (coords.), *Comentarios al Código Penal. Parte Especial. II* (Tirant lo Blanch, Valencia 2004); P. Esquinas

70. Nevertheless, consideration must also be given to the hypothesis that a physician deliberately and consciously *fails to assist* not just any sick person or the victim of an accident, such as in the cases merely mentioned, but his own patient, and as a result of this failure to act the patient dies or sustains irreparable consequences to his health. In these cases, jurists consider that an intentional or wilful offence does exist, the so-called offence committed by omission, which is the equivalent of an act committed through active (as opposed to passive) conduct. Depending on the circumstances and the specific case, an offence of homicide or wilful injury shall exist. Besides other requirements which need not be gone into here, the legal grounds for this criminal liability on the part of the physician are derived from the close relationship which exists between patient and physician as a result of the contract or other form of de facto connection (an example being the hospital doctor on duty who treats a casualty department patient). In these cases, in view of the privileged position enjoyed by the physician in relation to the life and health of the patient, he has a special duty to guarantee 'his' patient's legally *protected interests and this obliges him to provide his services in such a way as to ensure that no harm comes to these interests, provided, of course, that he is able to do so in the circumstances.*

B. Liability in Respect of Negligent Conduct

1. Juridical-Criminal Negligence: Features and Configuration in the Penal Code

71. In negligent liability the legally protected interest (in this case, the life, integrity and physical or mental health of the patient) is not harmed intentionally. Liability is based rather on the author's – whoever he may be – breach of certain duties of care or diligence, as a result of which the legal interest has sustained harm. The intended purpose of the author in such cases is of little interest or is irrelevant to criminal law; indeed, the purpose may even be highly useful to society (e.g., treating a patient). What is important is how the author has conducted himself, that is, the means and the use he has made of these means,[110] the lack of due diligence in his action which may have led to the unintended and perhaps even unforeseen outcome. Given the nature of this offence of negligence, it is this type of liability which generally speaking arises most frequently in professional acts, particularly unlawful acts committed by physicians.

72. The Spanish Criminal Code has been recently reformed by Organic Law 1/2015, of March 30, amending Organic Law 10/1995, of November the 23rd, on Criminal Code. This new regulation defines offences as 'intentional or negligent

Valverde, *El delito de denegación de asistencia o abandono de los servicios sanitarios. El artículo 196 del Código Penal* (Comares, Granada 2006), pp. 651–675.

110. *See* J. Cerezo Mir, *Curso de Derecho Penal Español. Parte General I. Introductión. Teoría jurídica del delito/I* (Tecnos, Madrid 1985), pp. 267 ff and p. 380.

actions or omissions punishable by Law'. As a consequence, negligence is considered as a key element in several offences. There are five cases that seem especially relevant in terms of health care workers liability:

(1) Homicide. Article 142.1 Penal Code states that 'Whoever causes the death of another by serious negligence shall be convicted of manslaughter and punished with a sentence of imprisonment of one to four years (…) When the manslaughter is committed due to professional negligence, the punishment of special barring from exercise of the profession, trade or cargo shall also be imposed, for a period of three to six years'. On the other side, number 2 of this same article states that 'Whoever causes the death of another by less serious negligence shall be convicted with a sentence of fine of three to eighteen months'.
(2) Abortion. According to Article 146 Penal Code, 'Whoever causes an abortion due to serious negligence shall be punished with a sentence of imprisonment of three to five months, or a fine from six to ten months'.
(3) Injuries. The Criminal Code states that whoever causes injuries that detracts from his bodily integrity or his physical or mental health, whoever causes to another person, by any means or procedure, to forfeit or lose the use of a major organ or limb, or a sense, or sexual impotence, sterility, serious deformity, to suffer a serious physical or mental illness, or a genital mutilation in any form or whoever causes another person to forfeit or lose the use of a non-major or limb, or a deformity due to serious negligence shall be punished (Article 152 Penal Code):
   (a) With a sentence of imprisonment from three to six months, in the case of the injuries described in Article 147.1 ('injury that detracts from his bodily integrity or his physical or mental health, shall be convicted of the offence of grievous bodily harm, with a sentence of imprisonment of six months to three years, whenever the injury objectively requires medical or surgical treatment for health purposes, in addition to qualified first aid');
   (b) With a sentence of imprisonment of one to three years, in the case of the injuries described in Article 149 (to forfeit or lose the use of a major organ or limb, or a sense, or sexual impotence, sterility, serious deformity or to suffer a serious physical or mental illness or to cause a genital mutilation in any form;
   (c) With a sentence of imprisonment of six months to two years, in the case of the injuries in Article 150 (to forfeit or lose the use of a non-major or limb, or a deformity).

Similarly, Article 152 states that 'when the injuries are committed due to professional negligence, the punishment of special barring from practice of the profession, trade or office shall also be applied, for a term from six months to four years'.

(4) Injuries to the foetus. According to the Spanish Criminal Code (Article 158), whoever, due to serious negligence was to cause a foetus an injury or disease that seriously damages the normal development thereof or causes such foetus a

serious physical or mental handicap shall be punished with a sentence of imprisonment of three to five months or a fine from six to ten months. When these acts are committed by professional negligence, the punishment of special barring from practice of the profession, trade or office for a term of six months to two years shall also be imposed. It is important to underline that the pregnant woman shall not be penalized under this provision.

(5) Gene manipulation. Article 159 of the Criminal Codes states that '1. Those who manipulate the human genes so as to alter the genome for purposes other than eliminating or decreasing serious flaws or diseases, shall be punished with a sentence of imprisonment from two to six years and special barring from public employment and office, profession or trade for seven to ten years. 2. Should alteration of the genome be perpetrated due to serious negligence, the punishment shall be a bfine from six to fifteen months and special barring from public employment and office, profession or trade from one to three years.' Therefore, it is clear that gene modification produced by negligence is banned by Spanish law.

The Spanish legislator has drawn a crucial distinction between minus serious and serious negligence. In principle, the difference[111] between them is that in the case of serious negligence the breach of duties of care is more inexcusable or clumsy compared with the less serious breach which leads to minus serious negligence.[112] However, our Criminal Code does not include an explicit reference on this issue. Thus, it will be a matter of Case Law to determine which conducts correspond to any of these different modalities in each offence, as it happened in the past.[113]

2. The Elements of Offences of Negligence: Aspects of Greatest Relevance to Medical Practice

73. Notwithstanding the clarification given above, it would appear that a literal reading of the Penal Code is insufficient to enable us to grasp the scope of liability in respect of negligence and its repercussions for physicians. It is thus up to those whose job it is to interpret the law (at the end of the day, the judges who have to apply it) to determine specific examples of the elements through which liability has to manifest itself in order to have legal-criminal relevance.

In the case of offences of negligence as described in the Penal Code, the following elements must always be present:[114]

111. Cerezo Mir, *Curso de Derecho Penal Español. Parte General I*, pp. 390 f.
112. The representation of the result or the absence thereof (conscious or unconscious fault) may be present in both; *see* Cerezo Mir, p. 392; S. Mir Puig, *Derecho Penal. Parte General* (10th ed., PPU, Barcelona 2015), p np. 294 and ff; Carmen Gómez Rivero, *La responsabilidad penal del médico* (Tirant lo Blanch, Valencia, 2nd edición, 2008), pp. 329–432.
113. See Supreme Court Rulings of 1 Dec. 1989, 29 Feb. 1996, 3 Oct. 1997, 25 May 1999, 29 Nov. 2001.
114. See A. Urruela Mora & S. Romeo Malanda, 'Tendencias actuales de la jurisprudencia española en materia de responsabilidad penal médica', pp. 35–74.

(1) failure to observe the duties of care entailed in professional practice;
(2) the causing of death or injury to the patient;
(3) causal link between the conduct of the physician and the result;
(4) the existence of an unlawful link between conduct and result, or objective imputation of the result.

Each of these elements will be examined in detail below, although we will focus only on the aspects which are of greatest relevance to the specific category of medical negligence.[115]

a. Failure to Observe the Duties of Care Entailed in Professional Practice

74. Let us look first of all at conduct in which due care is not exercised. This is certainly the most complex element or component part of the offence, and the one which proves most difficult to unravel. In practice, in the final instance whether or not an offence of negligence exists will depend on this element, although it should not be forgotten that the other component parts of the offence must also be present.

This requirement stems from the criminal rule which lies at the root of offences of negligence and which states that in their social life (in all areas of social life), citizens' behaviour must conform to certain duties or rules designed to ensure that legally protected interests or not endangered are harmed, particularly where major risk is involved (traffic, public transport, dangerous industries, nuclear energy, certain sports, etc.; but also in apparently harmless activities such as looking after plants hung from a balcony or window). This is what is known as 'the duty of care'. Thus, citizens or professionals (for our purposes here, physicians or health care professionals) whose conduct in the exercise of their profession conforms to these duties of care are in fact merely tailoring their conduct to the guidelines laid down by the rule. It is therefore necessary to compare the duty of care required in the particular sector of social life with the actual conduct of the author.

75. As is known, however, the precise legal content of this duty of care is not laid down specifically in the Law (a rather pointless task in any case, in view of the sheer number of conducts which are subject to certain duties of care) and thus it befalls the judge (with, of course, the appropriate expert advice on hand) to assess whether in a given case a duty of care has been breached. All physicians who treat a patient should observe minimum conduct guidelines to avoid committing a criminal offence, regardless of their level of training or their qualifications: the duty of care is an objective one. This was made clear in a ruling of the Supreme Court (2nd Chamber) dated 14 February 1991 when, in a health-related care, it stated that in order to constitute punishable negligence, the following was required: 'an act or omission performed in breach of rules or regulations of caution or precaution – as required by the circumstances of the event, place and time –, which aimed to foresee

115. *See* C.M. Romeo-Casabona, *El Médico y el Derecho Penal. I. La actividad curativa* (Bosch, Barcelona 1981), pp. 211 ff.

and, where appropriate, avoid damage or harm'. This criterion indicates the minimum level of necessary care or ability, below which there exists a duty to refrain from acting.

76. However, a number of authors raised the point that the duty of care should be established in accordance with individual ability, and assessment of this duty should be determined *not* from the standpoint of culpability, as the majority would hold, but should be based rather on the description of the offence included in the law. Put another way, the duty of care is only breached when the person, in accordance with his ability, could have foreseen the outcome, which means that the level of this duty will vary from person to person. This represents an individual or subjective duty of care.[116] This notion of the duty of care is extremely important in the medical profession, particularly with regard to professionals of much greater ability than others practising the same specialist branch, given that if they fail to make use of this extra-special ability they will be in breach of the duty of care which is within their reach; from an objective point of view, this situation would also affect those of below-average ability: they would not be liable (not having breached the duty of care) if they used all the diligence they are capable of using, even though this is below the average ability of colleagues. The question arises only in relation to individual ability and not (exceptional) knowledge, since the latter is taken into account in the appraisal of objective foreseeability. Only insofar as failure to use this ability can be determined objectively can a case be made for the existence of a breach of the duty of care, which would give rise in turn to an offence of negligence;[117] if this is not the case, in certain situations an intentional offence may exist, whereas the rest would not be punishable.[118]

77. Objectively due care is determined by the (intellectual) criterion of the objective foreseeability of the outcome (adequate causation), and is corrected and restricted by another (statutory) criterion, according to which only dangerous actions are prohibited, that is, actions which lead to an objectively foreseeable outcome and which an intelligent and judicious person would refrain from committing. This is the criterion followed by the Spanish Supreme Court in recent years.[119]

---

116. *See* E. Orts Berenguer & J.L. González Cussac, *Compendio de Derecho Penal. Parte General.* (5th ed., Tirant lo Blanch, Valencia 2015), p. 328; G. Quintero Olivares, *Parte General del Derecho Penal* (5th ed., Aranzadi, Cizur Menor 2015), pp. 437 f. (although with slight nuances). The issue is dealt with in greater depth in Cerezo Mir, *Curso de Derecho Penal Español. Parte General I*, pp. 381 f.; A. Jorge Barreiro, *La imprudencia punible en la actividad médico-quirúrgica* (Tecnos, Madrid 1990), pp. 41 ff.; Romeo-Casabona, *El Médico y el Derecho Penal*, I, pp. 215 ff.; A. Torio Lopez, 'El deber de cuidado en los delitos culposos' in *Anuario de Derecho Penal y Ciencias Penales*, 1974, pp. 25 ff.
117. Mir Puig, *Derecho Penal. Parte General*, p. 299.
118. For more details *see* Cerezo Mir, *Curso de Derecho Penal Español I*, p. 382. Jorge Barreiro, *La imprudencia punible en la actividad médico-quirúrgica*, p. 42, opts rather for the alternative of intentional or negligent homicide, depending on the case.
119. For instance, Supreme Court Ruling of 6 Jul. 2006.

(i) Technical Fault, Breach of Lex Artis *and of the Duty of Care*

78. It is difficult to describe in more specific terms the content of the duty of care as conceived objectively, due to the tremendous variety and complexity of the conducts which have to be appraised.

One could determine content on the basis of general laws which are applicable to cases which fit the legal description of the offence or ones of a similar nature. This set of technical rules and procedures is what is commonly known as *lex artis*, which naturally differs from sector to sector and from profession to profession. The implication of this is that a physician or health care professional who has been guided by the *lex artis*, by what his skill and judgement indicate to be appropriate at each moment and in each circumstance, generally speaking will not have breached his duties of care. This is an issue to which we shall return later.

Determining the existence or otherwise of a breach of the duty of care is also possible, although less frequent in the case of physicians, on the basis of technical or administrative provisions. As has been mentioned above, in such cases – and if injury is caused to the patient –, the offender shall have committed an offence of serious negligence or minus serious negligence involving a breach of regulations, depending on the circumstances.

79. A distinction must be drawn between three closely related although not completely identical notions which, if confused, could give rise to hasty and erroneous consequences. The three in question are breaches of the objective duty of care, technical error or fault and infringements of the *lex artis*.[120] Conceptually, the three are very similar, which is why it is crucial that as far as is possible the logical context of each should be clearly defined.

Technical error or fault, known also as professional error or fault, is a concept which is common also to other professions, most of which are of a technical or experimental nature (architects, engineers, etc.). Technical fault in medicine involves the *defective application of methods, techniques or procedures in the different stages of the action of the physician*[121] (examination, diagnosis, indication, administering of treatment). As used here, the concept of technical fault does not imply a legal appraisal but rather the de facto verification that a given medical situation is incorrect from the medical point of view. This neutral legal interpretation implies only that once it has been ascertained that an error resulting in harm has in fact taken place, it then becomes necessary to verify whether a breach of the duty of care has also occurred, given that it is possible for a technical error to exist without a breach of the duty of care. Technical fault or error, which is a scientific

120. See: D. Arias Madrigal, La responsabilidad penal en el ámbito médicosanitario: algunas consideraciones generales, en 'Revista de Ciencias Penales', vol. 2, nº 1, 1999, pp. 81–106; C. Gómez Rivero, La responsabilidad penal del médico, Tirant lo blanch, Valencia, 2004, pp. 329–336; E. Hava García, La imprudencia médica, Tirant lo blanch, Valencia, 2001; A. Jorge Barreiro, La imprudencia punible en la actividad médico quirúrgica, Tecnos, Madrid, 1990, pp. 145–150.

121. *See* Romeo-Casabona, *El Médico y el Derecho Penal, I*, pp. 233 ff.; M. Corcoy Bidasolo, *El delito imprudente* (PPU, Barcelona 1989), pp. 101 ff., Urruela Mora & S. Romeo Malanda, 'Tendencias actuales de la jurisprudencia española en materia de responsabilidad penal médica', pp. 35–74.

concept, does not entail negligence (legal concept) *eo ipso*,[122] in the eyes of the Law the decisive element is not the error in itself but rather the cause of any such error. To sum up, then, the existence of technical fault alone is of no value other than as an indication (as long as it is accompanied by a result of harm to the patient) which leads us to ascertain subsequently that objectively due care has or has not been breached. Thus, it will not always be possible to state that criminal liability exists if, in this respect, the offence does not conform to this requirement. Indeed, the Supreme Court has ruled that technical fault should only bring liability if the mistakes committed are of an extraordinary magnitude.[123]

Similarly, with regard to *lex artis* we may conclude the following:

(1) technical error or fault does not necessarily suppose a breach of *lex artis*;
(2) *lex artis* is not immutable nor does it exist in one form only, and thus it must be reconciled with individual freedom to use different methods and must remain open to new techniques and procedures, including less widely used ones;
(3) *lex artis* is valid solely (as has been stated above) for 'typical' situations, for example, those described in scientific literature, whereas it is not valid for exceptional or 'atypical' cases;
(4) it is not possible to determine an identity based on content for both technical regulations and legal rules at the same time: each group pursues its own particular ends and therefore a breach of one does not necessarily imply that of the other.

In conclusion, although the principle that physicians should observe the *lex artis* (in the broad sense referred to earlier) is still very much in force, a breach does not as yet entail a breach of the duty of care, although it often does constitute an indication thereof.[124] Indeed, on occasions (in atypical situations) a physician's observance of the duty of care may even require him to distance himself from the *lex artis*.

80. The above general considerations regarding the three concepts are shared also by case law when, for example, it is said that medical practice is 'subject to the *lex artis*, and that medical criminal liability does not originate from errors of diagnosis or lack of extraordinary expertise (given that infallibility cannot be made a requirement): rather, negligence arises when conduct does not conform to certain requirements and means … '.[125]

122. A. Quintano Ripolles, *Derecho penal de la culpa* (Bosch, Barcelona 1958), pp. 505 and 510.
123. See Supreme Court Rulings of 13 Nov. 2002 and 29 Feb. 2006.
124. See See Supreme Court Rulings of 23 Oct. 2001, 7 Oct. 1986, 4 Sep. 1991 and 1 Dec. 1989.
125. Supreme Court Ruling of 5 Feb. 1981, which uses these very terms and others. A Ruling of 7 Oct. 1986 develops the criterion further and summarises doctrine on medical negligence: '1. No incrimination for scientific error; 2. A lack of extraordinary expertise is not deemed to be punishable either. 3. Culpability stems from cases where the doctor could have avoided the conduct which led to the harmful outcome; 4. Immutable general considerations should be avoided in the search for punishable medical liability'.

(ii) Determining the Existence of a Breach of the Objective Duty of Care: Special Features

81. To begin with, account must be taken of certain aspects, such as how to assess a person's training or specialist knowledge (even though there is no specific ban on practising without the appropriate specialist qualification), the general need to update scientific knowledge and techniques, circumstances of time and place (e.g., rural area or hospital, etc.), the duty of so-called 'therapeutic information', etc.

Within the various phases of the curing process (anamnesis, diagnosis, prognosis, treatment, preventive or prophylactic measures) there are a number of particular circumstances to which consideration must be given when determining whether or not duties of care have been breached. In view of the amount of guess-work involved, greater leeway is allowable in diagnosis, although, as Supreme Court case law has held, this does not mean that criminal liability for negligence is completely ruled out.

b. Death of or Injury to Patient

82. In order for criminal liability in respect of negligence to exist, negligent conduct by the physician of the type explained above is in itself insufficient. A harmful material result to the patient is also required, since in medical practice only a material result offence is possible; this point was clarified by the Supreme Court ruling of 14 February 1991 referred to earlier, which stated that 'concrete damage and harm must be caused, and this must be a consequence of the negligent conduct in its twin facets, namely, the lack of foresight or the "duty to know" and the lack of care or the "duty to prevent"'. In any case, it is not always easy to determine whether harm has been caused to the patient on the basis of how his condition has evolved.

This result may take the form of harm caused to the health or integrity of the patient and, in some extreme cases, even loss of life. Consequently, inadequate action on the part of a physician who has failed to observe due care, but which has not led to one of the aforementioned events or situations, shall not give rise to criminal liability of any kind. Conversely, the existence of a result of harm or damage to the patient does not necessarily imply punishable negligence on the part of the physician, given that it must be proven that his behaviour effectively breached the duty of care, in the terms outlined above. The presence of a result such as one of those listed above merely opens the way to a subsequent analysis of the conduct of the physician or health care professional.

c. The Causal Link between the Physician's Conduct and the Outcome

83. Let us suppose that duties of care have indeed been breached and have resulted in harm being caused to the patient. This in itself is insufficient: it is necessary to ascertain whether the negligent conduct actually caused the result, that is, whether a causal link exists between the two, a point that has been stressed by the

Supreme Court ruling of 14 February 1991:[126] 'a corresponding relationship of causation, of cause and effect, must exist between the negligent action and the harmful result; this in turn will generate liability when the blame can be attributed to a specific person'. As was mentioned above, the subject's negligent action does not extend also to the subsequent outcome – this is a requirement of the offence – given that the subject's intended purpose was not to cause the result in question. This is why the causal link associating the action and the outcome – a link which must always exist – forms part of the legal description of the offence.[127]

This requirement has led to widespread difficulties as regards the furnishing of proof, and it is easy to understand that such difficulties arise most frequently in the field of health or medicine, given that medicine by definition is an inexact science involving a certain degree of guesswork and not everything is known about the physical and mental behaviour of human beings.[128] Hence, doubts as to the existence of this causal link shall lead to the person being acquitted, by virtue of the application of the principle of *in dubio pro reo* (presumption of innocence).

d. Unlawful Link between Action and Outcome: Objective Imputation of the Latter

84. In specialist literature and in case law it is considered that something else is required in addition to all the above.[129] Firstly, a closer link between action and outcome than a merely causal link is required: the result in question must have been a consequence of the failure to observe objectively due care.[130] Secondly, the result must be one which the regulations governing due care aimed specifically to prevent.[131]

126. See also Supreme Court Ruling of 29 Oct. 1994.

127. Cerezo Mir, *Curso de Derecho Penal Español. Parte General I*, p. 280; Guillermo Portero Lazcano, 'Responsabilidad penal culposa del médico: fundamentos para el establecimiento de la negligencia o impericia', *Rev. Latinoam.Der.Méd. Medic. Leg.*, 6 (2): Dic. 2001 – 7 (1), Junio 2002, pp. 89–96. *See also* Supreme Court Ruling of 20 May 1981.

128. On the determination of the causal link in accordance with the criterion of 'the loss of life expectancy', *see* J.A. Gisbert Calabuig, *Nuevos aspectos de la responsabilidad médica: el ejercicio de la Medicina de grupo o en equipo* (Real Academia de Medicina de Valencia, 1979) passim; Romeo-Casabona, *El Médico ante el Derecho*, pp. 83 f.

129. See María Ángeles Rueda Martín, *La teoría de la imputación objetiva del resultado en el delito doloso de acción* (Bogotá, Universidad Externado de Colombia, primera edición 2002), pp. 49–122. See also Supreme Court Ruling of 9 May 2011.

130. *See* Cerezo Mir, *Curso de Derecho Penal Español. Parte General I*, pp. 396 f; Mir Puig, *Derecho Penal. Parte General*, pp. 306 ff (in which further views and critical considerations are given); Romeo-Casabona, *El Médico y el Derecho Penal, I*, pp. 226 ff; Esteban Sola Reche, José Ulises Hernández Plasencia & Carlos María Romeo-Casabona, 'La responsabilidad profesional del médico en el Derecho español', en Carlos María Romeo-Casabona (editor), *Responsabilidad penal y responsabilidad civil de los profesionales* (Centro de Estudios Criminológicos-Universidad de La Laguna, Tenerife 1993), pp. 99–120.

131. *See* Cerezo Mir, *Curso de Derecho Penal Español. Parte General I*, pp. 399 f; Mir Puig, *Derecho Penal. Parte General*, pp. 306 ff (in which some further views and critical considerations are given); Romeo-Casabona, *El Médico y el Derecho Penal, I*, p. 228; Esteban Sola Reche, José Ulises Hernández Plasencia & Carlos María Romeo-Casabona, 'La responsabilidad profesional del médico en el Derecho español', en Carlos María Romeo-Casabona (editor), *Responsabilidad penal y responsabilidad civil de los profesionales*, p. 110. This second criterion of imputation by itself,

It is difficult to provide clear-cut examples in the field of medicine, and hence we shall resort to another field in an effort to better understand the first of the above-mentioned criteria regarding imputation. Let us suppose that when driving along a stretch of road a motorist breaks the speed limit. Ahead of him is a cyclist who is riding rather erratically; the cyclist is knocked down and dies. Let us consider the circumstances: the driver has breached his duty of care by exceeding the speed limit; a death results therefrom and certainly there can be no denying that he has caused that death. Is he guilty of an offence of negligence? Not in the eyes of the law, because the result did not stem from his negligent driving, and would have occurred equally if he had not broken the limit. We can take an example also from the field of health: during an operation an anaesthetist administers cocaine instead of the correct substance; the patient dies but the autopsy shows later that he would have died anyway given his serious condition. All the above requirements, including the causal link, are present here except for d) the unlawful link between action and outcome or the objective imputation of the result. Thus, the correct decision would be to clear the accused. Proving that the result would have occurred in any case, even if the duty of care had been observed, will depend to a large extent on the skill of the defence lawyer, although as long as it seems possible or likely,[132] as long as doubt exists, a court should give the benefit of doubt and find the accused not guilty.

3. Aggravated Liability in Respect of Professional Negligence or Lack of Expertise

85. As far as these aggravated offences are concerned, we have little to add to what we have stated elsewhere.[133] Lack of expertise and negligence refer to professionals although their meaning differs: professional negligence implies a breach of technical duties incumbent only on professionals in the course of their work;[134] however, it does not follow that all negligence on the part of a person who happens to be a professional will render him liable to an aggravated sentence (for this to be the case he must breach his duty of care also).[135]

Although this aggravation of the offence is questionable, bearing in mind that there are other activities in society which may be performed by professionals and

without the first, is advocated by E. Gimbernat Ordeig, 'Infracción del deber de diligencia y fin de la norma en los delitos culposos', in *Revista de Derecho de Circulación*, 1965, p. 675.

132. There has been a great deal of debate as to the degree of likelihood, or even certainty, which can be required. *See* C. Roxin, 'Infracción del deber y resultado en los delitos imprudentes', in *Problemas básicos del Derecho penal* (Spanish translation and notes by D.M. Luzón Peña) (Reus, Madrid 1976), pp. 147 ff.

133. *See* Romeo-Casabona, *El Médico y el Derecho Penal, I*, pp. 229 ff.

134. *See* J. Cordoba Roda, 'Zum Verkehrsstrafrecht in Spanien', in *Zeitschrift f.d.g. Strafrechtswissenschaft*, 1961, pp. 122 f.

135. *See* Supreme Court doctrine, which is similar, on such types of lack of expertise or professional negligence: rulings of 24 Nov. 1984, 21 Feb. 1986, 5 May 1988, 27 May 1988; 6 May 1990 (Barcelona Provincial Court).

laypersons alike (e.g., the driving of motor vehicles), it is not as wide of the mark as might at first seem (provided it is kept within the appropriate limits). Bear in mind also that certain professions cannot be practised by non-professionals, such is the case with physicians (and also architects, engineers, pharmacists, etc.), and that authorization to practise is dependent on the person holding the appropriate qualifications (presumption of aptitude). Thus, it is understandable that breaches of duties of care, as set out in technical regulations, or illegal practice by a person who does not have the necessary qualification should be viewed as being more serious. In the light of this consideration, then, there would be no grounds for an objective aggravation of liability.[136]

C. Teamwork in Medical and Health Care

86. Teamwork,[137] which is becoming increasingly common in hospital medicine, poses particular problems, although it can prove extremely important and useful as regards determining liability, bearing in mind that in criminal law liability is strictly personal (each person is answerable for his own conduct). In cases such as these, one may apply the criterion adopted by Spain's Supreme Court – in a road traffic case first of all – which has become known as the principle of trust, according to which each person taking part in an activity may trust that in their respective missions the others will act in accordance with their duties; the same goes for joint activities, under the principle of the sharing out of functions. In this way, a surgeon may trust that his anaesthetist is using the appropriate parameters and carrying out the necessary verifications in the course of the operation; that the nurse will hand him the appropriate instruments; for her part, the nurse may trust that the instrument or drug requested is the correct one (and the dosage indicated is correct); the internist can trust that the nurse will give the prescribed doses at the times indicated; both physician and nurse may trust that the medicine or drug has been made correctly by the laboratory and that the labels indicate the exact content and expiry date.

The sharing out of functions also means that superiors will not ask their subordinates to perform any tasks which exceed their level of training or their allotted work or which they themselves should do. If they do assign such work, it is their duty to supervise that their orders or instructions are carried out correctly.

---

136. *See* Cerezo Mir, *Curso de Derecho Penal Español. Parte General I*, pp. 393 ff. A critical view is taken also by J. Bustos Ramirez, *Manual de Derecho Penal. Parte General* (3rd ed., Ariel, Barcelona 1989), p. 236.

137. For an extremely thorough study of this issue, *see* Jorge Barreiro, *La imprudencia punible en la actividad médico-quirúrgica*, pp. 113 ff. *See also* Romeo-Casabona, *El Médico y el Derecho Penal, I*, pp. 247–252; G. Stratenwerth, 'Arbeitsteilung und ärztliche Sorgfaltspflicht', in *Eb. Schmidt-Fest* (*Vandenhoeck und Ruprecht. Göttingen, 1961*), pp. 383 ff.; D. Wilhelm, 'Probleme der medizinischen Arbeitsteilung aus strafrechtlicher Sicht', in *Medizinrecht*, 1983, pp. 45 ff.

III. Civil Liability

87. Civil liability (whether linked or not to an offence)[138] aims to afford reparation in respect of harm caused to someone and, where appropriate, to compensate for any damages caused by the punishable event. This usually takes the form of financial compensation, although other forms may occasionally be used. This type of liability may be based on the contractual relationship which exists between the patient and the health professional, in accordance with the provisions of Article 1101 ('Persons who, in the performance of their obligations, should incur in wilful misconduct, negligence or default, and those who in any way should contravene the content of the obligation shall be subject to compensation of any damages caused') and related articles of the Civil Code, or, alternatively, on so-called extracontractual fault which gives rise to extracontractual liability, governed by Article 1902 of the Civil Code ('The person who, as a result of an action or omission, causes damage to another by his fault or negligence shall be obliged to repair the damaged caused').[139]

The distinction between the two forms of liability as applied in the field of medicine has led to a great deal of doctrinal discussion, not to mention controversy.[140] Both doctrine and case law have given ample recognition to the existence of a contractual relationship between physician and patient where said relationship stems from an earlier legal relationship *inter partes*.[141] Although contractual medical cover is becoming increasingly common, the importance of situations where this exists – emergency operations, occasional gaps in contractual cover, etc. – makes it inappropriate to examine here the contractual basis of civil liability derived from medical practice.[142] Notwithstanding the different legal regimes of contractual and extracontractual liability[143] – the need to be of legal capacity to enter into a contract (in the case of the former type), time-limits for the lapsing of contracts, proof of fault, etc. – case law has on occasions approximated the two in rulings on reparations.[144] The theoretical grounds for this lies in the circumstance that here both types of liability come in to play, that is, it can be ascertained that the general duty of *alterum non laedere* has been breached, as has a duty stemming from contractual

138. On the legal nature of liability stemming from a physician's acts, *see* E. Llamas Pombo, *La responsabilidad civil del médico* (Trivium, Madrid 1988), pp. 92–109; on jurisdictional limits *see* L. González Morán, *La responsabilidad civil del médico* (Bosch, Barcelona 1990), pp. 19–32.
139. The starting point for contractual and extracontractual liability is the same, namely, the notion of reparation and compensation; on this point, *see* Supreme Court Ruling of 19 Jun. 1984. The same ruling outlines the differences between both types of liability, which are governed by different legal systems despite the fact that the basic goal involved is one and the same. On situations where both contractual and extracontractual liability may be involved, *see* L. González Morán, *La responsabilidad civil del médico*, pp. 36–48.
140. See Enrique Ruiz Vadillo, 'La responsabilidad civil y penal de los médicos (especial referencia a losanestesistas)', *Derecho y Salud,* vol. 3, núm. 1, enero-junio, 1995, p. 74.
141. On this point, *see* Supreme Court Ruling of 19 Jun. 1984.
142. As argued by E. Llamas Pombo, *La responsabilidad civil del médico*, p. 100.
143. *See* in this regard the Supreme Court Ruling of 30 Dec. 1980.
144. Note, for example, how the Supreme Court Ruling of 16 Dec. 1986 admits the possibility of extracontractual liability even where a contract exists.

obligations,[145] even though both become merged in one single claim for compensation. Moreover, as laid down in the Supreme Court Ruling of 11 November 1990,[146] these obligations are derived from another which is common to all health professionals, whether or not they are under contract, namely, the obligation which is not necessarily to ensure the recovery of the patient. Put another way, it is not an obligation which involves a specific result, but rather one involving means: the professional's obligation is not to cure the patient but rather to provide him with all the care required, in accordance with the state of the art in science.[147]

88. Which is all the more reason not to draw a distinction between contractual and extracontractual liability when considering cases of civil liability.[148] For our purposes here it will suffice to consider the common elements between the two, taking as our starting point Articles 1101 and 1902 of the Civil Code which deal with the failure to observe certain duties of care incumbent on the author.[149] The conditions or circumstances of this form of liability include the following:[150]

(1) *Harmful conduct*: this consists of an action or omission,[151] which leads to a result of harm to the patient. In order for this conduct to be relevant in terms of

145. *See* G. Garcia Valdecasas, 'El problema de la acumulación de la responsabilidad contractual y delictual en el Derecho español', in *Revista de Derecho Privado*, 1962, pp. 834 ff; L. González Morán, *La responsabilidad civil del médico*, pp. 36 ff; E. Llamas Pombo, *La responsabilidad civil del médico*, pp. 100 ff.
146. In line with the Rulings of 6 Nov. 1990, 7 Feb. 1990, 12 Jul. 1988 and 13 Jul. 1987.
147. See, for instance, Supreme Court Rulings of 24 May 1999; and De Ángel Yagüez, *Responsabilidad civil por actos médicos. Problemas de prueba*, pp. 27 ff.
148. In this regard, *see* Supreme Court Rulings of 24 Mar. 1952, 7 Feb. 1990 and 22 Feb. 1991.
149. Article 1101: 'Any person who, in the performance of his obligations, commits wilful misconduct or negligence or defers his obligations excessively, or who in any way transgresses the spirit of said obligations, shall be liable to compensate for any damage or harm caused by his actions'.

   Article 1902: 'Any person who through his actions or omissions causes harm to another either wilfully or negligently is obliged to make good the harm caused'. In addition to this statutory requirement one has to consider also Article 1903, which allows a claim to be brought against the centre or institution in which the physician provides his services. In this regard, the Supreme Court Ruling of 5 May 1988 is significant: 'there existed culpable action on the part of the institution (…) in consenting to the use of health equipment in a deteriorated condition without providing sufficient guarantees that it was working properly and could be used in such a delicate health situation. This was responsible for the death of the patient being treated; the harm sustained was clear and substantial and was the result of an undeniable relationship of cause and effect, which was directly attributable to INSALUD because of the poor state of the material used in the hospital'.
150. *See* Supreme Court Rulings of 6 Nov. 1990 and 11 Mar. 1991.
151. This active or omissive conduct must be voluntary. A degree of confusion surrounds the possibility of inferring civil liability from involuntary acts when the basis used is the antinomy which exists between 'voluntary behaviour' and 'negligent behaviour'. Attributing a harmful outcome to negligent behaviour supposes that the outcome was not intended by the author, although this does not mean that the behaviour itself was not voluntary; the author voluntarily breaches the duty of care, even though it is not his wish to produce the harm in question. Cf. E. Llamas Pombo, *La responsabilidad civil del médico*, p. 210; J.L. Lacruz Berdejo, *Elementos de Derecho Civil II*. Vol. Primero (Bosch, Barcelona 1985), pp. 498 f. A similar line to that taken here can be found in J. Santos Briz, *La responsabilidad civil. Derecho sustantivo y Derecho procesal* (5th edition revised and updated, Montecorvo, Madrid 1989), pp. 26–27. The distinction between voluntary and involuntary behaviour is not valid either to explain civil liability; *cf. infra*.

civil liability it must be unlawful, that is, it must transgress a legal rule based on the principle that one shall not harm others.[152] Moreover, 'the harm on which the alleged liability is grounded must be a consequence of an action or omission circumscribable to the scope of activities related to the health-medical profession'.[153]

In cases where the physician-patient relationship is governed by a contract, there is debate as to whether 'liability waiver' clauses should be deemed valid. However, the limitations imposed by Articles 1102–1104 – which invalidate waivers with respect to liability derived from fault or an intentional act – and Articles 1255[154] and 1258[155] of the Civil Code – which annul the validity of clauses which are contrary to the law, to morals or public order or which entail consequences that do not conform to good faith or proper usage –, substantially curb the efficiency of agreements which exonerate the professional from civil liability in cases where strict liability is involved.

(2) *The causing of harm*: although this element is extremely difficult to determine, in the field of health or medical care it entails so-called bodily harm (although in the broad sense, which includes also harm of a mental nature) as well as material and moral harm, mental and physical pain and loss of profit or earnings.[156] The harm caused must be real in all cases. Even more complex than the determination of harm is the question of how it can be assessed for the purpose of compensation: the importance of the harm caused depends on personal circumstances, which are difficult to compare in absolute terms for all patients alike. Hence, to a large extent it is the law, having weighed up the specific circumstances of the case, which has to establish the nature and *quantum* of any reparation to be awarded in respect of civil liability.[157]

(3) *Causal connection between the conduct and the harm caused*: this is a perfectly logical requirement and is explained above;[158] it might be appropriate here to recall once more the difficulties involved, although not so much those regarding the furnishing of proof (which we will examine in a moment) as those which arise in seeking a general criterion which will enable us to construct – or rule out – the causal connection satisfactorily. In the area of negligence, for example, Spanish case law has adopted the notion that causation should be deemed to exist if the harmful result would have been avoided with diligent conduct; although this criterion appears clear and defendable, it is somewhat imprecise as regards the weighing up the likelihood that the result would have been

152. On this point *see* Santos Briz, *La responsabilidad civil*, pp. 28 ff.
153. E. Llamas Pombo, *La responsabilidad civil del médico*, p. 211.
154. 'The contracting parties may establish any covenants, clauses and conditions deemed convenient, provided that they are not contrary to the laws, to morals or to public policy'.
155. Contracts are perfected by mere consent, and since then bind the parties, not just to the performance of the matters expressly agreed therein, but also to all consequences which, according to their nature, are in accordance with good faith, custom and the law.
156. *See also* J. Ataz Lopez, *Los médicos y la responsabilidad civil* (Montecorvo, Madrid 1985), pp. 323 ff.
157. In this regard *see* Ataz Lopez, *Los médicos y la responsabilidad civil*, pp. 327–29.
158. On this issue *see infra* and particularly Ataz Lopez, *Los médicos y la responsabilidad civil*, pp. 335–46; J. Fernandez Costales, *Responsabilidad civil médica y hospitalaria* (La Ley, Madrid 1987), pp. 154–59; Llamas Pombo, *La responsabilidad civil del médico*, pp. 239–44.

avoided.[159] Furthermore, a lack of diligence – which would enable the conduct to be viewed as being negligent – is often associated with causation, when it is more correct initially at least to analyse the two separately. Only after a causal link has been seen to exist between conduct and result is it appropriate to assess the matter of whether the action was negligent or not.[160] The so called cases of *wrongful conception* and *wrongful pregnancy* derived of an omission of or failed diagnosis have been considered a by courts as a source for civil responsibility.[161]

Perhaps it is for these reasons that case law is not guided by one single criterion alone in establishing the causal connection: although the *conditio sine qua non* formula is widely accepted, there is another current in case law (backed by a sector of doctrine) which stresses the failings of this principle. For example, it is not capable of settling correctly cases involving several causal processes which lead to harm being caused, and it would rule out finding possible grounds for objective liability, etc. – This second body of opinion prefers other criteria and is supported by the Supreme Court ruling of 11 July 1987, which sided with the theory of adequation. Having said that, the *conditio sine qua non* formula continues to afford the surest means of establishing the causal link between conduct and harm. This does not mean, however, that it is not possible to perfect the legal relevance of causation either by extending civil liability of cases of objective liability – given that the problem is one of culpability, that is, strict liability –, or by limiting it in accordance with the modern-day category of objective imputation.

Objective liability will be dealt with in the next section, although it is important to recall here that objective imputation is a category which covers a range of criteria, which can be used to rule out liability in respect of a conduct which has been considered previously to have been the cause of a harmful result. This is why objective imputation may be considered as acting in the opposite sense to objective liability, which broadens the scope of liability, whereas the former serves to limit the attribution of harmful results to conducts for which a causal connection can be established and thereby reduces the scope of civil liability. In this way, the ruling of the Supreme Court (2nd Chamber) of 11 February 1987 acknowledges that 'the causal link between the action and the result is not in itself sufficient, (…) it is necessary also to add to the notion of cause, as understood by the natural sciences and as translated into the doctrine of *conditio sine qua non* or equivalence of conditions, the legal-criminal relevance of any such causal connection'. Furthermore, objective imputation leads to the author being

159. *See* Romeo-Casabona, *El médico y el Derecho Penal, I*, p. 227; Cerezo Mir, *Curso de Derecho Penal español. Parte General I*, p. 396. Moreover, this criterion should be complemented (restricted) by that of foreseeability, even where the causal link between conduct and harmful outcome can be established; *see* Cerezo Mir, p. 396 and also the Supreme Court Rulings of 13 Jul. 1987 and 7 Jun. 1988 mentioned above.

160. Cf. Supreme Court (2nd Chamber) Ruling of 11 Feb. 1987.

161. See Emaldi Cirión. *El consejo genético y sus implicaciones jurídicas*, pp. 233 ff.; Supreme Court (1st Chamber) Ruling of 24 Sep. 1999. Rulings dealing with *wrongful birth*: 18 Dec. 2003 and of 18 May 2006.

made responsible for conducts which, strictly speaking, are not the actual causes of the harmful result – as is the case, for example, with acts of omission.[162] Objective imputation is being introduced into Spanish civil law doctrine particularly in view of its potential as a criterion which limits criminal liability and any derived civil liability consequences. However, at present moment it does not play a decisive role in the determination of the legal relevance of causal conducts in medical practice yet.

(4) *Culpability of the causer of the harm*: although civil law specialists acknowledge that there are two accepted meanings of the term fault – in the broad sense as comprising intention also, and in the stricter sense as the breach of certain duties of diligence and foresight[163] – it is used more frequently in the stricter of the two senses, and in particular in relation to the health professions to denote negligent conduct from which civil liability may be derived.[164] The sense of Article 1104 of the Civil Code is adopted therefore.[165] Moreover, and here one can discern the influence of French doctrine, the category of 'medical fault' has gradually been introduced into Spanish law to denote breaches of duties of diligence by medical professionals in the course of professional practice.[166]
Here again we encounter difficulties in attempting to arrive at a precise definition of what constitutes a breach of said duties. These difficulties stem from the relative nature of the two factors which are generally advanced by our case law as requirements for an act to be deemed to be blameworthy, namely, the degree to which the harmful result is foreseeable and avoidable.[167]
Objective liability is a crucial issue in civil liability and has considerable implications for medical practice. In order for it to be deemed to exist, and thus give rise to an obligation to make reparation, the causal link between the conduct and the harm suffices and no fault needs to be present. This could be taken to mean that the requirement of culpability is replaced by the assumption of risk in the performance of the dangerous conduct.[168] To date, this type of liability has been used only exceptionally in Spanish law, as we shall see shortly. However, the use of the reversal of the burden of proof may be understood as meaning that some Supreme Court rulings have opened the way to objective liability.[169]

89. This element increases further the importance of the problem of proof, a subject which is still very much open to debate today. We mentioned earlier that harm

162. *See* Cerezo Mir, *Curso de Derecho Penal español. Parte General I*, pp. 280–81.
163. In this regard *see* M. Traviesas, 'La culpa', in *Revista de Derecho Privado*, 1926, pp. 273 ff (reference taken from Ataz López, *Los médicos y la responsabilidad civil*, p. 274 and p. 370).
164. *See* Llamas Pombo, *La responsabilidad civil del médico*, pp. 213–30. In our opinion this is the sense in which one has to understand the 'element of intent' which, according to the Supreme Court (1st Chamber) Ruling, is required along with the causal connection in order for liability to be found to exist.
165. Article 1104; 'Fault or negligence consists in the omission of the diligence which is required by the person's obligations and which corresponds to the circumstances of people, time and place (…)'.
166. *See* Ataz López, *Los médicos y la responsibilidad civil*, p. 290.
167. Significant in this regard is the Fourth Principle of Law of the Supreme Court Ruling of 11 Mar. 1991.
168. On all these points *see* Ataz López, *Los médicos y la responsabilidad civil*, pp. 257–62.
169. See: Supreme Court Rulings of 23 Jun. 2005.

was a necessary circumstance for determining civil liability and that it was extremely complex to assess this in the context of a physician-patient relationship. Generally speaking, this relationship is created when an unwell patient goes to the doctor and seeks his help to improve his condition or to attenuate the negative effects of his illness or accident. The objectives, unfortunately, are not always achieved and hence the problem arises of how to assess a lack of improvement or a worsening of the patient's condition. Clearly, an evolution of the patient's health along these lines could well be due to the action of the physician and thus it has to be decided whether or not such action was found wanting. However, it should not be ruled out that the worsening state may be due to the very process of the illness or the accident sustained by the patient and could not have been halted by the physician's diligent action.[170] Thus, the other circumstances of civil liability come into play and certain general aspects must be proven: the existence of harm,[171] the nature of any such harm, the causal connection, and fault or lack of fault-depending on who has to furnish the proof – on the part of the physician.

A general principle of civil liability is that the existence of harm must be proven by the person alleging its existence, and it is up to the judge to appraise whether this is in fact the case.[172] Abundant examples exist in civil law case law of attacks on people's honour, privacy and personal image,[173] which show how interesting the perspective described here is, that is, splitting the concept of culpable harm into its two elements and conferring a separate identity on the problem of the determination of harm (of a moral nature in the above-mentioned case law examples). In the field of medical liability this perspective is justified in view of the conflict which exists between the two categories of bodily and moral harm: partial recovery of sight,[174] causing of blindness, worsening of one's physical appearance following plastic surgery designed to do just the opposite, etc.[175] and even death (from the point of view of the moral harm caused to next-of-kin).[176] The number of circumstances in which it would be necessary to ascertain and prove the existence of harm in order to make

170. *See* Ataz Lopez, *Los médicos y la responsabilidad civil*, pp. 340 ff.

171. It is quite a different matter if the harm is caused by an unlawful intervention. As was stated, the existence of harm is indicated by the impairment sustained by the patient's health, but this does not necessarily mean that it can be made good through civil liability. This acceptance can be inferred from Arts 1101 and 1902 of the Civil Code: the obligation to make good the harm arises when said harm is caused by someone who commits, for instance, negligence, that is, it arises when the harm is culpable; however, there exists also harm caused by non-culpable behaviour; cf. Santos Briz, *La responsabilidad civil*, pp. 140–41 (NB the meaning given in note 144 coincides with that considered here).

172. *See* González Morán, *La responsabilidad civil del médico*, pp. 118–9; De Ángel Yagüez, *Responsabilidad civil por actos médicos. Problemas de prueba*, pp. 5 ff; and Supreme Court Ruling of 14 Apr. 1999.

173. The need to lay down the precise content of such rights and guidelines for determining whether infringement constitutes moral harm led the Constitutional Court to give rulings (in sentences handed down on 23 Mar. and 5 Oct. 1987 and 2 Dec. 1988).

174. In Supreme Court Ruling of 6 Nov. 1990; the appeal was dismissed for lack of proof that the doctor concerned had acted negligently.

175. An abundance of examples of case law on bodily harm can be found in González Morán, *La responsabilidad civil del médico*, pp. 121–4.

176. Although it is not a case involving medical liability, it is cited as an example by González Morán, *La responsabilidad civil del médico*, pp. 115 and 117.

the physician answerable for unlawful conduct could well be endless. In the case of organ transplants, for example, how is one to weigh up the rejection of the organ which worsens the patient's pre-operation condition? How can the success or failure of plastic surgery be appraised? To what extent and in which cases does the violation of professional secrecy give rise to moral damage? And so on ...

For their part, the other problems – proof of the causal link and fault on the part of the physician – are addressed in the text of the ruling of the Supreme Court (1st chamber) of 11 March 1991,[177] in which it is stated that:

> The contractual or extracontractual obligation of physicians and health professionals in general is not necessarily to achieve the recovery of the patient. Put another way, they are obliged not to attain a given result but to use means: the professional is not obliged to cure the patient but rather to provide him with all the care required, in accordance with the state of the art in science. Moreover, more or less objective liability of all types is generally ruled out in the case of health professionals and their conduct, while the reversal of the burden of proof (which has been accepted by this Chamber with respect to harm arising out of circumstances of a different nature) is also excluded, and hence it is up to the patient to prove the existence of a causal connection or link and of fault.[178]

This and other rulings have firmly established the current of case law which places on the shoulders of the plaintiff the burden of proving each and every one of the requirements.

As was stated above, the reversal of the burden of proof may lead to the objectivation of liability: the plaintiff will not have to prove the negligence of the medical action which caused the harm.[179] Such cases are few and far between in Spanish case law;[180] for example, the Supreme Court ruling of 1 December 1987,[181] taking into account the difficulties a patient would face in proving fault on the part of the physician in the application of radiotherapy, reversed the burden of proof when, in establishing the latter's liability, it considered that it was sufficient to recognize the causal link between the injuries suffered by the patient and the harmful conduct –

177. Rapporteur Luis Martínez Calcerrada y Gómez. Prior to this, Supreme Court Ruling of 6 Nov. 1990, following others of 13 Jul. 1987, 12 Jul. 1988 and 7 Feb. 1990. One possible argument in this sense is that based on the liability which could be established in cases involving omission, where the causal link could not be determined.

178. On the reference to the reversal of the burden of proof in harm of a different origin, *see* Supreme Court Rulings of 29 Dec. 1975, 2 Apr. 1986 and 20 Mar. 1987, which base civil liability on the existence of a harm that can be indemnified and, where appropriate, the presumption of culpability in the causal behaviour.

179. The reversal of the burden of proof does not lead to objectivation of liability in the strict sense of the term: in fact liability shall not be deemed to exist where the defendant can prove that he acted diligently. However, where this, and culpability, cannot be proven, he will have to answer for the harm caused by his action and thus it is in this sense that one can speak of objective liability; cf. Ataz López, *Los médicos y la responsabilidad civil*, p. 259.

180. Cf. Supreme Court Ruling of 13 Jul. 1987 (rapporteur Santos Briz), cited by González Morán, *La responsabilidad civil del médico*, p. 93.

181. See also: Supreme Court Ruling of 19 Jul. 2001.

excessive doses of radiotherapy – without the defendant having proven that he had used all his diligence in using a means considered to be dangerous.[182]

Notwithstanding what has just been said, doctrine[183] tends to acknowledge that it is inappropriate to burden the patient with the task of furnishing the proof in cases involving medical liability. There are a number of reasons which explain this. Firstly, the patient or his heirs may find themselves in a situation of helplessness as a result of the harm caused by the medical action. Secondly, and more frequently, they will be unable to obtain the appropriate information concerning the entire medical surgical process undergone, they will not have access to proof and will be unable to identify those truly responsible when several persons have taken part in the treatment. Neither will they be in a position to assess all these elements properly. Above all they will face the insurmountable obstacle placed in their path by the 'cruel corporatism of professionals'.[184] For these reasons, and on the basis of the principle that each side should be allowed to fight with equal weapons – a principle laid down by the German Constitutional Court in its resolution of 1 April 1979 – Spanish doctrine has found in objective liability the remedy to attenuate the inequalities in the field of medical liability which stem from the principle that the onus to prove charges lies with the plaintiff. However, it is important to stress here that this form of the reversal of the burden of proof should not be taken to mean that strict liability or liability without fault is accepted fully – given that lack of fault would not necessarily prevent the physician from being held responsible. It is a case rather of the burden of proof being displaced in the direction of the person who is better placed to furnish evidence that he acted with the necessary diligence.

IV. The Liability of the Public Health Authorities

90. Where criminal liability in the strict sense does not exist, there are a number of cases in Spanish law in which someone who did not actually cause the harm is obliged to provide reparation. Thus, for example, – and as is laid down in the Constitution (Article 106) – the State is held to be liable for harm derived from the functioning of public services, which means that it has to acknowledge liability for the actions of professionals who provide their services in the different national health authorities.[185]

182. For more details on objective medical liability in case law *see* González Morán, *La responsabilidad civil del médico*, pp. 215–30.

183. *See* for instance González Morán, *La responsabilidad civil del médico*, pp. 92–94 and 207 ff.; Llamas Pombo, *La responsabilidad civil del médico*, pp. 423 ff. Also Santos Briz, *La responsabilidad civil de los médicos*, p. 673, in which he shoulders the patient or his heirs with the burden of proving both the negligence of the physician and also the causal link between the negligence and the harm. However, it is generally acknowledged that the injured party is not in a position to furnish full and convincing proof of the negligence, the harm caused and the causal connection between the two; *see* González Morán, p. 133.

184. González Morán, *La responsabilidad civil del médico*, p. 207.

185. *See supra.* Supreme Court (1st Chamber) Ruling of 22 Feb. 1991 (rapporteur Francisco Morales Morales), which is based on Art. 1903 of the Civil Code, establishes direct not vicarious liability, which can be demanded directly of the employer because of his own *culpa in vigilando* or *in*

A. Direct State Liability

91. Although provision is made in the Civil Code for civil liability on the part of the State (Article 1903 number 5), this is further reinforced by other administrative legislation such as Law No. 30/1992 of 26 November 1992 on General Government and the Common Administrative Procedure. Its Article 139.1 declares that private individuals shall be entitled to receive compensation from the State for all injuries suffered to their properties and rights, except in cases of force majeure, provided that said injuries are a consequence of the normal or non-normal functioning of public services. In all cases, any harm alleged must be real in nature, must be assessable in financial terms and must have been suffered by an individual or group of persons (Article 139.2). This type of liability is enforced using administrative channels and expires one year after the date of the event giving rise to the claim for compensation.

The fact that this liability is considered not to be a form of indirect responsibility or liability in respect of the actions of others, but rather as direct liability,[186] which is not grounded on the unlawful nature of the harmful act or the negligence of the public servant involved, means that we are once again in the sphere of objective liability.[187]

92. This then constitutes the basic legal rules governing cases of harm or injury caused in State-run hospitals. Liability is grounded not on a contract (even where one exists between patient and physician) but on the law itself, and as a result any such liability is extracontractual in nature.

93. It is clear that liability is based on the existence of injury, which, as we saw earlier, is a requirement laid down in Article 139 of the Act. Here again it may be understood that the concept of injury is a purely de facto one, and is accepted in a manner similar to the way the notion of harm is accepted by civil law, as was explained above ('injury' in the criminal law denotes an attack made on a legally protected interest and implies that the interest in question is undermined, even though this cannot always be assessed in monetary terms).

94. In some exceptional cases, the State has also assumed liability which is not catered for in current legislation. Such was the case when it assumed responsibility for the repercussions of the so-called toxic syndrome (where thousands of people were poisoned by adulterated cooking oil), by virtue of the RD of 19 October 1981

---

eligendo, regardless of the type of liability attributable to the material author of the deed. The ruling follows Supreme Court Rulings of 22 Jun. 1988 — which held INSALUD alone responsible for the lack of diligence of an unidentified nurse — and of 17 Jun. 1989 and 30 Jan. 1990.

186. *See also* González Morán, *La responsabilidad civil del médico*, p. 149, and Supreme Court Ruling of 11 Mar. 1991.

187. In this regard, Supreme Court Ruling of 16 Dec. 1987, which, 'without there being a clearly negligent action on the part of the professional, independently of whether said professional or other health professionals in the hospital incurred in organisational liability (…)', establishes the direct and objective liability of the hospital and INSALUD in respect of the serious harm caused to the patient; ruling cited by González Morán, *La responsabilidad civil del médico*, p. 218.

and 18 June 1982; a similar case was also with haemophilic patients infected of HIV caused by blood-transfusions (1993).

B. Liability on the Part of the Social Security System

95. Let us examine now the situation of a person covered by Social Security who makes a claim for liability in respect of medical assistance provided in a social security hospital.

It should be noted first of all that the Social Security is a public albeit autonomous body, although it is expressly excluded from the regime put in place for autonomous State-run institutions. As we shall see in a moment, this consideration is important for the question of the most appropriate avenue of jurisdiction to be used.

It is also important to point out that two very different types of legal relationship are involved in health care which is provided under the Social Security system. The first is the employer-employee relationship which exists between the health professional and the Social Security system, while the second is the (statutory) national insurance link between the Social Security and the person covered by the system. It is clear from this that no legal contractual relationship exists between the health professional and the patient. Hence, liability stemming from the actions of the former is extracontractual and is based on the above-mentioned statutory provisions of the Civil Code. This means that a claim may be made *jointly* against the Social Security system and the professional, under Article 1903 of the Civil Code (*see also* the rulings of the Supreme Court – Civil Chamber – of 20 February 1981 and 28 March 1983).

96. It is also possible to claim *directly* against the Social Security using the courts for labour disputes, on the basis of the national insurance link which exists between the system and those affiliated to it. Support for this can be found in Article 1 and Article 2(o) of the Law 36/2011, of 10 October which regulates the Labour Jurisdiction. Such claims would involve making the National Institute of Health directly liable for the supposedly incorrect granting of services it is obliged to provide (see rulings of the Supreme Court – Labour Disputes Chamber – of 20 November 1982 and 21 November 1983). As we have already seen, the fact that there is no legal relationship of any type between the physicians employed by the Social Security and the beneficiaries of the system, this avenue of direct liability (or the legal basis thereof) cannot be extended to include the employees of the system (although, as we have also seen, extracontractual liability remains an option).

Just as when the State is held to be directly liable (as was mentioned above in the previous section), the advantages afforded by this avenue of jurisdiction – Social Security liability – are clear for all to see. The physician who may have provided imperfect services is relegated to a secondary role and his professional competence and prestige are not compromised to the same extent. Furthermore, and bearing in mind the rather closed nature of the medical profession, it opens the way to greater objectiveness when it comes to determining the actual facts and furnishing means of proof. All of which means that the patient-beneficiary is afforded greater assurances that he will receive adequate compensation in respect of the harm produced. It should be said, however, that much will hinge on the flexibility and breadth of the criteria adopted by case law until such times as doctrine governing the matter becomes fully consolidated.[188]

C. *Vicarious Liability on the Part of the Administration*

97. We shall now examine briefly the question of vicarious liability on the part of the health authorities.[189] We speak of vicarious liability when the law holds one person responsible for the misconduct of another, although he is himself free from personal blameworthiness or fault.[190] Indeed:

> Vicarious liability is liability for the tort of another person. (…) The most common kind of vicarious liability is based upon the principle of respondeat superior. Under that principle, private and public employers are generally jointly and severally liable along with the tortfeasor employee for the torts of employee committed within the scope of employment. (…) But respondeat superior may apply to impose liability upon the employer for contracts made by an agent within his authority and also for many kinds of torts, including fraud and other torts that do not entail physical harms.[191]

In principle, all criminal offences give rise to civil liability. A decision regarding both criminal and civil liability is made in the criminal law procedure, save where the (private) accusation expressly indicates the contrary. The Penal Code makes provision for – or perhaps it would be more accurate to say that it can be deduced from the Code – vicarious civil liability of the State and other public health authorities in respect of offences or fault committed by employees who are found to be criminally liable and who are unable to pay the compensation awarded by a court. Indeed, its Article 121 states that:

> The State, Autonomous Communities, provinces, islands, municipalities and other public entities, as appropriate, shall be subject to subsidiary liability for damage caused by those criminally accountable for malicious or negligent felonies, when these are authorities, agents and employees of those bodies, or civil servants carrying out their duties or functions of office, as long as the damage

188. *See* for instance the Supreme Court Ruling of 1 Nov. 1991, with regard to 'a private hospitalisation contract. It adopted a criterion of fault, as opposed to the objectivation of liability and different to the criterion established for public hospital liability'; in Pedreira Andrade, 'Ejercicio de los derechos y reclamaciones de los usuarios. Diversas vías de actuación', in *Jornadas sobre los derechos de los pacientes* (Madrid 10–14 Dec. 1990, Instituto Nacional de la Salud), pp. 581–89. *See also* Supreme Court Ruling of 24 Apr. 1990 and the legal grounds provided by Art. 1089 of the Civil Code.
189. See: Pablo Salvador Coderch et al., 'Respondeat Superior I', *InDret,* Barcelona, marzo 2002.
190. John G. Fleming, *The Law of Torts* (Law Book Company 9th Edit., Sydney 1985), Ch. 19, p. 409.
191. Daniel B. Dobbs, *Law of Torts* (West Group, St. Paul 2000), Ch. 22, § 333, p. 905.

> is caused directly by operation of the public services they are entrusted with, without prejudice to patrimonial liability arising from normal or abnormal operation of those services, which may be demanded pursuant to the rules of administrative procedure and without double compensation arising in any case. If civil liability is claimed in criminal proceedings against the authority, agents and employees thereof, or civil servants, the claim must be filed simultaneously against the public administration or entity presumably subject to subsidiary civil liability.

Therefore, the institutions above mentioned must cover the civil liability of an insolvent health care professional as determined by a court. We should add also that vicarious civil liability is understood by Spanish courts in the objective sense, that is, that the institution or body deemed to be liable is answerable even where it has not been at fault (*in eligendo, in vigilando* fault is presumed to exist), and no proof that it exercised all diligence or care can be admitted.

§3. Quality Assurance: Review Boards

I. Quality Assurance

98. Like its neighbouring countries, Spain has based its health model on the notion of the coexistence of public and private action. However, it falls upon the authorities to guarantee the right to health protection (Article 43.1 CE), regardless of private sector involvement, because health is viewed as a public service;[192] these are the principles which have shaped medical care in Spain.

When speaking of quality assurance it is necessary to return once more to the constitutional principle contained in Article 43.2 of the Spanish Constitution, which defines the role of the public administrations in this regard as follows:

> the public authorities are charged with the organisation and assurance of public health through preventive measures and the necessary services and facilities. The Law shall lay down the rights and duties of all concerned.

The principle is taken up once again in Article 1.1. of the LGS, the goal of which is 'the general regulation of all actions to give effect to the right to the protection of health, as recognized in Article 43 and others of the Constitution'; Article 6.1.4 of the Law stipulates that the actions of public health authorities shall aim, among other things, to assure health assistance in all cases where a loss of health occurs; Article 9 sets out the duty of the authorities to inform users of public health services, or associated private services, of their entitlements and duties; Article 10 (which nowadays has to be complemented with the dispositions of the basic Law

192. *See* M. Beato Espejo, 'El sistema sanitario español: su configuración en la Ley General de Sanidad', p. 403 note 41. Fuller treatment is given in J.M. Rodriguez Pastrana, *El servicio público de la Sanidad: el marco constitucional*, pp. 26–39.

41/2002, of 14 November, on autonomy of patients and of rights and obligations in the field of clinical documentation) lists the rights of patients in relation with the various public health administrations; Article 30 deals with the intervention of the authorities in the inspection, control and appraisal of the activities and functions of all health centres and institutions; Articles 32–37 deal with health-related infringements and sanctions. More specifically, Articles 32 and 33 regulate the disciplinary powers of the Administration where civil and criminal actions are also involved; Articles 34 and 35 set out guidelines and principles governing the classification of infringements of regulations as minor, serious and very serious, while Article 36 lists the sanctions applicable in each case.[193]

Mention should be made at this point that Title V of the Law, governing pharmaceutical products, confers quality assurance powers on the Administration. These powers include the evaluation of the suitability of drugs, medicines and other health products (Article 95.1). Authorization of medicines and drugs is subject to their being safe and efficient, and of sufficient quality and purity; moreover, they must have been manufactured by suitably able natural or legal persons endowed. All these aspects must be guaranteed by the procedure for authorization, which extends also to other aspects such as tolerance, purity, stability and information, in accordance with statutory requirements (Articles 95.3 and 95.4). The Administration is also charged with drawing up standards governing the quality, production, storage, advertising and dispensing of drugs and medicines (Articles 98–103).[194]

These provisions are developed fully in the Law on guarantees and rational use of medicines and health products of 2006 in the version under Legislative Royal Decree 1/2015.[195] The explanatory memorandum to the Legislative Royal Decree 1/2015 states that 'pharmaceutical services includes medicines and medical devices, as well as a set of actions to ensure that patients receive and use them adequately to their clinical needs and in precise doses according to their individual requirements, for an adequate period of time with the necessary information for their proper use and at the lowest possible cost'. After setting forth a series of principles, the Legislative Royal Decree 1/2015 proceeds to lay down regulations relating to quality (Article 11), safety guarantees and others governing non-toxicity or tolerance (Article 12), efficacy (Article 13), identification (14), information (15), authorization procedure (16 and 17), exclusivity of data (18) and conditions of prescription and dispensing of drugs (19). Of note also is Chapter Six Title II which deals with pharmacoepidemiology and risk management (Article 55) and objectivity in the evaluation of security (Article 56). The latter article stipulates also which bodies are competent to draw up security control programmes.[196]

---

193. *See infra*.

194. *See* M. Beato Espejo, 'El sistema sanitario español', p. 413.

195. Legislative Royal Decree 1/2015 of 24 July which approves the refunded text of the Law on guarantees and rational use of medicines and health products of 2006.

196. The RD 1090/2015, of 4 December, which regulates clinical trials with medicines, the Ethics Committees on clinical trials with medicines and the Spanish register of clinical trials (Real Decreto por el que se regulan los ensayos clínicos con medicamentos, los Comités de Ética de investigación con medicamentos y el Registro español de estudios clínicos). Thus, it regulates the functions and responsibilities of participants in clinical trials and the requirements for authorization in the drugs and medicines sector accordingly to European provisions.

These provisions provide the basis for the control of health care activities.

99. In addition to the above, a further and complementary avenue through which quality control is assured in medicine, this time from the perspective of citizens as users of the health care system, is opened up by the Constitution itself. The opening paragraphs of Article 51 state that:

(1) The public authorities shall guarantee the defence of consumers and users by protecting, through efficient procedures, their safety, health and legitimate economic interests.
(2) The public authorities shall promote consumer and user information; they shall encourage the setting up of such organizations and shall hear them in matters affecting consumers and users, in accordance with the terms laid down by the Law.

These stipulations were developed further by the Consumer and User Protection Law 26/84 of 19 July 1984, which set out as its objective the defence of consumers and users, in accordance with Article 53.3 of the Constitution. The in force regulation in this field is the Royal Legislative Decree 1/2007, of 16 November, which approves the refunding text of the General Law for the defence of the consumers and users and other complementary laws. This defence is one of the general principles which shapes Spain's legal order. Notwithstanding, as we have seen above nowadays specific legislation on health quality has been implemented much deeply.

Chapter III Title I of the Law is devoted specifically to the protection of health and safety. Of particular note is Article 57 (Chapter II, Title V of Royal Legislative Decree 1/2007 *Judicial and extrajudicial proceedings of protection of consumers and users*) which puts in place a system of arbitration which is empowered to give binding decisions for the settlement of complaints or claims filed by consumers or users.

100. A concern and a central objective of the Spanish Health Care System is to ensure and improve the quality in which such services are implemented, and there is no doubt that ensuring patient safety throughout the care process is a key factor in achieving these objectives. The Quality Plan for the National Health System of 2010 presents a set of six major areas that seek to address the issues affecting the major principles and challenges of the Spanish health system:

(i) Protection, health promotion and prevention.
(ii) Promoting equity.
(iii) Development and Support for human resource planning in health care.
(iv) Promoting clinical excellence.
(v) Using information technology to improve care of citizens.
(vi) Increased transparency.

The Law on Cohesion and Quality of the National Health System has implemented the framework of the LGS in 2003,[197] which maintained the basic lines of the former, but modified and broadened the articulation of that law to reflect existent social and political reality. By 2003, all of the Autonomous Communities had gradually assumed purview in matters of health and had established stable models to finance the assumed purview. Therefore, the Law on Cohesion and Quality establishes coordination and cooperation of public health authorities as a means to ensure citizens the right to health protection, with the common goal of ensuring equity, quality and social participation in the National Health System. The law defines a core set of functions common to all of the autonomous health services. Without interfering with the diversity of forms of organization, management and services inherent in a decentralized system, it attempts to establish certain basic, common safeguards throughout the country. This law attempts to establish collaboration of public health authorities with respect to benefits provided, pharmacy, health professionals, research, health information systems and the overall quality of the health system.

Toward these ends, the law created or empowered several specialized organs and agencies, all of which are open to the participation of the autonomous communities:

- Agency of Evaluation of Technologies (Agencia de Evaluación de Tecnologías).
- Spanish Agency of Medicines and Medical Products (Agencia Española de Medicamentos y Productos Sanitarios),
- Human Resources Committee (Comisión de Recursos Humanos).
- Committee to Assess Health Research (Comisión Asesora de Investigación en Salud).
- Instituto de Salud Carlos III.
- Institute of Health Information (Instituto de Información Sanitaria).
- Quality Agency of the National Health System (Agencia de Calidad del Sistema Nacional de Salud).
- Observatory of the National Health System (Observatorio del Sistema Nacional de Salud).

The basic organ of cohesion is the Interterritorial Council of the Spanish National Health Service, which has great flexibility in decision making, as well as mechanisms to build consensus and to bring together the parties taking such decisions. A system of inspection, the *Alta Inspección*, assures that accords are followed.

This culture of increasing quality of the Spanish health care system has been focused to ensure patients' safety preventing harm of any nature and origin (caused by devices or medicaments or by health staff, derived from negligence or from a not-guilty accident). A way to get this purpose has been the implementation of a system of communication and recording of health related adverse events by the Spanish Ministry of Health as well as by a number of Autonomous Communities. The purpose of this system is not to prosecute and punish the authors, but just to

197. Law 16/2003 of 28 May, on Cohesion and Quality of the National Health System (Ley 16/2003 de 28 de mayo, de cohesión y calidad del Sistema Nacional de Salud).

learn from those events by analysing their cause-root to prevent they could be repeated.[198]

101. This system of control of medical services was historically complemented in Spain by further provisions concerning treatment provided in a public hospital or care centre. RD 571/1990 of 27 April which dictates norms on the peripheral structure of management of health services managed by the National Institute of Health, provided for the creation of Citizens Participations Commissions (Article 10.1), 'a body of community participation in the planning, monitoring and evaluation of the management and quality of care provided by the National Institutes of Health in the field of health care'. The functions of the Committee included (a) knowing and developing proposals for action assistance programs of the National Institute of Health in the health sector. (b) Knowing and developing proposals on the economic programs of the National Institute of Health in the Health Sector for each exercise. (c) Identifying and reporting the annual management report of the National Institute of Health in the health sector. (e) Receiving information and making proposals on personnel policy, the policy on services concerted with other entities, public or private ones, as well as on purchases and supplies of the National Institute of Health in the health sector. (f) Proposing to the bodies of the health sector to adopt whatever measures are appropriate to the adequacy of the activities of the National Institutes of Health to the needs of the health sector and, in general, those relating to improving the quality care (Article 10.3). Article 23 RD 521/1987 of 15 April governing the structure, organization and functioning of hospitals under the management of the National Institute of Health provided for the setting up of a Social Welfare Committee, a collegiate advisory body charged among other things with 'examining specific aspects which might improve care' (Article 23.2 c); finally, Article 32 provided for the creation of a Patient Care Service to channel and give written form to any claims which might arise. These claims were forwarded to the heads of the Division concerned, and replies should be given in writing and signed by the director or person appointed by him. Two representatives of Consumer and User Organisations seated on both Committees.[199] It should be pointed out, however, that in practice the application of the Decree provisions was far from satisfactory: in 1989 only 28% of the Social Welfare Committees had been set up and were working; Patient Care Services received 13,005 complaints – less than 1% of the total number of activities carried out in hospitals.[200] It is considered that the 'chief cause of the low number of complaints would appear to be people's misgivings that lodging a complaint serves any useful purpose'.[201]

Nowadays once the institutional Health System in place in Spain was fully decentralized by mean of Law 16/2003 of 28 May, on Cohesion and Quality of the

198. C.M. Romeo-Casabona & A. Urruela Mora, *El establecimiento de un sistema nacional de notificación y registro de eventos adversos en el sector sanitario: aspectos legales*, Granada, Comares, 2010, pp. 27 ff.

199. Cf. F.J. Elola Somoza, *Crisis y Reforma de la Asistencia Sanitaria Pública en España* (1983–1990), p. 195.

200. Figures taken from the 'Memoria Fundacional de S.G. de Gestión de la Atención Hospitalaria de 1989' (Hospital Care Management Report for 1989), cited by F.J. Elola Somoza, *ibid.*

201. F.J. Elola Somoza, *ibid.*

National Health System, Autonomous Communities had completely assumed purview in matters of health and had established stable models to finance the assumed purview, and consequently the basic regulations in this fields are the ones issues by each of the Spanish Autonomous Communities.

II. Review Boards

102. One of the most important recommendations of the Helsinki (1964) and Tokyo (Helsinki II, 1975) Declarations was the setting up of independent committees to oversee medical research protocols, particularly where experiments involving human beings are concerned. In the United States these recommendations led to the creation of Institutional Review Boards, which have had a major influence on the regulations governing Clinical Trials Committees throughout the world, and also on recent Spanish provisions.[202] These committees were set up primarily to review medical research protocols and those governing the consent of subjects once they have been duly informed of the importance, consequences and risks entailed in the treatment or operation to be undergone.[203]

The review carried out by the Committees prior to the clinical test is designed to protect the patient by ascertaining whether he has given his/her free consent and also the scope of any such consent, the appropriateness of the information given, particularly with regard to potential risks and benefits. The overall aim is to ensure that he is not subjected to any experimentation to which he has not given his/her express consent and authorization and that his/her rights are protected. The rights of the researchers involved are protected also in that a clear framework of responsibility is created. The same is true also of the host institution, whose reputation is thus kept intact.[204] Appraisal and control by Committees of this type are strictly scientific and legal-administrative in nature. They do not enter into the ethical considerations of the test performed. On this last point, notice has been drawn[205] to the confusion which traditionally existing in Spanish legislation between Clinical Trials Committees, which limit themselves to the purely scientific and medico-legal aspects, and Bioethics Committees, whose job it is to settle conflicts of values which arise in the course of medical practice. Article 60 of the Legislative Royal Decree 1/2015 of 24 July which approves the refunded text of the Law on guarantees and rational use of medicines and health products of 2006, under the heading 'Guarantee of respect for the ethical principles', stipulates that no clinical test may be performed without a preliminary report drawn up by a Clinical Research Ethics Committee, which shall be independent of the instigators of or the researchers involved in the test and of the health authorities and shall be duly authorized by the competent body of the corresponding Autonomous Community, which shall notify such authorization to the Spanish Agency of Medicines and Medical Products. The

202. F. Abel, 'El Comité de ética', in *Labor Hospitalaria*, no. 209, 1988 (3), p. 210.
203. F. Abel, 'El Comité de ética', p. 207.
204. *See Ensayos Clínicos en España* (Monografías Técnicas 17, Ministerio de Sanidad y Consumo, Dirección General de Farmacia y Productos Sanitarios, Madrid 1990), p. 17; F. Abel, 'El Comité de ética', *cit.* p. 210.
205. F. Abel, *ibid.*

Committee shall weigh up the methodological, ethical and legal aspects of the proposed protocol, as well as the anticipated risks and benefits of the test. Clinical Research Ethics Committees shall be made up of, at the very least, an interdisciplinary team comprising doctors, hospital and primary care pharmacists, clinical pharmacologists, nursing staff and non-health professionals, of whom at least one shall be a jurist.

103. The attribution of scientific-legal and ethical supervisory functions had already been included in the Ministerial Order of 3 August 1982, which developed Royal Decree 944/1978 governing clinical trials on human beings of pharmaceutical and medicinal products. The Order itself was updated several times during the last two decades, and nowadays the in force regulation in this field is the Royal Decree 1090/2015, of 14 December, which regulates clinical trials with medicines, the Ethics Committees on clinical trials with medicines and the Spanish register of clinical trials which sets out in Article 12 the general functions of the Ethics Committees on clinical trials with medicines, namely, to weigh up the methodological, ethical and legal aspects of the proposed protocol and to issue an opinion; to assess the substantial changes in approved clinical studies and issue the corresponding report; and to track the study, from its approval until the reception of the final report.

104. By 1988, the Ministry of Health had authorized the setting up of 143 Clinical Trials Committees.[206] In 2015 106 Clinical Research Ethics Committees do exist in Spain.

§4. Biomedical Ethics Committees

I. Introduction

105. Biomedical Ethics Committees were regulated for the first time in Spain by a Royal Decree of 1978, which named these committees 'Clinical Trials Committees' (Comités de Ensayos Clínicos, CEC). This is the first legal text that established that all drug clinical trials were to be evaluated by these committees and, therefore, all centres that would perform such studies should have a CEC. From that moment on, the Spanish Parliament has passed a gross number of acts referring somehow to Biomedical Ethics Committees.[207] Indeed, it was only a month before this writing that a new Act on this topic was passed, Royal Decree 1090/2015, of 4 December, which regulates clinical drug trials, Research with drugs Ethics Committees and the Spanish Clinical Trials Register.

---

206. Information taken from *Ensayos Clínicos en España* (1982–1988), p. 53.

207. See C.M. Romeo-Casabona & P. Nicolás Jiménez, 'Research Ethics Committees in Spain', en *Research Ethics Committes, Data Protection and Medical Research in European Countries* (Deryck Beyleveld, David Towned, and Jessica Wright, Eds.) (Sheffield Institute of Biotechnological Law and Ethics, Ashgate 2005), pp. 233–244.

106. This situation has brought us into a legal framework that is confusing, as there are at least three main types of committees, regulated in different acts, and some special bodies such as the Spanish Committee of Bioethics. Indeed, the nomenclature used in the statutory provisions governing such committees is, at the very least, confusing. The three main types of Committees are the Research Ethics Committees (Comités de Ética en Investigación, CEIs), Health Care Ethics Committees (Comités de Ética Asistencial, CEAs) and Animal Research Ethics Committees (Comités de Ética de Experimentación Animal, CEEAs), but some other names, such as Clinical Research Ethics Committees (CEICs), will remain for a time (at least two years).

For a long time, the so-called CEICs have been the most prominent type of CEIs and, therefore, we will focus our attention on them in this document. In the near future, they will disappear, as Royal Decree 1090/2015 will divide them into two categories: CEIs and Committee for Research Ethics drug (CEIm). Therefore, CEICs will only last, as such, for two years. However, it is plausible to dedicate space to them for two reasons: they will be ruling for those two years, and they will be highly related to the new types of Ethics Committees.

II. Clinical Research Ethics Committees (CEIC)

107. Clinical Research Ethics Committees were initially created by Royal Decree of 1978, which named these committees 'Clinical Trials Committees'. Afterwards, the naming was changed by Law on Medicinal Products (1990) and its subsequent development by the Royal Decree 561/1993, a regulation that also established some of the still ruling principles regarding to CEICS: the inclusion of lay members in the Clinical Research Ethics Committees and the full implementation of good clinical practice guidelines, the documentation to be included in the dossiers to be submitted to the Committees, etc.

These regulations established that the competent authorities to authorize clinical research ethics committees are the Autonomous Governments. Thus, they become institutional or local committees and others of regional level, without implying a hierarchy between them. As a consequence, there are a lot of CEICs over the country. In some regions there is only one CEIC (i.e., Galicia, Navarra, Aragon), in other regions there are many CEICs, mainly located in hospital centres (i.e., Catalunya), and, finally, in other regions (i.e., Madrid, Andalucía) there are both, regional and hospital site CEICs. Accredited CEICs have to be notified to the Spanish Agency of Medicines and the Coordinating Centre of Ethical Committees. On 2004 Royal Decree 223/2004 transposing the European Directive (20/2001/CE) implemented the 'Single Opinion' for multicentre clinical drug trials whereby it is only necessary the approval of one CEIC (CEIC of reference) for each EU Member State.[208]

108. On 26 July 2006, the Medicinal Product and Medical Devices Act 29/2006 replaced the Law on Medicinal Products, becoming the most important law in terms

208. See Eurec, 'Clinical Research Ethics Committees in Spain', at: http://www.eurecnet.org/information/spain.html.

of the regulation of the Committees. This currently active law (on the version of the Legislative Royal Decree 1/2015 of 24 July which approves the refunded text of the Law on guarantees and rational use of medicines and health products of 2006) includes in its Article 60 a detailed description of the CEICs functions, which can be summarized in the following bullet points:

– No clinical trial will be conducted without prior favourable report of the Clinical Research Ethics Committee, which will be independent of the promoters, researchers and health authorities. The committee must be accredited by the competent body of the Corresponding Autonomous Community, which ensures the independence of the former. Accreditation must be communicated to the Spanish Agency for Medicines and Medical Supplies by the competent body of the respective Autonomous community.
– CEICs will be formed at least by an interdisciplinary team composed of physicians, primary care and hospital pharmacists, clinical pharmacologists, personal nurses and individuals outside the health professions, of which at least one will be a graduate in law and a specialist in the field.
– CEICs will weigh methodological, ethical and legal aspects of the protocol proposed, and balance risks and benefits arising prospective trial.
– CEICs may require full information on the sources and amount financing for testing and distribution expenses in, among others, the following paragraphs: reimbursement of patient expenses, payments for special analyses or technical assistance, purchase of appliances, equipment and materials, and payments to hospitals or centres where research is developed through the use of their resources and compensation to investigators.

109. The Spanish legal framework on this topic has recently been updated. This situation was strictly linked to the approval of Regulation (EU) No. 536/2014 by the European Parliament and by the Council on 16 April 2014 regarding clinical trials on medicinal products for human use. It was also linked to the repeal of Directive 2001/20/EC, which introduced changes in the regulation of the CEIs. This regulation was ambiguous. On one hand, it laid the concrete organization of the Ethics Committees in the hands of the EU Member States. To this purpose, number 18 states that:

– 'It should be left to the Member State concerned to determine the appropriate body or bodies to be involved in the assessment of the application to conduct a clinical trial and to organize the involvement of ethics committees within the timelines for the authorization of that clinical trial as set out in this Regulation. Such decisions are a matter of internal organization for each Member State. When determining the appropriate body or bodies, Member States should ensure the involvement of laypersons, in particular patients or patients' organizations. They should also ensure that the necessary expertise is available. In accordance with international guidelines, the assessment should be done jointly by a reasonable number of persons who collectively have the necessary qualifications and experience. The persons assessing the application should be independent of the sponsor, the clinical trial site, and the investigators involved, as well as free from any

other undue influence.' Similarly, its Article 4 states that 'The ethical review shall be performed by an ethics committee in accordance with the law of the Member State concerned.'
- However, it also introduced a very important condition: that the Member States shall ensure that the timelines and procedures for the review by the ethics committees are compatible with the timelines and procedures set out in that Regulation for the assessment of the application for authorization of a clinical trial. Obviously, this condition involved the necessity to address some changes in the national legal frameworks on Ethics Committees.

110. The main consequence of this new regulation in the Spanish legal framework on the CEIs was the approval of Royal Decree 1090/2015 on 4 December, which regulates clinical drug trials, the CEIm and the Spanish Clinical Trials Register. This new act introduces fundamental changes in the regulation of the CEIs. The most important of which is the division of the CEI into two different types:

(a) CEI: an independent body built based on a multidisciplinary composition, whose main purpose is to ensure the protection of the rights, safety and welfare of the subjects participating in a biomedical research project. It will also offer a public guarantee regarding the opinion on the documentation of the research project considering the views of lay people, in particular, patients or patient organizations.
(b) CEIm: the CEI that is also accredited to issue an opinion on a clinical study using drugs and clinical research on health products in accordance with the terms of Royal Decree 1090/2015.

What does this new classification involve? It is worth to mention that in 2007 the Law 14/2007, of 3 July, on Biomedical Research created a specific type of Research Committee, the Research Ethics Committees. According to Article 12.1:

> 1. The Research Ethics Committees of those centres that undertake biomedical research shall be duly accredited by the corresponding authority of the autonomous community to which they belong or, in the case of centres that belong to the General Administration of the State, by the corresponding authority of such, in order to assure its independence and impartiality.

The main functions of the Research Ethics Committees were:

(a) To evaluate the qualification of the main researcher and that of the research team as well as the feasibility of the project.
(b) To consider the methodological, ethical and legal aspects of the research project.
(c) To balance the anticipated risks with the benefits arising from the study.
(d) To oversee compliance with the procedures that provide assurance of the traceability of samples of human origin, notwithstanding the provisions in the legislation on the protection of data of a personal nature.

(e) To inform, after an evaluation of the research project, of all biomedical research that implies interventions on human beings or that use human biological samples, notwithstanding other reports that must be created. No research project may be authorized or developed without prior approval by the Research Ethics Committee.
(f) To develop codes of good practice in accordance with the principles established by the Spanish Bioethics Committee and to manage conflicts and proceedings generated by its noncompliance.
(g) To coordinate its activities with that of similar committees of other institutions.
(h) To oversee confidentiality and to exercise other functions that may be assigned by the regulation in the development of this Law.

This new type of Committee was meant to fill a legal vacuum in relation to the ethical evaluation of research projects in human subjects, different from clinical drug trials. They were to review of all types of research projects involving humans, including drugs clinical trials and health products, studies using biological identified or identifiable samples, embryonic material, as well as when handling personal data. According to the LIB, the CEI may also act as an external ethic committee of biobank, ethically evaluating applications for the transfer of samples and data associated with them. The resolution of a CEI is binding, in case of being negative.[209]

111. In practise, however, they were never created. Instead, the responsibilities fell to the already existing CEICs, which assumed their functions. Now, it seems that, according to Royal Decree 1090/2015, which regulates clinical drug trials, the CEIm and the Spanish Clinical Trials Register, CEICs will become CEIs but will only be able to address the functions of the CEIs that were not related to monitoring and evaluating clinical trials with drugs or health care devices. Instead, this role will be played by the CEIm, which will replace the former CEICs in terms of their functions, mainly evaluating each of the clinical drug trial protocols to be performed in its scope of action and geographic area. Thus, the distinction seems clear: while CEIm might oversee all types of research, CEIs will only be able to address research unrelated to clinical trials with drugs or health care devices.

In summary, CEICs are still the most important oversight bodies of methodological adequacy, ethical goodness and regulatory compliance regarding research on human subjects. They consist of an independent multidisciplinary group of people whose main role is to impartially assess research projects involving humans in order to guarantee the protection of participants, ensuring that all projects meet methodological requirements, respect basic ethical principles and human rights, and comply with the law.[210] However, the Spanish Legal Framework has recently introduced dramatic changes, and these CEICs will split into two main types of committees in two years: CEIs and CEIm, which will replace the former CEICs in evaluating each

209. See: Eurec, 'Clinical Research Ethics Committees in Spain', at: http://www.eurecnet.org/information/spain.html.
210. See: Eurec, 'Clinical Research Ethics Committees in Spain', at: http://www.eurecnet.org/information/spain.html.

drug clinical trial protocols to be performed in its scope of action and geographic area.

III. The Spanish Committee on Bioethics

112. The Spanish Committee on Bioethics was created by Law 14/2007, of 3 July, on Biomedical Research. It is an entity composed of twelve members, which is independent and of a consulting nature on matters related to the ethical and social implication of biomedicine and the health sciences. It is assigned to the Ministry of Health and Consumption. According to Article 78, its main functions are:

> a) To issue reports, proposals and recommendations for the State and autonomous public powers in matters with relevant ethical implications. b) To issue reports, proposals and recommendations on matters that the Committee considers relevant, relating to the ethical and social implications of biomedicine and the health sciences. c) To establish general principles for the drafting of good practices codes for scientific research that shall be developed by the Research Ethics Committees. d) To represent Spain in the supranational and international forums and organisations that deal with bioethics. e) To draft an annual memorandum of activities. f) Any other functions that are attributed to it, through regulations develop under this Law.

The Law also states that the Spanish Committee on Bioethics shall collaborate with other State and autonomous committees that have counselling functions on the ethical and social implications of biomedicine and the health sciences and shall promote communication amongst these bodies, notwithstanding their respective functions. The reports, proposals, recommendations and other documents drafted by the Spanish Committee on Bioethics are usually published for general knowledge and diffusion, in full compliance with constitutionally recognized fundamental rights.

IV. The Commission on Guarantees for the Donation and Use of Human Cells and Tissues

113. There is a very special Ethics Committee that plays an essential role in the Spanish Legal Framework. We are referring to the Guarantees Commission for the Donation and Use of Human Cells and Tissues, which was created by Law 14/2007, of 3 July, on Biomedical Research. It composed by twelve members and aimed at providing counsel and guidance on research and experimentation with human embryonic biological samples and to contribute to the updating and dissemination of scientific and technical knowledge in this matter. Its main functions are: (a) To assure the scientific, ethical and legal guarantees that may be demanded in relation to the research mentioned in Article 35 and to annually evaluate the results. (b) To provide, upon request of the State health authorities and the autonomous communities, reports on biomedical research with human embryonic cells and tissues and their clinical applications in the field of regenerative medicine. (c) To provide a compulsory report on research projects that require transborder flows of embryonic material. In the case of a research project with embryonic stem cell lines from non-EU member countries, the Commission shall only issue its report when the project incorporates the documentation that accredits the origin, procedures and guarantees in the obtaining and treatment of stem cell lines and the regulation of the country of origin on this matter.

Part II. The Physician-Patient Relationship

Chapter 1. General Description

§1. Rights and Duties of Physicians and Patients

I. General Context

114. Traditionally, the relationship between physicians and their patients in Spain has been based on trust, although the former are renowned for their overtly paternalistic approach. Over the years Spain has become increasingly sensitive to the need for effective protection of patient rights, and particular concern has been paid to respect for the principle of patient autonomy and more 'humane' treatment, something which has been conspicuously absent in hospitals. Moreover, the growing involvement of medical activities in disputes of a moral nature and the increasing complexity of medical practice have created the need for recognition of physicians' specific rights and duties, as well as those derived from their relationship with their patients.

In this regard it is important to stress the impetus provided by the Spanish Constitution, which is scrupulously loyal to the principle of respect for people's individual rights and is open to social and ideological pluralism. This disposition has found its way through to a wide range of sectors of society, although it took considerable time for the process of the incorporation of these rights into the legal order to mature, and lead eventually to the passing of three capital acts: the LGS of 25 April 1986; the Convention for the Protection of Human Rights and Dignity of the Human Being with regard to the Application of Biology and Medicine: Convention on Human Rights and Biomedicine (commonly known as the Oviedo Convention), which came into effect in Spain on 1 January 2000, following its ratification by Parliament; and Law 41/2002, of 14 November, on the autonomy of patients and rights and obligations with regard to clinical information and documentation. On the other hand, the recognition, protection and respect of the rights of patients and physicians do not depend exclusively on their being enshrined by the community as worthy ethical values. Rather, as shall be shown below, they are first and foremost civil or constitutional rights of patients[211] and physicians as citizens; this means that it is up

211. *See* J. Escrihuela Morales, 'Los derechos del enfermo', in *Jano*, n. 664, 1985, p. 1279; C.M. Romeo-Casabona, 'Configuración sistemática de los derechos de los pacientes en el ámbito del derecho español', in *Jornadas sobre los derechos de los pacientes 1990* (INSALUD, Madrid 1992), pp. 173 ff.

to the legal order to provide legal support for patient and physician rights. Thus, it is necessary first to examine the question of how and where these rights have become enshrined in positive Law.

115. The Spanish Constitution of 1978, which underpins the country's political and legal system, contains a series of provisions from which it is possible to discern both the core of the legal-health structure, as conceived by the Constitution, and also a set of individual rights. Some of these manifestations are of particular importance for hospital patients. A number of the aforementioned rights are considered to be public rights and freedoms to which privileges and reinforced constitutional guarantees are applicable, especially where they are given the status of fundamental rights (Articles 53.1 and 2, and Article 54 of the Constitution), in which case direct protection may be provided by ordinary courts and even, in certain cases, the Constitutional Court (Article 53.2); other rights, meanwhile, are derived from obligations contracted by the authorities via the Constitution, based on the principles which govern the State's economic and social policy. Protection of these rights results from the contents of the laws drawn up to give effect to them (Article 53.3).

Of the aforementioned laws, there are several which have direct implications for health, and more specifically hospital care. The list provided here is by no means exhaustive and should not be viewed as reflecting priorities of any kind:[212]

(1) The right to equality before the law, with no discrimination on the grounds of birth, race, sex, religion, opinion or any other personal or social condition or circumstance (Article 14 of the Constitution).
(2) The right to life and to physical and moral integrity; in no circumstances can a person be subjected to torture, or to inhuman or degrading punishment or treatment (Article 15).
(3) The right to freedom and security (Article 17.1).
(4) The right to ideological and religious freedom and freedom of worship (Article 16.1).
(5) The right to one's honour, and to personal and family privacy, to one's image, and to legal restrictions on the use of computerised information (Article 18.1 and 4).
(6) The right to secrecy in communications (Article 18.3).
(7) The right to strike (Article 37.2).
(8) The right to health protection (Article 43.1).
(9) The right to have public health organized and protected by the authorities (Article 43.2), with special consideration to be given to persons suffering physical, sensory and mental handicaps (Article 49), the elderly (Article 50) and consumers and users (Article 51.1).
(10) The right to health and physical education (Article 43.3).

Having listed the rights which affect patients, it is appropriate to refer specifically to two crucial legal provisions. The first enshrines freedom, justice, equality

212. *See* L.C. Martínez Aguado, *Los derechos del paciente en el hospital publico* (unpublished dissertation) (Zaragoza, 1986), p. 26.

and political pluralism as superior values of the legal order (Article 1.1), while the second states that the dignity of a person, his inherent rights, the free development of his personality, respect for the law and for the rights of others, all constitute the foundations of political order and social peace (Article 10.1). In spite of the enormous complexity surrounding the interpretation of both provisions as regards their direct applicability (Article 1 at least) and their scope as statutory regulations placed alongside the fundamental rights enshrined in the Constitution (and even the hierarchical relationship between them), all experts acknowledge that they are crucial at least as principles which help interpret the aforementioned fundamental rights and which exercise a major influence on the content of these. It should not be forgotten that these values inevitably take on even greater importance in the case of hospital patients.

II. Rights and Duties of Physicians

A. Objection on the Grounds of Conscience

116. Objection on the grounds of conscience by physicians and other health care professionals arises chiefly with regard to abortion and in particular where professionals, as specialists or because they are assigned to certain services, find themselves compelled to carry out a legal abortion contrary to their ideological views, religious beliefs or personal ethics. The problem of the right to object on such grounds arises mainly in public hospitals (such as those belonging to the Social Security system), although it may also affect (albeit to an extremely lesser degree) private centres. Objection on the grounds of conscience has also arisen on occasions with regard to non-therapeutic sterilization or, more rarely, in connection with certain forms of assisted reproduction.

In Spain, the right to object for reasons of conscience is related with the fundamental right to 'ideological and religious freedom', established in Article 16.1 of the Spanish Constitution: 'The ideological and religious freedom of individuals and communities is guaranteed, expression of which is limited only insofar as it may be necessary to maintain the public order protected by law.' However, it is not unanimously accepted that conscientious objection may be considered as being an autonomous right linked to the right to ideological and religious freedom. However, the Parliament clearly has the power to regulate this in order to solve specific conflicts by exempting a person from certain legal obligations, provided the objector can prove the existence of a dilemma between his/her legal obligations and moral convictions. This does not mean that the system must protect any kind of objection, but that such protection must be reserved for sufficiently important issues. It would be just as unacceptable to sacrifice the conscience of the objectors, as it would be to ignore the interests and assets protected by the rules giving rise to objection.[213]

213. Comité de Bioética de España, 'Opinion of the Spanish Bioethics Committee on Conscientious Objection in Medical Care', 2011, p. 6, at: http://www.comitedebioetica.es/documentacion/docs/en/Conscientious%20objection%20in%20medical%20care_CBE_2011.pdf.

The Spanish legal framework did not pay real attention to this issue. For instance, it was not addressed in the law which legalized abortion in 1985 (Organic Law 9/1985, of July 5, amending Article 417 of the Criminal Code). It was neither regulated by the LGS which, although at pains to include patient rights, did not follow suit with regard to the rights of health care professionals. The first legally binding document facing this issue, apart from case studies, was the Code of Medical Ethics of 1990, which stated that:

1. It is ethical for a physician, on the grounds of his ethical or scientific beliefs, to refrain from participating in abortions or in issues relating to human reproduction or organ transplants. He shall notify without delay the reasons for his actions, and where necessary will offer appropriate treatment for the problem on which he has been consulted. At all times he shall respect the freedom of the persons concerned to seek the opinion of other physicians.
2. The physician must not be conditioned by actions or omissions which are immaterial to his own right to object on the grounds of conscience. In all cases, the College of Physicians shall provide all necessary advice and help to the physician (Article 27).

Therefore, it can be stated that for a long time objection on the grounds of conscience by physicians and other health care professionals was only ground on the basis of Constitutional Court Ruling 53/1985 (11 April), legal principle n. 14 (relating to the depenalization of abortion, which explicitly recognized it as a fundamental right, alleging that the right to conscientious objection 'exists and may be exercised' regardless of whether or not it has been expressly recognized in Parliament. Afterwards, several rulings confirmed the High Court statement. For instance, a ruling by the Territorial Court of Oviedo[214] recognized in 1988 the right to object on grounds of conscience in relation to abortion. In this ruling it stated that 'doctors on call, who are conscientious objectors, cannot be forced to perform medical acts of any kind which lead directly or indirectly to abortion, either prior to or during termination of the pregnancy'. However, the ruling goes on to add the restriction that 'physicians shall provide all necessary assistance to patients admitted for such a purpose in all other situations or pathological states which may arise, even where these are a direct consequence of the abortion performed'. Similar criteria were applicable to conscientious objection in relation to other medical activities, provided that failure to act does not at the same time entail serious danger to the life or health of the patient.

In the last years, the Spanish Organic Law 2/2010 of 3 March on sexual and reproductive health and voluntary interruption of pregnancy gave a concrete answer to this issue. It confirmed case law, granting the rank of law to conscientious objection to abortion. Therefore, it can be stated that there is at present a legal recognition of conscientious objection to abortion, pursuant to section 19.2 of the Organic Law 2/2010, which, when stipulating that the medical service for this purpose must be provided at establishments within the public health network, adds:

214. Ruling of the Territorial Court of Oviedo (Court for Administrative Disputes), 29 Jun. 1988.

> The health care providers directly involved in the voluntary interruption of pregnancy shall be entitled to exercise conscientious objection, with no detriment to the access to and quality of the assistance due to the exercise of conscientious objection. Refusal to carry out an interruption of pregnancy for reasons of conscience shall at all times be a personal decision of the medical staff directly involved in performing that voluntary interruption of pregnancy, which must be expressed in advance and in writing. Health care providers shall, in any case, provide adequate medical attention and treatment to women requiring them before and after an abortion (s. 19.2)

Soon afterwards, the Spanish Bioethics Committee made several recommendations for the regulation of conscientious objection in lawful medical care, or for the regulation of specific cases within this field:

> 4.1. Conscientious objection must be exercised by individuals. It must be exercised by individual persons, this right cannot be exercised in a collective or institutional manner. 4.2. Hospitals cannot invoke conscientious objection at an institutional level. Private hospitals that are approved and their services contracted by the Social Security can exclude the objected service from their contract. 4.3. The person exercising objection must be involved in the service. The regulation must specify the possible extent and scope of the objection, which medical practitioners or other employees in medical or pharmaceutical centres are entitled to allege conscientious objection, respecting the principle of equality. The opinion of those medical practitioners and other health care providers must be taken into account when establishing these provisions. 4.4. The objection must be specific and refer to specific actions. The objection cannot be extended to all care cases deriving from possible incidents produced by the medical service giving rise to the objection and forming part of the usual obligations of health care providers. 4.5. Hospitals must have the necessary information on the objectors to enable them to guarantee hospital management and ensure the necessary health care provisions. 4.6. 'Subsequent objection' and reversible conscientious objection are accepted, because life is a dynamic process in which the opinions of the individuals might change. 4.7. It must be possible to check the coherence of the objector's actions with his/her ideology and beliefs within his/her overall activity in the medical profession. It would not be coherent to object in the public health system and not in private practice. 4.8. The recognition of conscientious objection is consistent with the establishment by Parliament of an alternative service by the objector. This service would be established to avoid any imbalance in the provision of medical services. 4.9. The Spanish Bioethics Committee understands that both the compliance with the law and the objection must be performed in a responsible way and that the provision of the services established by law must be guaranteed at all times.[215]

215. Comité de Bioética de España, 'Opinion of the Spanish Bioethics Committee on conscientious objection in medical care', 2011, p. 6, at: http://www.comitedebioetica.es/documentacion/docs/en/Conscientious%20objection%20in%20medical%20care_CBE_2011.pdf.

117. To sum up, it could be stated that Spanish Legal Framework recognizes the objection on the grounds of conscience by physicians and other health care professionals[216] as a fundamental right. The right to object on grounds of conscience may be invoked by health care professionals (physicians and others) who find themselves involved in a process of abortion (or other medical practice contrary to their conscience). However, in this last case there are certain limitations imposed by rules governing offences of failure to give help and offences committed by omission, which are implicit in the Penal Code; one of the limitations imposed by the Constitution in Article 16, and one which is specified in the Organic Law on religious freedom of 5 July 1980, is 'the safeguarding of safety, *health*, and public morals' (Article 3, paragraph 1), although there is some discussion as to whether the word 'health' denotes public health alone or that of the individual also. The possible interpretations – in the restricted or broader sense – could well alter the scope of the right. Objection should be limited to acts designed to destroy the foetus.[217] Thus, it is clear that physicians shall provide all necessary assistance to patients admitted for such a purpose in all other situations or pathological states which may arise, even where these are a direct consequence of the abortion performed. Similar criteria are applicable to conscientious objection in relation to other medical activities, provided that failure to act does not at the same time entail serious danger to the life or health of the patient.

B. *The Right to Strike*

118. The right of health professionals to strike is also recognized by the Spanish Legal Framework. However, it is ruled by an extremely ancient law Royal Decree-Law 17/1977 of 4 March,[218] which was passed prior to the Constitution of 1978. Intentions to amend it have been made afterwards, but none of them has been successful. Some concrete issues, such as the assurance of minimum services in public hospitals during strikes have been ruled afterwards. In general, they provide patients an adequate protection on their fundamental right to health care. Regrettably, isolated cases of patients dying as a result of not receiving treatment during a strike have been reported in this country. If proven, the cases should give rise to, at the very least, criminal liability for negligence.

C. *The Right of Exclusive Practice*

119. The high degree of scientific and technical qualification required for medical activities justifies the fact that practice is limited exclusively to qualified physicians. Excluded from practice are those who are not qualified as physicians or

216. I. de Miguel Beriain, 'La objeción de conciencia del farmacéutico: una mirada crítica', *Revista de Derecho UNED*, nº 6, 2009, pp. 173–198.
217. Cuerda Riezu, *ibid.*; Garcia Aran, 'La objeción de conciencia del médico en relación a la interrupción del embarazo', p. 128.
218. The right to strike is regulated generally in Royal Decree-Law 17/1977 of 4 March.

specialists, those who have not registered with the corresponding professional college and are not expressly authorized by the authorities to engage in certain practices. All this makes up the exclusive right of practice granted to physicians, a right which is afforded criminal protection against illegal practice by unauthorized or insufficiently qualified persons. As was explained earlier (Part I, Chapter 2) the illegal practice of medicine is included as a punishable offence (called literally encroachment or impersonation) in the Criminal Code.

120. Another aspect of exclusive practice is the ban on the *issuing of prescriptions* by unauthorized persons. Social Security or Municipal Welfare prescriptions are deemed to be 'official documents' and hence unauthorized issue is considered by the courts to be forgery (Penal Code, Article 392).[219] However, the prescriptions of private practice physicians working for private hospitals or for private health care companies are not deemed to be official documents, although forgery is also punishable if it causes harm of harm is intended. Harm of this type has been perceived by the courts on occasions. 'Where the name, book of prescriptions and signature of a physician who has not actually made out the prescription have been used, it must be considered that the physician's prestige, professional reputation and action have been damaged, because the unscrupulous use of his name and title is sufficient to cause moral harm and affect the reputation and professional honour to which he is entitled' (Supreme Court Ruling, 2nd Chamber, of 22 January 1981). Nowadays, most forgeries of prescriptions are still committed by drug addicts to obtain psychotropic substances in chemists.[220]

D. Duties of Physicians

121. A physician's most important duties arise from his recognition and respect of the corresponding rights of patients, as we shall see below. There are, however, a number of more specific statutory duties which must be observed.

122. Duty to denounce the commission of offences. The Spanish Criminal Procedure Act imposes certain duties on physicians regarding the obligation to notify the appropriate authority of any offences which a physician detects either when treating a patient or in other circumstances (Articles 259, 262, which are related to the general obligation to report an offence and 355, which is directly related to their obligation to report a harm).

This duty to notify offences which come to the attention of the physician in the course of his work has been criticized a great deal from the point of view that if, in so doing, he betrays his patient he is in breach of his duty of secrecy towards the latter, and is also betraying the confidential relationship which should exist between the two. In such cases a conflict of duties arises (the duty to report the offence and the duty of confidentiality towards the patient) and the problem thrown up is which is of greater value. The solution is by no means easy, although we would side with

---

219. *See* Rulings of Supreme Court (2nd Chamber) of 18 Apr. 1989 and 22 Apr. 1991.
220. *See* Ruling of Provincial Court of Valencia, 18 Jan. 1990.

the duty of confidentiality since it relates to respect for personal privacy, which is recognized by the Constitution as being a fundamental right (Article 18.1).

123. Duties to assist. To begin with, the duty of human solidarity obliges a physician to act to help others, either as a result of his professional status, as a public servant, or as an ordinary citizen just like any other. A physician who fails to act in such cases may be criminally liable. According to Article 196 of the Criminal Code:

> A medical practitioner who, while under obligation to do so, were to refuse health assistance or abandon the provision of health services, when refusal or abandonment were to cause serious risk to personal health, shall be punished with the penalties of the preceding Article, in the upper half and with that of special barring from public employment and office, profession or trade, for a term of six months to three years.

However, as far as the aforementioned offence is concerned, convictions of physicians are extremely rare;[221] in some cases physicians have been convicted of failing to visit the home of a patient when under a duty to do so.[222]

III. Rights and Duties of Patients

124. The primary legal sources of patient rights at national level in Spain are the General Law on Public Health of 1986 and the Basic Law 41/2002 on the Autonomy of the Patient and the Rights and Obligations with regard to Information and Clinical Documentation. The rights of patients were originally introduced in the Spanish Legal Framework by LGS of 1986. This Act, still in force, set out in Article 10 and Article 11 a series of rights and duties of patients[223] and users of public (and, in some cases, private) health services. These are truly subjective and claimable rights. The most important ones are:

- The right to one's personality, to human dignity and intimacy, and the right not to be discriminated against on the grounds of race, gender, sexual tendencies, etc.
- The right to information concerning health services to which they are entitled and concerning any requirements governing the use thereof.
- The right to confidentiality in respect of all information concerning their medical condition and their stay in public health institutions and in private institutions which co-operate with the public system.
- The right to be notified if the prognosis, diagnosis and therapeutic procedures applied to them is likely to be used as part of a teaching or research project. In no way shall the project entail any additional danger to their health and in all

221. Rulings of Supreme Court (2nd Chamber) of 22 Oct. 2015.
222. Rulings of Supreme Court (2nd Chamber) of 21 Jun. 1989 and 2 Oct. 1989.
223. *See* Romeo-Casabona, 'Configuración sistemática de los derechos de los pacientes en al ámbito del derecho español', pp. 178 ff.

cases the patients' prior written consent must be sought and authorization given by the physician and the management of the health institution concerned.
- The right to have a physician assigned to his case. The physician's name shall be notified to the patient and he shall serve as his main health care interlocutor. In the absence of the physician appointed, responsibility shall be assumed by another member of the team.
- The right to participate, through community institutions, in health activities, in accordance with the terms laid down in the present Law and any statutory provisions which develop the Law further.
- The right to make use of channels created to enable patients to lodge complaints or propose suggestions within the appropriate time-limits. In either case the patient shall receive a written reply within the stipulated time-limit.
- The right to choose his physician and other qualified health care professionals in accordance with the conditions laid down in the present Law, as well as in any provisions drawn up to develop the Law further and those regulating the functioning of health care centres.
- The right of a patient to obtain drugs and medicines and health products considered necessary to promote, conserve or restore his health, in accordance with the terms laid down by the State Administration.

The Law also established the main obligations of citizens towards health institutions and bodies (Article 11):

(1) To comply with general health regulations governing the population and also with any specific health service regulations.
(2) To treat facilities with care and to co-operate in the up-keep of health care institutions.
(3) To ensure that appropriate use is made of the services provided by the health care system, in particular the use of services, procedures for certifying sick leave and permanent disability, and therapeutic and social services.

125. Afterwards, several Acts have complemented the LGS, introducing new rights or modifying those already mentioned, as far as at the end of the nineties it was quite clear that the list of rights included in the LGS had proven to be insufficient, mainly due to a change of attitude towards health care relations and a correlative need for defining these rights and their content. This need was covered by two main tools. The first was the Convention for the Protection of Human Rights and Dignity of the Human Being with regard to the Application of Biology and Medicine: Convention on Human Rights and Biomedicine (commonly known as the Oviedo Convention), which came into effect in Spain on 1 January 2000, following its ratification by Parliament. Notwithstanding the direct applicability of the Convention, the ratification of the Convention encouraged a reform of the existing legislation on health care. A reform was necessary not only because some aspects of the existing legislation were in contradiction with the Convention, but also because some of the new rights provided for in the Convention were not yet acknowledged in the Spanish health care legislation.[224]

This reform was addressed by Basic Law 41/2002 on the Autonomy of the Patient and the Rights and Obligations with regard to Information and Clinical Documentation, which partially repealed the LGS of 1986, particularly as regards the provisions on patient rights. It regulates matters which the LGS of 1986 had fallen short in its attempt to regulate, such as the right to health information, informed consent, health documentation, clinical records and other clinical information. This Law likewise classifies the ways in which capabilities may be limited and attributes physicians with authority over the evaluation thereof. Therefore, this Law, a primary law nation-wide, meant a major advancement in physician-patient relations.[225] Indeed, the purpose of this law is to regulate the autonomy of the patient and the rights and obligations with regard to information and clinical documentation of patient, users, professionals as well as public and private health centres and services (Article 1). Its Exposition of Reasons (Explanatory Memorandum) states the following:

> (…) this Law completes the provisions enunciated by the General Health Act as general principles. In this regard, it reinforces and provides special treatment for the right to autonomy of the patient. In particular deserving of special mention is the regulation on prior instructions which, in accordance with the criterion set down in the Oviedo Convention, considers the wishes of the patient stated in advance within the scope of informed consent.

According to the Act, patient rights include:

(a) Right to informed consent. The right of a patient to informed consent is one of the basic patient rights in Spain. The Patient Rights Law defines an informed consent as the free, voluntary and conscious decision of a patient, stated in the full use of his faculties after receiving proper information, so that an action concerning his health can be undertaken.[226] Of course, it includes the patient's right to take part in the decision-making process and the right to refusal of treatment.
(b) Right to information about health as a right independent of the right to informed consent. Article 4 of the Act recognizes a double right of the patient (the positive and the negative aspect): the right to know all the information about his/her health with the purpose of any action that may be carried out on it; and the right not to know, that is, to be respected in the decision to not receive any information as long as the individual requests so.
(c) Right regarding access to medical files. All patients or users of health care services have the right for a record to be kept of the information gathered during

224. Eurogentest, Patient Right in the EU Spain European Ethical – Legal Papers N°15, P.7, at: http://www.eurogentest.org/fileadmin/templates/eugt/pdf/spain.pdf.

225. See C. García Ortega et al., 'Patient autonomy and information and clinical documentation-related rights within the context of Spanish Law 41/2002', *Revista española de salud pública*, 78:4, pp. 469–479.

226. See Centre for Biomedical Ethics and Law, KatholiekeUniversiteit Leuven, *National Patient Rights Legislation. Spain*, at: http://europatientrights.eu/countries/ratified/spain/spain.html.

all their provided health care services. They also have a whole right to gain access to this record.

(d) Right to intimacy. Article 7 of the Law states the right of all people to have the confidential nature of information about their health respected and that no one may access this information without previous authorization as established by law.

126. Apart from all these fundamental acts, there a number of Laws and Royal Decrees ruling some specific issues. For instance, rules of patients related to genetic testing are included in Basic Law 14/2007 of 3 July 2007 on Biomedical Research, which contains a comprehensive regulation regarding genetic analyses.

A. *Respect for Human Dignity and Equality*

127. The LGS is expressly linked to the Constitution, as is made clear in the first section of the rights it lays down (Article 10.1), which alludes specifically to respect for dignity and personality (Article 10.1 of the Constitution). It adds also intimacy and equality (non-discrimination), which are also enshrined as rights by the Constitution (Articles 18.1 and 14, respectively): '[all persons have the right] to respect for their personality, human dignity and intimacy, and not to be discriminated against on the grounds of race, social background, sex, morals, or economic, ideological, political or trade union grounds'; this statement may be viewed as the main axis of the patient rights which Article 10 of the LGS then lists. References to human dignity were also included both in the Oviedo Convention (which considers as its main purpose to 'protect the dignity and identity of all human beings and guarantee everyone, without discrimination, respect for their integrity and other rights and fundamental freedoms with regard to the application of biology and medicine') and Basic Law 41/2002 on the Autonomy of the Patient and the Rights and Obligations with regard to Information and Clinical Documentation (Article 2, devoted to basic principles).

Lastly, human dignity takes on even greater relevance with regard to research and experimentation involving human beings, as we shall see in a moment; however, personal dignity cannot be considered independently but rather only from the point of view of its bearing on other fundamental rights, and thus it is with regard to these rights that one has to ascertain whether dignity has been harmed.[227]

B. *Rights of Access to Health Care*

128. The Spanish Constitution of 1978 guarantees the right to health care and health protection. According to Article 43.1, 'It is incumbent upon the public authorities to organize and watch over public health by means of preventive

227. Constitutional Court Ruling of 27 Jun. 1990, n. 4.

measures and the necessary benefits and services. The law shall establish the rights and duties of all in this respect'.

The Spanish health care system is a totally decentralized system. Following the decentralization of the Spanish nation, different health care powers were transferred to the regional level. In practice, however, decentralization reform was completed in 2002 and resulted in the governance of the system being decentralized to all seventeen Autonomous Communities.[228]All of them have important legislative and implementation powers in the fields of public health, community care and most social services. There is no hierarchy between the central government and the regional government in matters that have been transferred.[229] This means that even if all Spanish citizens share the same constitutional right to health care access, in practice the quality of the service might be different depending on their Autonomous Community and the resources affordable by the Autonomous Health Care Administration (even if Article 3 of LGS states the opposite, see below).

129. The most relevant Spanish Law in terms of Health Care access is LGS. It stipulates that all Spaniards and foreigners resident in Spain are entitled to health protection and health assistance (Article 1.2); there are provisions also covering non-resident Spaniards and foreigners (Article 1.3). As a result, all Spanish citizens who fall ill have the right to health assistance, a provision which is of crucial importance to patients, even if it does not actually stated thus in Article 10 of the LGS.

The Law also states that public health assistance shall extend to the entire population, that access to facilities and services shall be on the basis of effective equality and that health policy shall aim to do away with territorial and social imbalances (Article 3). Where considerable delays are encountered in the public system, or where the treatment is not available, a patient who uses a private health service or physician is entitled to claim full reimbursement of any expenses incurred; however, the courts require that the assistance required must have been requested in the first place and have been refused. It does not suffice for the patient to allege refusal on the basis that considerable delay would have been encountered, save in emergency cases involving risk to the patient's life, which made it necessary to seek the services of other physicians.[230]

A number of the rights included in Article 10 of the LGS derive directly from this right to health care: information concerning health services to which patients are entitled and any requirements governing the use thereof (Article 10.2); the right to have a physician assigned to their case (Article 10.7); the right to participate in health activities (Article 10.10); the right to make use of channels for complaints and suggestions (Article 10.12); the right to choose one's physician (Article 10.13); the right to obtain drugs and other medicines under conditions of equality (Article 10.14). Beyond these, the LGS establishes the duty of the authorities to provide users with information concerning public (or associated) health services and their

---

228. A. Durán, J.L .Lara & M. Van Waveren, 'Spain: Health System Review', in V. Bankauskaite (ed.), *European Observatory on Health Systems and Policies,* Vol. 8, nº 4, 2006, p. 19.
229. Eurogentest, Patient Right in the EU Spain European Ethical - Legal Papers N°15, P.7, at: http://www.eurogentest.org/fileadmin/templates/eugt/pdf/spain.pdf.
230. Supreme Court Rulings of 12 Dec. 1991 and 15 Jan. 1992.

rights and duties (Article 9), and to ensure that when needed the assistance provided is adequate.

C. Patients' Rights to Self-determination

130. General principle. There is no disputing nowadays a patient's right to decide with respect to his own treatment. This implies the need for consent on his part (or, where he is not in a position do so, that of his legal representative) once he has received the necessary information ('informed consent') and also his right to refuse consent if he considers it appropriate for his personal interests. The Spanish Legal Framework is built on the basis of the Oviedo Convention and Basic Law 41/2002 on the Autonomy of the Patient and the Rights and Obligations with regard to Information and Clinical Documentation.

131. The right to refuse life-saving treatment. One of the most controversial rights included in the Law involves the possibility that a patient may refuse treatment on which his life depends (Article 2.4). The problem usually arises with moribund patients, and shall be examined in the section which deals specifically with such patients (Chapter 2, §3).

132. Refusal of a blood transfusion on religious grounds. Major difficulties can arise when adults refuse certain forms of treatment for reasons of religion, for example, when Jehovah's Witnesses refuse blood transfusions.[231]

Beliefs and religious behaviour of this kind can pose serious care and legal conflicts when refusal is accompanied by serious risk to the life of the member of the religious group, such as, for example, one who is bleeding severely following an accident or who is to about to undergo an operation which is likely to require a blood transfusion (this possibility is catered for in some foreign hospitals which, if they have time, take a sufficient amount of the patient's own blood – self-transfusion – prior to the operation for use if needed; Jehovah's Witnesses do not seem to object to this solution).

Respect for the patient's religious freedom, where treatment contravenes his religious beliefs or dictates of conscience, such as blood transfusions in the case of Jehovah's Witnesses, must be taken into account by physicians if they wish to avoid subsequent liability (offence of coercion, for instance). Respect for the wishes of a patient poses no major problems and should prevail if the physician has foreseen the situation and can offer alternative, albeit more difficult and risky, forms of treatment.

231. *See* M. Bajo Fernández, 'La intervención médica contra la voluntad del paciente', in *Anuario de Derecho Penal y Ciencias Penales*, 1979, pp. 492 ff; by the same author, 'Agresión médica y consentimiento del paciente', in *Cuadernos de Política Criminal*, 1985, pp. 127 ff; L. Martín-Retortillo Baquer, 'Derechos fundamentales en tensión (¿Puede el juez ordenar une tranfusión de sangre en peligro de muerte, aún en contra de la voluntad del paciente?)', in *Poder Judicial*, 1984, pp. 31 ff; C.M. Romeo-Casabona, *El Médico y el Derecho Penal, I*, pp. 372 ff.

The situation is vastly different where no therapeutic options are available to replace or mitigate a life-saving blood transfusion. The fundamental issue here is whether the refusal can be deemed to constitute a suicidal attitude. Jehovah's witnesses stress that they are not suicidal nor are they exercising the 'right to die' when they refuse a transfusion.[232] Such arguments are acceptable and easy to explain: their view is that they wish to live but without transgressing their religious beliefs, a stance which is deserving of respect. However, when no other therapeutic alternative exists and the blood transfusion is considered to be the only means of eliminating the immediate danger to the life of a patient of that religious persuasion and if, in order to remain faithful to his religion, he continually refuses to undergo a transfusion, it must be acknowledged that in adopting such a stance the patient is contemplating the possibility of death, and thus, if he is aware that there is no other means of saving his life, the patient is expressing a desire (albeit an indirect one) to die. This acceptance of death, from a legal standpoint, is equivalent to a suicidal attitude,[233] which is equally to be respected from the ethical standpoint, in that it seems from a personal valuation based on individual conscience. From a legal perspective, the correct solution is awkward given that at stake is an interest of particular value, to which the legal order affords reinforced protection. However, insofar as the decision is a conscious one taken by an adult after great thought and without undue pressure, it should be respected and even supported by the Constitution (Arts. 15, 16 and 18).

133. The *right to move freely* and the right to security (Article 17.1 of the Constitution) can prove to be particularly complex when the patient is suffering from certain illnesses. Similarities may be drawn with the European Convention for the Protection of Human Rights and Fundamental Freedoms of 1950 (Article 5 e, considers that detention is lawful in the case of the lawful internment of a person liable to spread a contagious disease, or a mentally deranged person, an alcoholic, drug addict or vagrant), and the International Covenant on Civil and Political Rights of 1966 (Article 12.3). Both international instruments have been signed and ratified by Spain.

The Spanish Constitution states that no person may be deprived of his freedom, except in situations set out in the Constitution itself and in cases provided for in law (Article 17.1). As a result, in situations of emergency or need the competent health authorities are empowered to protect public health by adopting examination, treatment, hospitalization or control measures, under the conditions laid down in the Organic Law on Special Public Health Measures of 14 April 1986, without such measures being deemed to infringe constitutional rights.[234] In this respect, Basic Law 41/2002 includes exceptions to the need for consent (Article 9.2).

232. *See also* Bajo Fernández, 'La intervención médica contra la voluntad del paciente', p. 498.
233. J.L. Díez Ripollés, 'La huelga de hambre en el ámbito penitenciario', in *Cuadernos de Política Criminal*, n. 30, 1986, p. 609; Romeo-Casabona, *El médico y el Derecho Penal, I*, p. 375.
234. On this and the following situation, *see* E. Cobreros Mendazona, *Los tratamientos sanitarios obligatorios y el derecho a la salud* (HAEE/IVAP, Oñati 1988), pp. 334 ff, and 369 ff.

D. The Right to Information

134. Although it is closely bound up with consent to the medical act, it should not be forgotten that the right to information is justified in its own right and is wholly independent of all others. Information given to a patient entails a number of considerations. The first is clearly tied to consent, as was mentioned above; only after a patient has been given the relevant material information will he be in a position to give conscious and valid consent. However, the right to information goes beyond this and need not even be linked to a voluntary act on the part of the patient, as in acknowledged by Article 9 of Basic Law 41/2002, where it is stated that the information in question need not always be conceived as being a prior condition for a patient to choose freely and give his consent. It implies also that the patient has the right to know about his condition and the treatment process, as well as the right to be given therapeutic information. Reference is made also to his right to receive a discharge report on leaving hospital (Article 20), and to be granted access to his health or clinical records (Article 18). However, in view of the close ties between information and consent to a medical act, we will dwell on the subject for a moment.

§2. Informed Consent

135. As we have already mentioned, informed consent is another patient right which has been naturalized in Spanish legislation, particularly in the Oviedo Convention and in Basic Law 41/2002. According to Article 5 of the Oviedo Convention, 'An intervention in the health field may only be carried out after the person concerned has given free and informed consent to it. This person shall beforehand be given appropriate information as to the purpose and nature of the intervention as well as on its consequences and risks. The person concerned may freely withdraw consent at any time.' This approach was reinforced by Basic Law 41/2002, which includes informed consent as one of its basic principles.[235] According to the second paragraph of its Article 2, all actions within the scope of health require in general the prior consent of patients or users of health services. The consent, which must be obtained once the patient has received prior information, shall be given in writing when a law provides this. The same article (paragraphs 3 and 4) determines that the patient has the right to decide freely between the clinical options available, once he has received proper information. This includes the right to freely refuse a treatment. The Law also declares that all professionals involved in care activities are obligated not only to perform their techniques correctly, but also to comply with the duties of information and clinical documentation. They are also obligated to respect the decisions taken freely and voluntarily by the patient (Article 2 (6)). The third article of the Patient Rights Law defines an informed consent as the free, voluntary and conscious decision of a patient, stated in the full use of his faculties after receiving proper information, so that an action concerning his health can be undertaken.

235. See Eurogentest, 'Patient Right in the EU Spain', *European Ethical – Legal Papers*, N°15, p. 10, at: http://www.eurogentest.org/fileadmin/templates/eugt/pdf/spain.pdf.

Basic Law 41/2002 dedicates its fourth chapter to regulate the autonomy of the patient. According to the first paragraph of Article 8 any action regarding the health of a patient requires the free and voluntary consent of the concerned party, once the patient has assessed the options inherent to the case and after he received the information provided for in Article 4 which regulates the right to health care information. The Law establishes as a general rule that the informed consent must be given orally, unless otherwise stipulated by law, a solution that has been welcomed by practitioners and scholars as the LGS of 1986 required a written consent in all cases. However, this was not workable in practice and was even unnecessary in many health care processes.[236]

The same Law describes the cases in which written informed consent is compulsory: in case of surgical operation, invasive diagnostic and therapeutic procedure, and in general when the application of procedures implies risks or drawbacks having a notable and foreseeable negative repercussion (Article 8.2). The written consent has to contain sufficient information on the application procedure and on its risks. The physician has to assess the need for a written consent on the basis of the degree of incertitude as regards the result of the intervention (Article 10 (2)).

It is worth to mention that the Law establishes two exceptions to the requirement of informed consent, which clarify Article 8 of the Oviedo Convention ('When because of an emergency situation the appropriate consent cannot be obtained, any medically necessary intervention may be carried out immediately for the benefit of the health of the individual concerned'). The physician shall in the first place be able to conduct clinical interventions which are essential for the health of the patient without the informed consent of the patient in case there exists a risk to public health. In the second place the informed consent does not have to be obtained when there is an immediate serious risk for the physical or mental integrity of the patient and it is not possible to obtain his consent, consent of the family or the consent of persons tied to the patient for de facto reasons.[237]

136. Some observations are necessary with regard to consent-related information. In general, information is a requirement which conditions the validity of subsequent consent to the medical act; however, the act need not necessarily lead to treatment or intervention, which is why information in its own right is construed as an autonomous right enjoyed by the patient, regardless of whether he is to give his consent. On the other hand, consent and information are frequently linked and hence the two rights are not entirely unrelated given that when the patient has to give his consent he must know what he is consenting to and needs information to do so. Moreover, whoever provides him with the information should be person(s) who will treat him or perform the intervention (Article 4.3 Basic Law 41/2002).

236. See Eurogentest, 'Patient Right in the EU Spain', *European Ethical – Legal Papers*, N°15, p. 7, at: http://www.eurogentest.org/fileadmin/templates/eugt/pdf/spain.pdf.

237. See Centre for Biomedical Ethics and Law, KatholiekeUniversiteit Leuven, *National Patient Rights Legislation. Spain*, at: http://europatientrights.eu/countries/ratified/spain/spain_right_to_informed_consent.html.

Very little needs added to what has been said above, especially with regard to the need for information, the amount of information, disclosure, understanding ('comprehensible information'), form ('verbal and written'), and persons to whom it shall be given (the patient and his next-of-kin, although, in the case of the latter, without violating the respect for the privacy of the patient), etc., given that everything can be inferred from the aforementioned paragraphs of Basic Law 41/2002.

From the legal standpoint, and in the light of the explicit wording of the Basic Law 41/2002, the duty to inform admits an only exception, the so-called 'therapeutic privilege' (Article 5.4). According to this clause, information is not provided to the patient due to therapeutic reasons. Keeping this in mind, it could be said that in the Spanish legal framework restrictions on the right to information on the grounds of therapeutic privilege can be justified to a certain extent. This clause is based on a simple reason: although the physician is obliged to give clear and adequate information to his patient, it is possible for him to give partial or gradual information only, provided that in doing so his intended purpose is not to fraudulently evade his duty and that in his sound judgment, and in view of the specific circumstances of the case, he considers that full information might seriously impair the patient's recovery and hinder beyond repair the success of the treatment. Where information is restricted, the patient should be given an approximate idea of the seriousness of his condition, and under no circumstances should he be totally misinformed. Brief or limited information given to a patient should in all cases by accompanied and compensated for by fuller information given to the next-of-kin, since at the end of the day they will have to serve as substitutes for or complement the self-determination of the former.

137. As was stated above, there can be no doubt that an adult patient who has received adequate information, that is, a patient who is conscious of the repercussions of his decision, is entitled to refuse treatment. To sum up, physicians must respect a patient's refusal of treatment where the latter is aware of the repercussions of his decision. If, in spite of this – and notwithstanding opposition on the part of the patient or, in the case of an incompetent patient, his guardian, next-of-kin or those close to him – a physician chooses to intervene, and performs surgery or any other form of treatment requiring hospitalization, he shall be held to be criminally liable as the author of arbitrary curative treatment, provided that all the measures taken were of a clearly curative nature (otherwise liability would probably be more serious, if the patient's personal integrity were undermined), or even for having unlawfully deprived the patient of his freedom, if the appropriate authorization was not sought and obtained from a judge. An attack of this nature on the patient's personal freedom shall be liable to punishment under the offence of coercion (or that of unlawful detention, depending on the case). Physical or moral compulsion must be present or actual deprivation of freedom – displacement – of the patient for the purpose of carrying out the intervention shall be required; if this is not the case, civil liability may be claimed. Spanish criminal courts, however, have not tried any of the above cases, except for a number involving the involuntary confinement in psychiatric hospitals of mentally ill patients or violent or threatening persons, where it was deemed that the offences of coercion and unlawful detention, respectively, were applicable.[238]

§3. Privacy

138. The right to personal privacy is the one that traditionally has been disregarded most frequently in hospitals, a situation which reflects perhaps the little importance attached to it by society. However, awareness of this right is currently on the increase due mainly to its inclusion in the Constitution (Article 18.1, which states that the law shall restrict the use of data processing in order to protect the honour and the personal and family privacy of citizens, as well as the full exercise of their rights), LGS, Basic Law 41/2002 and Organic Law 15/1999 on the Protection of Personal Data.[239] Various aspects can be inferred directly or indirectly from this right.

139. In the first place, it entails going only as far as is strictly necessary in a medical examination (e.g., questions concerning the patient's private, family or social life) needed to arrive at a correct diagnosis. Above all, however, it alludes directly to the *corresponding duty of confidentiality*, to professional secrecy, which was afforded scant protection in our legislation until recently and is still inadequately protected in certain fields, among them the field of health. This duty covers all aspects relating to an illness, including hospitalization, and, if a patient so requests, obliges the physician to keep information secret from next-of-kin (even though next-of-kin are listed among those who should receive information in Basic Law 41/2002: Article 5.3). Contrary to what is often understood, the duty is binding on *all* health care professionals, regardless of rank or function, and not just nurses and physicians. The LGS is also very clear as to this right to confidentiality (Articles 10.1 and 10.3).

This constitutional right to privacy, together with the right to one's image, which is of equivalent rank (Article 18.1 of the Constitution), prohibits the publication in scientific works (and, of course, in the media) of photographs or other information likely to reveal the identity of the patient without the latter's prior consent. The duty of confidentiality is not applicable only where expressly laid down in the law[240] or where authorization is granted by a judge on legal grounds.

140. A true test of the right to privacy is posed by the *computerised processing of personal information* concerning hospital patients or out-patients. Such technology, with all the advantages it affords, is here to stay and throws up a greater

238. Supreme Court Rulings of 16 Apr. 1959 and 24 Oct. 1978, respectively.

239. C.M. Romeo-Casabona & P. Nicolás, 'The implementation of Directive 95/46/EC in Spain', in D. Beyleveld et al. (eds.), *Implementation of the Data Protection Directive in Relation to Medical Research in Europe* (Ashgate, Aldershot 2004), p. 357.

240. *See* Cobreros Mendazona, *Los tratamientos sanitarios obligatorios y el derecho a la salud*, p. 267.

likelihood that patients will become more vulnerable to invasions of privacy.[241] In Spain, this topic is ruled by Organic Law 15/1999 on the Protection of Personal Data. Its Article 3 defines personal data as 'any information concerning an identified or identifiable natural person', while processing of data is defined by (c) of the same article as operations and technical processes, whether or not by automatic means, which allow the collection, recording, storage, adaptation, modification, blocking and cancellation, as well as assignments of data resulting from communications, consultations, interconnections and transfers.

Personal data which refers to health is in accordance to Article 7(3) considered to be data with special protection. It may be collected, processed and assigned only when – for reasons of general interest – the data subject has given his explicit consent or it is provided for by law. The personal data concerning health may also be processed when this is necessary for purposes of preventive medicine or diagnosis, the provision of medical care or treatment, or the management of health care services. Such data processing has to be effected by a health professional who is subjected to professional secrecy or by another person who is also subjected to an equivalent obligation of secrecy. Article 8 of the Organic Law 15/1999 on the Protection of Personal Data is entitled 'Data on health'. According to this provision public and private health care institutions and centres and the corresponding professionals may process personal data relating to the health of persons consulting them or admitted to them for treatment, in accordance with the provisions of the central or regional government legislation on health care.[242]

141. Freedom and confidentiality of patients' correspondence and communications, although both are included as fundamental rights in the Spanish Constitution (Article 20.1 and 18.3, respectively) and are protected by criminal law.

142. Ideological and religious freedom and freedom of worship are entitlements of hospitalized patients also, notwithstanding the fact that the LGS prohibits only discrimination on grounds of ideology (Article 10.1). This right means that patients shall be allowed to engage in acts of worship of their religious persuasion and also that they shall not be obliged to undergo treatment which contravenes their beliefs. Where this is not possible, and as long as they are competent adults, they are entitled

---

241. *See* F. Madrid Conesa, *Derecho a la intimidad, informática y Estado de Derecho* (Publ. Universidad de Valencia, Valencia 1984), passim; F. Morales Prats, *La tutela penal de la intimidad: privacy e informática* (Ed. Destino, Barcelona 1984), passim; F. Morales Prats, 'Confidencialidad, intimidad e informática: la protección de los datos del paciente. Perspectiva jurídico-penal', *Jornadas sobre los derechos de los pacientes 1990* (INSALUD, Madrid 1992), pp. 131 ff; C.M. Romeo-Casabona, *Poder lnformático y Seguridad Jurídica* (Fundesco, Madrid 1988), pp. 25 ff; C.M. Romeo-Casabona, 'La reforma penal ante las nuevas tecnologías de la información', in *Informática e Diritto*, 1987, pp. 115 ff; C.M. Romeo-Casabona & E. Domínguez Garcií, *El Derecho ante las nuevas tecnologías en el ámbito sanitario* (Report commissioned by the Ministry of Health and Consumer Affairs, La Laguna 1991); E. Sola Reche, 'La protección penal de la intimidad informática', in *Anales de la Facultad de Derecho de la Universidad de La Laguna*, no. 11, 1991, pp. 179 ff.

242. See Eurogentest, 'Patient Right in the EU Spain', *European Ethical – Legal Papers*, N°15, p. 28, at: http://www.eurogentest.org/fileadmin/templates/eugt/pdf/spain.pdf.

to refuse treatment. This right is not enforceable in the case of a minor whose parents refuse treatment, as was explained above with reference to Jehovah's Witnesses. Here again account should be taken of the problems raised by the right to do as one pleases with one's life when the treatment refused is of a life-sustaining nature.

Although the LGS does not explicitly recognize freedom of worship, this is recognized in the Constitution (Article 16.1) and in a series of other statutory provisions, beginning with Organic Law 7/1980, of 5 July, governing Religious Freedom, which guarantees freedom to practise acts of worship, the right to receive religious assistance of one's own persuasion and the non-imposition of other religions (Article 2.1 d); moreover, the rights recognized by this law are afforded constitutional guarantees (Article 4). Religious assistance in hospitals[243] is assured as follows: of the *Agreements between the Spanish State and the Holy See*, the one governing 'Legal Affairs'[244] provides for measures of religious assistance in hospitals:

> 1. The State recognizes and guarantees the exercise of the right to religious assistance of citizens interned in prisons, hospitals, psychiatric hospitals, orphanages and similar public and private centres. 2. Catholic religious assistance and the pastoral activities of priests and other members of religious orders in the aforementioned public centres shall be regulated by common agreement between the Church and State authorities. In all cases, people's right to religious freedom and respect for their religious and ethical principles shall be safeguarded (Article 4).

§4. SECRECY

143. The obligation to respect medical secrecy is both laid down in Article 199(2) of the Spanish Criminal Code, the Oviedo Convention, Basic Law 41/2002, LGS, and the Organic Law 15/1999 on the Protection of Personal Data.

The Spanish Criminal Code states (Article 199) that:

> 1. Whoever discloses secrets of others that he obtains knowledge whereof through his trade or labour relations, shall be punished with a sentence of imprisonment from one to three years and a fine from six to twelve months. 2. Professionals who, in breach of their obligation of secrecy or reserve, reveal secrets of another person, shall be punished with a sentence of imprisonment of one to four years, a fine of twelve to twenty-four months and special barring from that profession for a term from two to six years.

243. Recognition has existed for some time of patients' right to spiritual assistance in hospitals belonging to the Social Security system: General Regulation governing the regime, government and services of Social Security health care centres (Ministerial Order of 7 Jul. 1972, Art. 148.5).

244. Signed on 3 Jan. 1979, and ratified on 4 December of the same year (*Official State Journal*, 15 Dec. 1979).

According to it, in the last years several physicians who broke professional secrecy have been condemned to prison. If the offender is not a member of the health care team authorized to access the data, then it is Article 197 which should be invoked, as far as it states that:

> 1. Whoever, in order to discover the secrets or to breach the privacy of another, without his consent, seizes his papers, letters, electronic mail messages or any other documents or personal belongings, or intercepts his telecommunications or uses technical devices for listening, transmitting, recording or to play sound or image, or any other communication signal, shall be punished with imprisonment of one to four years and a fine of twelve to twenty-four months.

In the case of health care laws, it is worth to mention that Article 16 of Basic Law 41/2002 regulates the access by health care professionals and of those persons who – although not being health care professionals – carry out their tasks in the context of health care. According to the first paragraph of this provision the health care professionals who conduct the diagnosis or treatment of the patient, have access to the clinical record as a fundamental instrument for the proper care of the patient. Each health care centre has to establish the methods which allow access at all times to the clinical record by the professional caring for the patient (Article 16 (2)). The management and the administration personnel of the health care centre may only access data of the medical file related to their own functions (Article 16 (4)), even if it still unclear if these functions might provide them with exhaustive information about patient's health or not. Furthermore, the patient's medical file may also be accessed by health care personnel who carry out functions of inspection, evaluation, accreditation and planning in the performance of their functions (Article 16 (5)). According to Article 16(6) all personnel who access the data of a medical file during the course of their work, have to maintain confidentiality. According to Article 16(3) access to the clinical record for judicial or epidemiological purposes or for purposes of public health, research or teaching is governed by the provisions of the Organic Law 15/1999 on the Protection of Personal Data.[245] This Act (Organic Law 15/1999 on the Protection of Personal Data) dedicated its articles number 10, 11 and 12 to regulate data secrecy, data disclosure and third party access to data, detailing the conditions to access to patient's information. Finally, its Article 44.4.b) renders processing or surrounding health care data a very serious infringement and Article 45 states it could be punished with a sanction from EUR 300,000 to EUR 600.000.

It is finally worth to mention that civil protection of professional secrecy in medical practice exists in the form of the Organic Law on civil protection of the right to honour, personal and family privacy and to one's own image of 5 May 1982, which in Article 7.4 considers that the disclosure of private data concerning a person or family which is learned in the course of professional or official activities constitutes unlawful invasion of privacy. In the previous section on patient privacy we referred to the repercussions of this right for the physician's duty of secrecy.

---

245. See Eurogentest, 'Patient Right in the EU Spain', *European Ethical - Legal Papers*, N°15, p. 26, at: http://www.eurogentest.org/fileadmin/templates/eugt/pdf/spain.pdf.

144. Nevertheless, it is necessary to highlight that the Spanish Legal Framework imposes an obligation on health care staff to facilitate information to the health authorities or their agents (Article 35, B.5 and C.5 LGS), an obligation which must be rendered compatible with the duty of the confidentiality imposed by the very same Law. Similarly, the duty to report any offences which come to their knowledge is incumbent upon physicians also, as we saw earlier, despite the fact that this represents a clear restriction on the duty of secrecy.[246] Indeed, it is worth to mention that the Spanish Penal Code (Article 450) states that:

> 1. Whoever is able, by his immediate intervention and without risk to himself or another, and does not prevent a felony being committed that affects the life, integrity or health, freedom or sexual freedom of persons, shall be punished with a sentence of imprisonment of six months to two years if the offence is against life, and that of a fine from six to twenty-four months in the other cases, except if the offence not prevented is subject to an equal or lower punishment, in which case a lower degree punishment than that for the actual felony shall be imposed. 2. The same penalties shall be incurred by whoever, being able to do so, does not resort to the authority or its agents in order for them to prevent a felony of those foreseen in the preceding Section when informed that it is about to be, or is being committed.

Therefore, it seems that a health care worker who knows that a patient is planning to commit a felony that affects the life, integrity or health, freedom or sexual freedom of persons is obliged to avoid it personally or by resorting the authority or its agents. However, it is important to highlight that this obligation only exists when a felony is foreseen. It does not directly involve the same duty in the case of a general danger. Indeed, this is a much more conflictive case.

§5. Complaints

145. Introduction. A patient whose rights are violated may seek protection from the courts and request compensation for any harm sustained, especially in serious cases. Patients or their relations, as users of health care, can avail themselves of a number of avenues to submit complaints regarding assistance or the manner in which they are treated during their stay in hospital.

The Spanish Legal Framework on this issue is built on the basis of the Oviedo Convention and LGS, which constitute the most important legally binding documents on this topic as far as Basic Law 41/2002 did not address it at all. According to Article 23 of the Oviedo Convention, 'The Parties shall provide appropriate judicial protection to prevent or to put a stop to an unlawful infringement of the rights and principles set forth in this Convention at short notice'. Article 24, on the other side, stated that 'The person who has suffered undue damage resulting from an intervention is entitled to fair compensation according to the conditions and procedures

246. *See* Part II, Ch. 1, §1, 2 and §6.

prescribed by law'. These statements have been reflected somehow in Article 10.12 of the LGS, which states that all patients have the right to make use of channels for complaints and suggestions. In practice, all health service centres in the Autonomous Communities should have guidelines stating the rights and obligations of the users of health care services, the available services at the centre, their characteristics and the procedure for submitting suggestions or complaints.[247]

146. Complaints concerning the violation of patient rights.[248] The LGS establishes a list of health user rights in Article 10, which has been adequately complemented and/or amended by Basic Law 41/2002, as previously mentioned. If they are to be exercised effectively, a disciplinary system is needed to ensure respect for these rights and to punish health care professionals who violate them. One initial possibility is to lodge a complaint against the hospital through the Patient Care Service.

When violation constitutes an offence, or gives rise to civil liability[249] on the part of the professional or direct or vicarious liability of the Administration, the patient may take the appropriate legal action.[250] In other cases, the confusion surrounding the issue makes it difficult to decide which system of infringements and sanctions should apply. However, we should not forget the health authorities' own means of corrective action to deal with violations of or disregard for certain rights, the disciplinary powers of Colleges of Physicians and the relevant disciplinary aspects which may be inferred from the Legal Statutes of Social Security Medical Personnel and the Consumer and User Protection General Law.

§6. Access to Medical Records

I. Patient Access to Hospital Records

147. Spanish law resolved the issue of patients' access to their hospital records by granting unrestricted access under the LGS, which stipulates that hospital or health records 'shall be made available to patients' and that 'the authorities shall adopt measures to guarantee these rights and duties' (Article 61). This regulation was amended by Basic Law 41/2002, which regulates patient rights regarding the medical file in its fifth chapter. According to Article 15 of this Law, all patients or users of health care services have the right for a record to be kept – in writing or in the most suitable technical medium – of the information gathered during all their provided health care services:

---

247. A. Durán, J.L. Lara & M. Van Waveren, 'Spain: Health System Review', in V. Bankauskaite (ed.), *European Observatory on Health Systems and Policies*, pp. 38–39.
248. *See* A. Pedreira Andrade, 'Ejercicio de los derechos y reclamaciones de los usuarios', pp. 199 ff.
249. For example, for breaches of privacy 'resulting from the disclosure of private data concerning a person or family which come to be known in the course of the professional or official activity of the person who discloses them', the specific regime contained in Art. 7.4 of the Organic Law on the protection of honour, personal an family privacy and one's image of 5 May 1982 is applicable.
250. *See* Part I, Ch. 3, §2.

> The clinical record is defined in Article 14 (1) as the set of documents related to care processes for each patient, with an identification of the doctors and other professionals who have intervened. This provision also stipulates that the aim of a clinical record is to obtain the maximum degree of integration of the health data of the patient, at least in each health centre. The medical file has to be elaborated by the professionals who are directly involved in the treatment (Article 15(3)). Each health centre has to file the clinical records of its patients in such a way that their security, their correct keeping and the possibility of retrieval of information are guaranteed (Article 14(2)). According to Article 15 (4) the clinical record has to be kept in accordance with the criteria of unity and integration in order to facilitate the best and most appropriate knowledge of the patient's health care data by physicians. The medical file of a patient has to be kept for an appropriate time which has to be at least five years starting from the date of discharge in each process of medical care (Article 17 (1)).[251]

Basic Law 41/2002 also regulates the right to access the medical file. Its article 16, the right of the patient or his duly accredited representative to access his medical file is guaranteed by Article 18. According to the first paragraph of this provision the health care centres have to regulate the procedures which enable the patient to exercise this right. The right to access the medical file cannot be exercised to the prejudice of a third party's right to confidentiality of his data noted in the medical file for the therapeutic interest of the patient, nor to the prejudice of the right to confidentiality of the subjective annotations made by the professionals who elaborate the clinical record (Article 18 (3)).

The medical file has to include all information considered to be significant for the truthful and updated knowledge of the health condition of the patient. Article 15.2 of the Law describes the minimum content of the medical file, which includes: (a) documentation relating to the clinical-statistical sheet; (b) authorization for admission (only required in case of hospitalization or if so provided); (c) report for emergency (only required in case of hospitalization or if so provided); (d) anamnesis and physical exploration; (e) the evolution; (f) medical orders; (g) the inter-consultancy sheet; (h) reports on complementary explorations; (I) informed consent (only required in case of hospitalization or if so provided); (j) the anaesthesia report (only required in case of hospitalization or if so provided); (k) the surgery report or delivery register (only required in case of hospitalization or if so provided); (l) the pathological report (only required in case of hospitalization or if so provided); (m) the evolution and planning of nursing care; (n) the therapeutic application of nursing; (o) the graph of constants (only required in case of hospitalization or if so provided); (p) the clinical report for discharge (only required in case of hospitalization or if so provided).

148. Two comments need to be made with regard to this statutory provision. First, in referring to hospital records in a general sense, regardless of whether they

251. See Eurogentest, 'Patient Right in the EU Spain', *European Ethical – Legal Papers*, N°15, p. 23, at: http://www.eurogentest.org/fileadmin/templates/eugt/pdf/spain.pdf.

are stored in computer or in written form, the provision covers all forms in which records may be kept; hence, the right of access to the record as recognized in Basic Law 41/2002 extends also to any information stored in a computer.

Secondly, a question mark surrounds exactly which parts of the record a patient is entitled to from the point of view of the precautions provided for in comparative law to avoid negative consequences for a patient who is granted direct access which is not 'filtered' by the physician. Similarly, the requirements of the physician who wishes to safeguard his own privacy if the record includes his subjective opinions concerning the patient have been borne in mind, as far as our legislation describes a file entitled 'subjective notes', which is devoted to store this type of information. Indeed, Basic Law 41/2002 clarifies that the right to access the medical file cannot be exercised to the prejudice of a third party's right to confidentiality of his data noted in the medical file for the therapeutic interest of the patient, nor to the prejudice of the right to confidentiality of the subjective annotations made by the professionals who elaborate the clinical record (Article 18(3)). Thus, it is perfectly possible to reconcile the recognition of access to the hospital record ('shall be made available') with the presence of highly subjective components (the physician's subjective appreciations concerning the patient's attitude or behaviour and his reactions), which might affect the physician's own privacy

II. Third Party Access to Data

149. First of all, it must be stated that, according to Organic Law 15/1999, Article 12, third party access to data shall not be regarded to constitute data disclosure when such access is necessary to provide a service whose recipient is the controller. Patient relatives cannot gain access to the data without prior authorization by the patient. However, Article 18(4) establishes that the clinical record of a deceased patient may be accessed by family members or persons related to the patient by de facto reasons, unless the patient has expressly prohibited such access, and this was duly accredited. This provision also stipulates that a third party may access relevant data of the medical file when his health is at risk.[252] However, it is not clear whether such access can only be granted when the clinical record belongs to a deceased patient or whether such access can be extended to the clinical record of any patient.[253] The right to access the medical file cannot be exercised by family members or third parties when it concerns subjective annotations made by the professional who elaborated on the clinical file or when the obtained information would affect the privacy of the patient or would be harmful to third parties.

252. See Eurogentest, 'Patient Right in the EU Spain', *European Ethical – Legal Papers*, N°15, p. 23, at: http://www.eurogentest.org/fileadmin/templates/eugt/pdf/spain.pdf.

253. M.T. Requejo, 'Legal Analysis of the Spanish Basic Law 41/2002 on the Autonomy of the Patient and the Rights and Obligations with Regard to Clinical Information and Documentation', *European Journal of Health Law*, 2003, p. 266.

III. Access for the Purposes of Inspection, Statistics or Science

150. Access for purposes of inspection, statistics or science is clearly a possibility, particularly in the case of computerized information, which can contribute greatly to scientific activities (teaching or research, for instance), inspections or the compiling of statistics.

Article 8 of the Organic Law 15/1999 on the Protection of Personal Data is entitled 'Health-related data'. According to this provision public and private health care institutions and centres and the respective professionals may proceed to process personal data relating to the health of the individuals visiting them treated by them, pursuant the provisions of central or regional government legislation on health care.

Similarly, Article 11 c) of Organic Law 15/1999 on the Protection of Personal Data authorizes data disclosure 'when surrender involves public authorities and its purpose is further processing for historic, statistical or scientific purposes'.

IV. Access to Records for Judicial Enquiries

151. Hospital records can be of crucial documentary importance as elements of proof in legal processes.

In the case of a criminal process, the accused may be either the physician or the patient. In the latter case, physicians and hospital authorities in general can allege professional secrecy which, as is known, is afforded scant guarantees in our legal order, a situation which has posed problems for certain professions, notably journalism and medicine. It has already been mentioned above that the Constitution of 1978 stipulates that it is up to the law to regulate the cases in which, on the grounds of professional secrecy, a person shall not be obliged to give testimony with regard to alleged offences (Article 24.2). To date, however, no law has done so, although in view of the fact that this legal principle is placed alongside other fundamental rights in the Constitution it has been suggested by some that professional secrecy may be used as a direct argument not to hand over hospital records to a judge.[254] It is doubtful whether this can in fact be done, since – as the Constitution itself indicates – the law shall determine the situations in which it is possible. In practice, physicians do collaborate with judges in criminal processes, provided that the ruling asking for their cooperation describes the information requested in detail and justifies its necessity adequately.

The situation seems rather more complex when records have to be handed over in proceedings in which the physician himself is the defendant, probably on charges of alleged negligence in treating one of his patients (the person to whom the records refer). It has been argued on occasions that the physician is not obliged to deliver up the records on the basis of his right not to testify against himself (Article 24.2 of the Constitution); neither is the hospital, since it is merely the depository of the

254. In this respect, *see* R. de Angel Yagüez, 'Problemas legales de la historia clínica en el marco hospitalario', p. 5.

records.[255] However, it does not seem to us that a physician incriminates himself by handing over the records, given that such records and any interpretations which are made of them are merely one of the elements which, taken together with the other elements of proof, will lead the judge to decide whether or not he was at fault. Furthermore, as part of his fundamental rights the patient is entitled to receive effective protection by courts and judges in exercising his legitimate rights and interests, and under no circumstances can he be placed in a situation of defencelessness (Article 24.1 of the Constitution). This means that access to the full records is legitimate. Where the request for access is made by the patient's next-of-kin (e.g., where a patient dies during treatment and his death leads the family to take legal action), it should be noted that no right of access is actually recognized in their case, although it should be granted for the same reasons outlined just now, so that they may take the appropriate legal action.

In the case of other civil, labour or administrative proceedings, account must be taken at all times of the patient's right to confidentiality and the protection of his privacy – which, as we have seen, is reinforced in matters pertaining to health –, so that no hospital records are made available to a judge without the patient's consent. Similarly, the patient's right of access to his records must be taken into account. Note also that on occasions he may stand to lose from such access, while on others access will be to his benefit.

255. As understood by R. de Angel Yagüez, 'Problemas legales de la historia clínica en el marco hospitalario', p. 6.

Chapter 2. The Physician-Patient Relationship in Specific Terms

§1. The Minor Patient

I. The Relevance of the Wishes of the Minor Patient

152. The relationship between the physician and a minor patient poses specific problems, relating chiefly to the obtaining of consent for treatment and any other measures required, as well as to ensuring that the minor is not subjected to abusive conduct. Two main statutes must be considered, namely, the Civil Code and the Basic Law 41/2002, of 14 November, on the Autonomy of the Patient and the Rights and Obligations with regard to Information and Clinical Documentation, whose purpose is to regulate the autonomy of the patient and the rights and obligations with regard to information and clinical documentation of patient, users, professionals as well as public and private health centres and services.

The age of political and civil majority in Spain is eighteen (Articles 12 of the Constitution and 315 of the Civil Code). However, before reaching this age a minor has the capacity to carry out certain acts, which means that he or she must give his/her valid consent to such acts. This is true, notwithstanding the Civil Code's statement that 'parents with rights of parental authority are the legal representatives of their non-emancipated minor children' (Article 162). The Code goes on to list a number of exceptions where this provision does not apply, including one which is of interest to us here: acts relating to the rights to personality or others which the child, in accordance with the law and his/her level of maturity, may carry out for himself. What this means is that parents (with rights of parental authority) are the legal representatives of their non-emancipated children, except with respect to acts relating to rights of personality if the children concerned are capable of acting on their own behalf. Clearly, if a child is to undergo medical treatment these rights are affected and thus in order to determine whether the child is able to decide for himself it is necessary to take account of what is known as his/her natural capacity for judgment, regardless of biological age. Put another way, what counts is the child's real capacity to understand the nature and the effects of the treatment about to be given.

In addition to this general rule established in the Civil Code, Article 9.3.c) and 4 of Law 41/2002 also stipulates that consent by representation cannot be granted in case of minors unless these are not intellectually or emotionally capable of understanding the medical act, and only if they are not emancipated or if they are under 16 years of age. Nevertheless, in case of interventions that involve serious risks for the patient's health or life – according to the judgment of the physician – the Minor's Legal Representatives must be give the consent although the minor must be heard and his or her opinion must be taken into account.[256]

Where, according to law, a minor does not have the capacity to consent to an intervention, this may only be carried out with the authorization of his or her

256. See S. Romeo Malanda, 'El valor jurídico del consentimiento prestado por los menores de edad en el ámbito sanitario', pp. 1 ff.

representative or an authority or a person or body provided for by law. The opinion of the minor shall be taken into consideration as an increasingly determining factor in proportion to his or her age and degree of maturity.

In accordance with Article 9.6 of Law 41/2002, the representative has to give his consent according with the circumstances, in proportion to the needs of the patient, at all times in favour of the patient and with respect to his personal dignity. To the degree possible, the patient has to participate in the decision-making process throughout the health care process (Article 9.7 of Law 41/2002).

Admittedly, there are practical difficulties involved in ascertaining the degree of maturity of a minor patient, although this will only be necessary when the minor and his/her parents disagree with respect to acceptance of the physician's orders. In such cases, as we have mentioned above, parents are obliged to act in the best interests of their children (as the Civil Code puts it, they must 'at all times aim to benefit their children, in accordance with their personality'), although they are afforded support in the sense that in the exercise of their parental authority they can seek the help of the authorities (Article 154 of the Civil Code).

Where disagreement exists between the parents and the physician, and if the latter considers that the parents' attitude is clearly harmful to the child, as happens when parents reject treatment without good cause, he may intervene directly, in view of the state of necessity (Article 20.5 of the Penal Code and 9.6 of Law 41/2002), as long as the situation is urgent and the patient's life is under threat; where treatment is not urgent he may seek the help of the judicial authorities, which will issue the appropriate instructions, and may even restrict or withdraw parental authority. Paediatricians have a special role to play when they are asked to treat children who have clearly been physically abused by their parents. In addition to the aforementioned option open to the paediatrician, he is legally obliged to notify the judicial authorities so that the necessary criminal proceedings may be taken (Article 262 of the Criminal Procedure Code).

153. Parental duties, among them the duty to provide religious education, oblige them to do all that is necessary to benefit the health and life of their children, until they come of age and can exercise for themselves their religious freedom and take personal responsibility for their decisions. Refusal to allow a minor to be treated on religious grounds (e.g., refusing permission for a blood transfusion) constitutes an abuse of parental authority in that parents' freedom to choose between different values and is not admissible in this case since it affects the children and suits not the children's interests but rather those of the parents. In such circumstances, the physician is obliged to act to protect the life of his/her patient and any intervention will be supported by the legal authorities.

Spanish Constitutional Court Judgment 154/2002, of 18 July,[257] deals with a situation in which the minor himself refuses the life-sustaining treatment because it contravenes his/her religious beliefs (blood transfusion). The Constitutional Court

257. The full text of the Judgment in English can be consulted in: http://www.tribunalconstitucional.es/es/jurisprudencia/restrad/Paginas/JCC1542002en.aspx.

has held that 'the exceptional recognition of the minor's capacity as regards certain legal acts (. . .) is not sufficient in order, by way of comparison, to recognize the legal effectiveness of an act – like the one being considered here – which, as it negatively affects life, has, as essential notes, to be definitive and therefore irreparable'. Some legal scholars, however, tend to consider that the patient's wishes should be accepted.

As to the behaviour of the parents in these scenarios, these same Judgments also states that they are not required to behave (whether asking for or approving the transfusion, or convincing their son to accept it) in a manner which is against their conscience or religious convictions and 'the teachings which, in a regular, normal and ordinary use and exercise of their religious freedom have been transmitted to their son for a long time before the accident took place or the first symptoms of the illness became evident'.

II. Minor's Lack of Capacity to Consent to Treatment

154. The physician must follow the rules mentioned above regarding natural capacity for judgment. Where this capacity does not exist, the minor must be assisted by his/her parents or legal representatives. If, for any reason, the minor cannot be assisted by these people and where the situation is urgent the physician may intervene immediately; in other cases, he shall consult other relatives or persons close to the minor (Article 9.3(a) of Law 41/2002).

Spain's legal order stipulates explicitly that the actions of a minor's legal representatives in exercising their authority shall 'at all times aim to benefit their children, in accordance with their personality' (Civil Code, Article 154, paragraph 2). This means that parents or guardians must always conduct themselves in accordance with the interests of the minor child for in their charge and not to further their own interests. The Civil Code also provides that where a conflict of interests arises between parents and child, the former may not exercise legal representation of the latter in the situations or acts relating to the conflict. Needless to say, all this is directly applicable to decisions concerning medical treatment provided to a minor. Let us consider briefly some of the most salient aspects involved.

In case of separated parents, Article 156 of the Civil Code states as follows:

> Parental authority will be exercised jointly by both parents or by only one with the express or tacit consent of the other. All acts that either of them may perform according to social use and according to the circumstances, or in situations of urgent need, will be valid. In the event of disagreement, either of the two can resort to a Judge who, after hearing them both and the child, if he had sufficient judgment and, in any event, if he were holder than 12 years of age, will attribute the authority to decide to the father or the mother, without a subsequent right to appeal … If the parents live separately, the parental authority will be exercised by the one with whom the child lives. However, the Judge may, upon reasoned request by the other parent and in the interest of the child, attribute parental authority to the requesting parent so that said authority can

be exercised jointly with the other parent or so that the functions inherent in the exercise thereof may be distributed between the father and the mother.

155. Newborn and very young children are not in a position to express their preferences because they have not formed their own opinions. Legally speaking, with newborn babies medical action will have to be based on the possibilities of attaining the goals of medicine, that is, to improve the child's health or keep him alive, and *not* on the likely quality of life he will enjoy in the future. If the medical goals are attainable, even though the quality of life of the child will be less than perfect, the physician is legally obliged to act (e.g., Down's syndrome sufferers with an organic pathology); if the objectives appear unattainable there is no obligation to intervene (anencephalia). Where doubts exist with regard to prognosis, the benefit of the doubt should always be given and treatment provided (e.g., reanimation).

156. Another complex scenario of lack of competence arises when a psychiatric hospitalization of minors is requested. The general procedure is contained in Article 763 of Law 1/2000 of 7 January, on Civil Procedure. This article is also applicable to the hospitalization of minors for reasons of a mental disorder, but in this case Article 763.2 states that commitment will take place at a mental health institution that is suitable to the minor's age, subject to a report on the minor from the health care services. Hospitalization requires court authorization, which will be prior to commitment, unless there are urgent reasons that make it necessary before receiving authorization. Should this happen, the head of the centre will report to the competent Court within a period of twenty-four hours. And the Court will have to ratify the measure within seventy-two hours after having become aware of the commitment.

III. Specific Cases

157. The above exposition constitutes the general rules. However, consideration should also be given to exceptional or specific cases which generally speaking do not involve curative actions as such. In effect, Article 9.5 of Law 41/2002 provides that the practice of clinical trials and the practice of assisted human reproduction techniques are subject to specific regulation and to the general regime of legal age. According to Article 5.6 and Article 6.1 of Law 14/2006, of May 26, on Assisted Reproduction Techniques, donors of gametes must be over the age of eighteen, as must any woman on whom the techniques are to be used. In addition, Article 4.3 and Article 5 of Royal Decree 1090/2015 of 4 December, governing clinical trials with medicaments, the Research Ethics Committees with medicaments and the Spanish Registry of Clinical Studies (in compliance with Article 32 of Regulation (EU) Nº 536/2014 of the European Parliament and of the Council of 16 April 2014 on clinical trials on medicinal products for human use, and repealing Directive 2001/20/EC), set out the requirements to undertake clinical trial on minors, namely, informed consent of the parents or legal representative; the minor has received information according to its capacity of understanding; some direct benefit for the group of patients is obtained from the clinical trial and only where such research is essential to validate data obtained in clinical trials on persons able to give informed consent or by other research methods; the Ethics Committee, with paediatric expertise or after taking advice in clinical, ethical and psychosocial problems in the field of paediatrics, has endorsed the protocol; etc.

Article 9.5 of Law 41/2002 also imposes the requirement for underage girls to obtain permission from their parents or legal guardian specifically for the voluntary interruption of pregnancy.

It should be noted that certain age-restrictions apply to the so-called 'prior medical instructions' or 'advanced directives'. Article 11.1 of Law 41/2002 provides that only persons who are of legal age are allowed to express their wishes through a document of prior instructions. Thus, although a minor who has attained the age of 16 years can take actual health care decisions autonomously, he cannot take health care decisions in advance before he has attained the age of 18 years.

158. Moreover, a minor under the age of 18, or his/her legal representatives on his or her behalf, cannot consent to become live donors of a transplant organ (Article 4, a and b of Law 30/1979, of 27 October, on the Removal and Transplantation of Organs); there is however one exception which covers donations of bone marrow: given that it is a tissue which can regenerate itself, donation poses no – or should pose no – major risks for the donor and is extremely suitable for use between brothers and sisters, although the exception is not limited expressly to such relations (Article 7.1 of Royal Decree–Law 9/2014, of 4 July, on setting standards of quality and safety for donation, procurement, testing, processing, preservation, storage and distribution of human cells and tissues and approving the coordination and operation rules for being used in humans). Neither can minors donate blood (Article 6.1 of Royal Decree 1854/1993, of 22 October, regulating minimal conditions for Blood Donations and Blood Banks).

A person under the age of eighteen, or any such person's legal representatives, cannot consent to sex reassignment surgery and sterilization (Article 156 Penal Code), except where this is for strictly therapeutic reasons, in which case the general regulations governing curative actions are applicable.

§2. The Mental Patient and Involuntary Placement

159. Treatment of mental patients or mentally deficient persons poses several legal problems,[258] ranging from admission to a hospital to (informed) consent to treatment. One question which must be decided beforehand is whether or not, for the purpose of consent (or authorization), these two aspects are linked or are entirely separate.

258. For a more detailed study *see* C.M. Romeo-Casabona, 'El tratamiento jurídico del enfermo mental en el Consejo de Europa y sistemas de garantías en el derecho español', in *Actualidad Penal*, 1991, pp. 329 ff.

Spanish legislation has a set of legal provisions that aim to protect the rights of patients who are incapable of giving their personal consent to receive medical treatment, including in that fundamental rights and freedoms.[259] The Kingdom of Spain signed and ratified the Convention on the rights of persons with disabilities.[260] This Convention has been in force in Spain since 3 May 2008.

We shall examine briefly the conditions of admission to and treatment in a hospital according to the different potential situations with respect to the validity of the mental patient's consent, namely, whether or not he has been declared incompetent by a judge, whether internment is urgent and whether he is to be treated for an organic or mental illness.

I. Voluntary Admission and Treatment

160. There can be no denying that psychiatric patients who are admitted of their own accord to a mental health institution are entitled to receive information, give informed consent and also to refuse treatment. It is quite possible that the extent or the nature of the patient's illness do not prevent him/her (i.e., he/she is not incompetent) from taking decisions such as to contact of his/her own accord a mental health institution or other centre with such facilities and ask to be admitted for treatment. His/her decision must be accepted and residential treatment provided if it is indicated medically, given that in such cases the principles of consent bases on the person's natural capacity for judgment and his/her grasp of the importance of his/her decision are applicable.[261]

Where the patient's condition and mental health worsen, or where his/her pathological picture on admission was already serious even though no significant deterioration is observed, the question arises as to what should be done if he refuses to continue treatment and wishes to be released from care but from the medical point of view continuation is advisable and his/her mental condition causes his/her fitness to take the appropriate decisions to be doubted. He would then be in the same position as an incompetent patient and the same criteria would therefore apply: if the patient decides he wishes to leave hospital but is prevented from doing so by the medical practitioner or the hospital management, notification must be given to a judge, who shall decide as appropriate. The situation is exactly the same as that of the involuntary internment (or, to be more accurate, extending internment)[262] of an allegedly incompetent person for reasons of emergency. It should be stressed that the hospital's decision to prevent the patient from leaving should not be based on

259. See on this M Aznar López, *Internamientos civiles y derechos fundamentales de los usuarios de centros sanitarios, sociales y sociosanitarios*, Comares, Granada, 2000, pp. 94 ff.

260. As adopted in New York on 13 Dec. 2006, and its Optional Protocol (Instrument of Ratification published in the Spanish Official State Bulletin of 21 Apr. 2008).

261. Circular No. 2/1984 from the Attorney General's Office acknowledges the validity of these voluntary admissions, although it expresses considerable reservations and urges caution concerning the persistent use thereof and the possibility that they conceal admissions made under duress.

262. S. García Zarandieta, 'Internamientos psiquiátricos', in *Privaciones de libertad y derechos humanos* (Ed. Hacer, Barcelona 1987), p. 50.

the need for treatment but on any potential risks which his/her release might entail for his/her own or others' health or life.

II. Involuntary Admission and Emergency Treatment

A. Treatment of Physical or Mental Illnesses

161. If admission is urgent and the physician considers that treatment is urgently required because the patient's life is in danger but the latter is unable to give valid consent or he/she is legally unfit this consent for the treatment shall be given by the patient's legal representatives. If the patient has no legal representative, consent shall to be given by those persons having family or de facto links to him or her.[263] Finally, if the patient's family or guardian is unavailable, the physician must admit the patient and may intervene to treat a health related problem. In this regard, he will be protected by the provisions governing exemption from liability in situations of urgent necessity; this possibility is catered for expressly by the Law on Basic Regulation of Patient Autonomy, which authorizes the physician to intervene without the required consent of the persons mentioned as above when there is an immediate and serious risk for physical or mental health (Article 9.2, b). The procedure is fully justified to avoid irreparable health consequences to the patient as a result of the increasing risk caused by the delay in obtaining for prior consent. To sum up, the physician should act as he would with any other patient in a similar emergency situation, and in this case the patient's mental illness has no bearing on the decision.

162. If in the situation described just now the mental patient or mentally deficient person is conscious and refuses admission and treatment, but his/her mental capacity does not permit him/her to take decisions because he/she is incapable of grasping the importance of his/her refusal and of his/her situation, intervention is possible under Article 9.2,b of the LAP, provided that, as in the previous case above, no next-of-kin or guardian is available (Article 9.3,a).

Nevertheless, Organic Law 6/1984 on the habeas corpus procedure (Article 1 b) does not exclude the possibility of a patient or his/her representative seeking a judge's ruling on the legality of the confinement, both in this case and in others mentioned below.

The procedure established in Law on Civil Procedure (*see* below) should be used also in cases where confinement of a mental patient is necessary for the treatment of somatic illnesses which have no bearing on his/her supposed mental incompetence. This would certainly safeguard the patient's interests better, because treatment would be not subject to prior the authorization of the judge and medical intervention should thus not be delayed, as being an emergency situation.

263. *See* Art. 9.3, a) and b) of LAP (Law 41/2002, of 14 November, on Basic Regulation of Patient Autonomy).

B. *Involuntary Admittance of a Person Due to his/her Mental Disorder*[264]

163. The Law on Civil Procedure[265] contains the premises and requirements for an involuntary admittance of a person due to his/her mental illness. Thus, the former regulation of this matter in CC (Article 211) has been changed.

The premises for admittance are as follows: Prior judicial authorization is required in all cases where the patient is unable to give his/her valid legal consent to the admittance or his/her valid legal refusal of admittance. While it is not expressly stated in Law, the admittance must be motivated by the need to treat the patient's serious mental illness or to prevent him/her from harming himself or others.

In emergency situations, the patient may be involuntarily admitted without prior judicial authorization. Under these circumstances, the medical-manager of the centre where the patient has been admitted shall make a request to the judge to ratify the authorization for their admittance, within a period of twenty-four hours. Notification must include details of the interned patient, the circumstances surrounding and leading to the decision, and the reasons substantiating the request for confirmation by the judge of the measure taken. It must also include an estimation of the foreseeable length of stay, where this can be predicted in the short or medium term.

The court must give its decision within a seventy-two hour period from when it was informed of the admittance. The judge shall authorize or refuse authorization in accordance with the procedure of voluntary jurisdiction provided for in the Civil Procedure Code.

There is a *legal procedure for authorising or ratifying the admittance* established by law:

(1) The court shall undertake the following activities before authorising or ratifying the admittance: (a) consider the opinion on the admittance of the party affected by the decision, the Public Prosecution Service and any other person whose appearance is deemed appropriate or is requested by the party affected by the measure. (b) Examine the person whose admittance is in question.[266] (c) Receive the patient's medical report. (d) Undertake any other checks that shall be deemed appropriate.
(2) The party affected by the measure shall be entitled to representation and defence.
(3) There shall be recourse to appeal against the decision adopted by the court regarding the admittance.

---

264. Aznar López, *Internamientos civiles y derechos fundamentales de los usuarios de centros sanitarios, sociales y sociosanitarios*, pp. 83 ff.

265. Act 1 /2000 of 7 January, on Civil Procedure (CPA), Art. 763.

266. *See* Rulings of Supreme Court (1st Chamber) of 2 Feb. 1988 and 12 Jun. 1989 (commented upon by R. Bercovitz Rodriguez-Cano, 'El examen por el Juez del presunto incapaz en el procedimiento de incapacitación', in *Poder Judicial*, No. 15, 1989, pp. 141 ff) for references to details of the examination used to determine incompetence; to a large extent the criteria may be extended to cases of compulsory confinement.

Admittance conditions and duration. Physicians caring for the patient shall send periodic reports (every six months or more frequently on the court's request) to the court regarding the need for the measure to remain in place. The court may request these or other reports at other times. Every time the court receives these reports it shall decide whether the patient should continue to be admitted or not. The doctors caring for the patient may request the court to cease the admittance when they consider that it is no-longer necessary.

Once confinement has been authorized, the judge is obliged by law to *review the situation of the internee*. This is one of the most important guarantees laid down in current legislation. He/she shall gather information regarding the need to extend the period of confinement when he considers it appropriate, but at least every six months he/she will receive the reports mentioned above, and he/she shall then give a ruling on whether internment should be continued or ended (Article 763.4, 3 LEC). This form of personal monitoring by the judge is independent of and cannot be replaced by the information on the situation of the incompetent patient which the guardian is obliged to submit annually to the judge (Article 269.4 CC).

Clearly, the *ending of confinement* must be authorized by the judge after his/her (at least) six-monthly review of the situation, at which time he/she is legally obliged to take the appropriate decisions regarding the continuation or not of internment. Notwithstanding this, when physicians who are caring the internee assume that it is no more necessary to maintain the placement, the patient will be discharged, and shall immediately inform the competent court (Article 763.4, 4 LEC).

The admittance of minors will be always performed in a health facility appropriate to their age, having before a report of child welfare services. To meet the appropriate decision in this field of mental illnesses in relation to consent to treatment by minors themselves or their legal representatives is a complex matter, for which legal provisions of LAP (Article 9.3, a) will be followed.[267]

In the case of a mental patient who has been tried by a court *relating to the commission of an offense*, the court may decide on placement in a psychiatric facility for treatment, for a maximum period not exceeding the time it would have taken in prison by the ruling if the person prosecuted had been found responsible of the offence (Article 101.1 of Penal Code in relation to Articles 20.1 and 95). The court can, however, under Article 97 of PC, review its decision and order to stop further confinement and replace it by other preventive measures or to cease the imposition of any of them. The prosecutor may ask for a statement of disability by the civil court, if appropriate. From this statement of disability authorities concerned may proceed with admittance measures set out above (First additional provision of PC).

C. *Intervention by Next-of-Kin and Guardians*

164. Still in the hypothetical cases outlined above, if the next-of-kin or persons close to the patient are available (as indicated by Article 9.2, b of the LAP) they shall give consent on behalf of an unconscious patient, save where he/she has already been certified as being incompetent and has a guardian, in which case

267. *See* further on this above, Ch. 1, §2.

consent should preferably be given by the latter.[268] However, the preference of the guardian is not exclusive, or, put another way, if the guardian is not available, next-of-kin or other persons *in facto* close to the patient may decide. If the patient is conscious but (legally or de facto) 'incompetent' to take decisions, the same procedure shall be used for organic illnesses, both for admission (clearly, the guardian does not need a judge's permission to intern the patient in anything other than a psychiatric unit or special training or education centre) and for treatment. Lastly, where involuntary confinement is necessary to treat mental illness, the procedure to be followed shall be that laid down by LEC for involuntary internment of a (conscious or unconscious) patient, as described above.

III. Involuntary, Non-urgent Admission and Treatment

A. *Treatment of Organic Illnesses*

165. In non-urgent situations where treatment is necessary, and if the patient is not competent to take decisions, the physician should seek consent from the guardian, next-of-kin or persons close to the patient (Article 9.3, a and b of the LAP). This should be understood as referring both to unconscious patients and also supposedly incompetent persons or ones who have already been certified as being incompetent (judicially modified capacity established in Sentence). As was stated above, these rules are valid for general interventions or medical treatment where confinement is not related to the cause of incompetence, that is, cases not involving persistent physical or mental deficiencies or illnesses which prevent the person from acting on his/her own behalf and avoid making harm to himself or to another.

B. *Treatment of Mental Illnesses*

166. Where the aim is to detain a supposedly incompetent person against his/her will (in a psychiatric hospital or other health care institution in order to treat the illness which has caused the incompetence) and the case is not of urgent necessity, the patient's next-of-kin should apply beforehand to the judge for authorization for confinement, in accordance with the conditions and procedures laid down in the Civil Procedure Act (Article 763 referred to above).

167. To sum up, consent to treatment need not always be given by the person who takes the decision regarding admission or confinement. Under normal circumstances treatment decisions shall be taken by the next-of-kin or persons close to the patient or by the guardian where appropriate, while decisions concerning

268. A similar opinion is held by F. Bueno Arus, 'El consentimiento del paciente en el tratamiento médico-quirúrigico y la Ley General de Sanidad', in *Estudios de Derecho Penal y Criminología* (UNED, Madrid 1989), p. 170.

confinement shall be the responsibility of the judge. This separation of powers might well place the physician in a curious position if, for example, a judge authorizes detention but the next-to-kin do not give the go-ahead to the treatment proposed by the physician.[269] On the other hand, doubts surround who should consent to treatment when a judge has ordered the detention in a psychiatric institution of a deranged person who has committed an offence; in principle, consent would be given by the next-of-kin or the guardian, because the rights recognized by the Patient's Autonomy Act (LAP) apply to 'both public and private health care services' (Article 1st).

In any case, the legal authorities may intervene in treatment-related disputes or conflicts concerning respect for the wishes of the patient when, in spite of his/her illness, he/she is competent to give consent. A similar situation may arise also where a judge orders detention (which presupposes that the internee cannot act on his/her own behalf) but the patient refuses the proposed treatment, if at that time he has sufficient capacity to understand the nature of his/her decision.

§3. The Dying Patient

168. Where a patient is terminally ill, that is, on the verge of death, the physician is faced with two questions: how far should he go in taking curative or symptom-relieving measures without breaching his duties or bringing forward death in a punishable way? Secondly, how should he appraise the wishes of his patient, in particular when the latter decides (where he is in a position to do so) to refuse all forms of treatment, including life-saving treatment?

I. Treating a Dying Patient

169. With terminally ill patients who are close to death, the most relevant duties of health care professionals and staff of health care institutions are to provide moral assistance and help them die in a dignified manner, without discriminating against them by basing treatment on the possibility that they will recover. Particularly humane treatment is an absolute must in such circumstances, and every access must be to given family members and to persons who can provide the spiritual help corresponding to the patient's religious beliefs. The patient must also be allowed to take decisions relating to his material interests (work, property, last will and testament), and even to be discharged if he so wishes, and where his condition and family circumstances so warrant, so that he may return home and die in the company of his loved ones. All these measures derive from his rights as a patient. When no treatment can bring about improvement or recovery, helping the patient die properly through the use of drugs or other means to alleviate his state of helplessness is not

269. In this regard *see* J.J. Carrasco Gómez, *Responsabilidad médica y Psiquiatría* (Colex, 2nd Edit., Madrid, 1998), pp. 181 ff.

only lawful[270] but is also one of the physician's duties. It has been said that breaches of this duty by a physician could even lead to an offence of failing to fulfil the duty to provide help. Indeed, Article 196 of the Spanish Penal Code states that:

> *A medical practitioner who, while under obligation to do so, were to refuse health assistance or abandon the provision of health services, when refusal or abandonment were to cause serious risk to personal health, shall be punished with the penalties of the preceding Article, in the upper half and with that of special barring from public employment and office, profession or trade, for a term of six months to three years.*

170. Generally speaking, the giving of drugs or other pain-relieving measures which entail a negligible and unintended shortening of the patient's life (known as indirect euthanasia) is considered lawful, as is the gradual increase in doses of certain painkillers (morphine, for instance) when the patient's body becomes increasingly insensitive to them, even where the increased doses risk depressing the respiratory apparatus to the extent of causing failure.[271] In such cases no offence of wilful homicide shall exist, because the authors' intended purpose is not to shorten the patient's life but rather to alleviate his suffering. Although some would argue here in favour of possible intentional homicide,[272] i.e., that the physician foresees that the result – bringing forward of death – may occur but continues anyway, we consider that it should be ruled out given that in truth the physician is not really allowing for that eventuality but is taking the necessary steps to relieve pain, without at the same time shortening the patient's life in a manner which might be determined causally.[273] Indeed, the most conflictive case of a treatment shortening the patient's life –terminal sedation- has been considered as acceptable by the current Code of Medical Deontology (2011), Article 36.5.

171. Possible negligent homicide, where the result was foreseen or at the very least foreseeable, shall depend on whether the physician has complied with his duties of objective care and stayed within the limits of permissible risk, in

270. M. Bajo Fernández, *Derecho Penal (Parte Especial). Delitos contra las personas* (Ceura, Madrid, 2d. ed. 1991), p. 96; J. Bustos Ramírez, *Manual de Derecho Penal, Parte Especial* (Ariel, Barcelona 1986), p. 50; C.M. Romeo-Casabona, 'El marco jurídico-penal en la eutanasia en el Derecho español', in *Revista de la Facultad de Derecho de la Universidad de Granada*, No. 13, 1987, p. 191.
271. I. De Miguel Beriain, 'El Derecho al final de la vida: rechazo al tratamiento, limitación del esfuerzo terapéutico, sedación en la agonía, auxilio al suicidio y eutanasia' Capítulo 26 en A. Palomar Olmeda, y J. Cantero Martínez (Dir.), *Tratado de Derecho Sanitario. Volumen I,* Cizur Menor, Thomson Reuters-Aranzadi, 2013, pp. 887–918.
272. Cf. E. Gimbernat Ordeig, 'Eutanasia, Constitución y Derecho Penal', in *Jano*, n. 920, 1990, pp. 987 f., who considers that the offence of participation in suicide (Art. 409, or omission of the duty to give help, Art. 489 *ter*, depending on the circumstances) exists, although he subsequently argues that there are grounds to justify such action and therefore the conduct should not be punished.
273. G. Arruego Rodríguez, 'La naturaleza constitucional de la asistencia sanitaria no consentida y los denominados supuestos de "urgencia vital"', *REDC*, n. 82, 2008.

accordance with how a judicious colleague would act in similar circumstances.[274] This conduct is determined by subjecting the physician to the requirements of the indication of the therapeutic measure and of *lex artis*. Treating pain is without doubt one of the functions of medicine, as attested by the existence in some hospitals of pain units whose specific job is to treat pain in extreme cases and also by the creation of hospices. Consequently, the judicious giving of drugs or use of equipment to control or alleviate pain in terminally ill patients does not entail a breach of the duty of objective care, nor does the eventual shortening of life constitute a punishable offence of negligence.[275]

Bear in mind also that although it is possible in theory, in practice it is extremely difficult to determine precisely this shortening of life. The most viable solution, in our opinion, would be to consider that in cases such as the above the physician is exculpated on the grounds of the state of justifiable necessity, in that the risk of shortening the patient's life is of less significance than the effective and necessary relief of pain. This view is fully shared by the Code of Medical Deontology (2011), which states that 'The physician has a duty to attempt the cure or improvement of patient's health whenever possible. When it is no longer possible, it remains the obligation of the physician to implement appropriate measures to achieve his/her welfare, even when this might result in a shortening of life' (Article 36).

II. Respecting a Patient's Wishes regarding the Cessation of Treatment

172. Both the European Convention for Protection of Human Rights and Dignity of the Human Being with regard to the Application of Biology and Medicine, ratified by Spain in 2000, and Law 41/2002, basic law regulating the autonomy of the patient and the rights and obligations in terms of information and clinical documentation, establish as a general principle that all health care interventions may only be carried out with the consent of the person affected after receiving the appropriate information. Moreover, they both declare that an intervention in the area of health care may only be carried out after the affected person has given his/her free and unequivocal consent. Thus, is can be stated the bioethical principle of autonomy of will, in the sense of not being allowed to act upon the health of a person without their consent, is laid out in an international document that has become part of the Spanish legal framework. Therefore, if a patient asks his physician to suspend or discontinue treatment his wish should be respected, particularly where recovery is completely ruled out.

The question arises here of whether the physician may be liable for omitting to give treatment, a situation which has been raised in connection with so-called passive euthanasia, or for retiring life support measures. Where there is no hope of

274. A. Torío López, 'Instigación y auxilio al suicidio, homicidio consentido y eutanasia como problemas legislativos', pp. 191 f.

275. M. Bajo Fernández, *Derecho Penal (Parte Especial). Delitos contra las personas*, p. 96; A. Torío López, 'Instigación y auxilio al suicido, homicidio consentido y eutanasia como problemas legislativos', p. 193.

recovery the patient's wishes can be said to pose no problems whatsoever. However, where treatment is crucial to keeping the patient alive during the (pre)terminal phase of his illness and death is not imminent, and where failure to give the treatment or to maintain life support measures will accelerate the process, the answer is rather more complex.

According to Law 41/2002, basic law regulating the autonomy of the patient and the rights and obligations in terms of information and clinical documentation, the patient is entitled to refuse treatment, although in this regard the Spanish legal framework imposes a series of restrictions where the right is not enforceable, for example, where public health is placed at risk, where the patient is incompetent to take decisions, and where treatment is so urgent that delay might cause irreversible injuries or entail risk of death (Article 9.2). The first two restrictions are self-explanatory, unlike the third which is ambiguous and might be construed as suggesting that life-saving treatment cannot be refused. It also raises problems concerning the duty to protect the patient's life in certain circumstances, some of which have already been examined above[276] and are affected also by the arguments which we shall look at now.

173. Article 15 of the Spanish Constitution is crucial to this issue. It states that 'everyone has the right to life and to moral and physical integrity; under no circumstances can any person be subjected to torture or to inhuman or degrading punishment or treatment (. . .)'. Clearly, then, life is the basis on which the exercise and enjoyment of all other rights to which human beings are entitled rest, and this circumstance justifies the special protection afforded to life in our legal order. It does not need to be stressed, therefore, that the scope of protection extends to all individuals, particularly those in a critical situation or who are at a disadvantage: incurable or terminal patients, invalids, the elderly, mentally ill or mentally deficient persons. The provision poses several problems of interpretation, some of which have been resolved by the Constitutional Court's ruling[277] on an appeal lodged by prisoners who went on an indefinite hunger strike until the prison authorities met their demands. Of most interest for our purposes here is the question of whether or not there exists a constitutional right to do as one pleases with one's own life, an issue which has a direct bearing on the lawfulness of euthanasia and refusal to accept treatment on the grounds of religion or conscience or for other personal reasons. A great deal of debate surrounds this highly complex and controversial grey area and the entire constitution needs to be examined in order to arrive at a satisfactory answer.

To begin with, it cannot be inferred from Article 15 of the Constitution alone that a person is entitled to do as he pleases with his own life, since the provision serves first and foremost as the guarantor of the right to life. Neither does it empower third persons to intervene in the lives of others.[278] However, precisely as a result of this

276. *See above*, Ch. 1, §1.

277. Constitutional Court Ruling of 27 Jun. 1990.

278. In this regard, *see* Constitutional Court Rulings of 27 Jun. 1990 (n. 7) and 19 Jul. 1990 (n. 5); *see also*, prior to these rulings, C.M. Romeo-Casabona, 'Los derechos del enfermo a la luz de la Constitución española', in *Todo Hospital*, n. 62, 1989, p. 29.

role of guarantor (vis-à-vis the State and third persons), it cannot be inferred either that there is a duty to live against one's wishes, that is, that the State's obligations allow it to intervene when someone has expressed his desire not to carry on living.[279] Lastly, a rereading of Article 15 in the light of the superior value of freedom (Article 1.1 of the Constitution) and of respect for human dignity (Article 10.1) leads us to conclude that the absence of a duty to live against one's wishes becomes not a right but rather the freedom to do as one pleases with one's own life. A further conclusion to be derived from this is that a physician cannot continue to treat a patient against his wishes, even if this means that his death will be hurried along.

174. Thus, to discontinue or interrupt treatment of a person who has no objectively determinable prospects of continuing to live does not run contrary to the notion of the dignity of the person. Rather, the exact opposite is true. To do otherwise could well be tantamount either to using the patient as an instrument for the physician's own interests or even to unnecessary and aggressive treatment ('acharnement thérapeutique'), in violation of the ban on inhuman and degrading treatments (Article 15 of the Constitution), which in turn is a specific violation of human dignity.[280] The Constitutional Court ruling of 27 June 1990 (Ground of the Judgment no. 9) states that no torture or inhuman or degrading treatment exists 'where authorisation is given for medical intervention, such as that challenged by the appellants [force feeding], which in this case was not ordered to inflict physical or mental punishment or to cause harm to the integrity of those subjected to the treatment, but rather to prevent where medically possible the irreversible effects of voluntary starvation and to mitigate or lessen the harm caused to the body'. The ruling goes on to state that 'the fact that force feeding, aimed at preventing the deaths of the appellants, cannot be deemed as constituting inhuman or degrading treatment due to the nature of the goal pursued, does not mean that it may not be considered as such, due to the means used to achieve this goal or in the sense that it prolongs suffering without in the process managing to prevent death'. It may be deduced from this that adequate treatment to maintain life is neither inhuman nor degrading, which is not the case when it serves only to prolong suffering without preventing (but merely delaying) death.

175. In the light of the above considerations, Law 41/2002, of 14 November, on the autonomy of patients and rights and obligations with regard to clinical information and documentation, where it does not recognize the right to refuse emergency treatment when delay might cause irreversible injuries or entail risk of death (Article 10.9), should be interpreted in the restrictive sense, i.e., that intervention by a third party may be ruled out if the patient does not wish to continue living.[281] The

279. See G. Mendes De Carvalho, *Suicidio, eutanasia y Derecho Penal. Estudio del art. 143 del Código penal español y propuesta de lege ferenda* (Comares, Granada 2009).

280. *See* C. Alvarez-Linera, 'El derecho a la vida y a la integridad. Prohibición de la tortura', in *La Ley*, n. 1763, 1987, pp. 1 ff; F. Bueno Arús, 'Límites del consentimiento en la disposición del propio cuerpo desde la perspectiva del Derecho Penal', in *Poder Judicial*, 1985, p. 14; Romeo-Casabona, *ibid.*

281. R. Junquera De Estéfani (director), *Bioética y bioderecho: reflexiones jurídicas ante los retos bioéticos* (Comares, Granada 2008), pp. 129–154.

Constitutional Court would appear to share this view when it rules that 'one thing is the decision of the person who assumes the risk of dying through an act of his own volition which affects him and him alone, in which case it could be held that compulsory medical assistance or any other means of preventing the fulfilment of this wish is unlawful; however, a totally different case is that of persons who in a special context of imprisonment . . .'. 'Thus, this constitutional right [to physical and moral integrity] shall be affected when medical assistance is imposed upon a person against his wishes, which may be based on a variety of reasons and not just a desire to die; coercive medical assistance shall, therefore, constitute a restriction which vulnerates the fundamental right, unless justification for the assistance can be found in the Constitution'.[282] A revised constitutional interpretation of the aforementioned Law would imply that even in this case refusal of treatment is possible, and that the exception included in the law refers only to cases in which the patient is unable to give consent (e.g., an unconscious patient) and his next-of-kin or persons close to him are unavailable to give it on his behalf; thus, in view of the situation of life-threatening danger (or irreversible injuries) treatment is proceeded with without first awaiting the consent that would otherwise be required. Put another way, and in criminal law jargon, the physician may intervene because he is legally protected by the existence of a situation of necessity.

176. The refusal of life support measures by a patient raised a different issue, as, in this case, it was doubtful whether these measures constituted a treatment or whether their retirement should be considered an act or a mere omission. Some Spanish authors believed that they constituted a medical treatment and their retirement, even if asked for by the patient, should be considered an act. Thus, the entire conduct should be qualified as euthanasia and be punished by the terms shown below. Most of the doctrine, instead, considered that life support measures, even hydration, were a form of medical treatment.[283] Therefore, the decision on their retirement relied on the patient, according to Law 14/2002, and health care workers could not impose their own criteria onto the patient. This same criterion was adopted by the Spanish judiciaries in the cases of Ramona Estévez and Inmaculada Echevarría, as both patients refused life support measures (in the case of Ramona Estévez, it was not her, but her family who made the decision).

III. Euthanasia

A. *Lawful Conduct in Relation to Euthanasia*

177. Earlier, in discussing the terminally ill, we outlined the requirements governing the actions of physicians in such situations. These may include the administration of drugs that may, as a side effect, reduce the lifespan of the patient (indirect euthanasia). This would not constitute an offence so long as the physician

282. Constitutional Court Ruling of 27 Jun. 1990, legal principles 7 and 8 respectively.
283. A. Couceiro, 'El enfermo terminal y las decisiones entorno al final de la vida', en A. Couceiro (Ed.), *Ética en cuidados paliativos* (Tricastela, Madrid 2004), pp. 263–304.

acts in accordance with *lex artis*. It was even argued that the doctor should respect the patient's decision to discontinue treatment, a situation that brings us into the realms of what is known as passive euthanasia.

178. Passive euthanasia. Passive euthanasia raises extremely complex issues. What is crucial from the criminal law perspective is the prior establishment of the different 'acts' (omissions) which entail passive euthanasia. Unfortunately there is disagreement in the literature as to where these limits lie.

179. In the first place we must identify, delimit and legally appraise the concept of orthothanasia, which, while similar in certain respects to passive euthanasia, has a completely different meaning. The word orthothanasia means 'justified death in the sense of death that occurs at the right moment'.[284] Orthothanasia, therefore, consists in the 'cessation of special treatments intended to revive the incurably ill when in a state of profound irreversible coma, in the terminal phases of an illness, those whose lives are being maintained artificially or who are on the point of death' (Roskam). Orthothanasia is clearly lawful in the situation where the patient has died though some bodily functions continue because they are artificially maintained by machines that control respiration and circulation. These are patients who have suffered brain death (irreversible lack of all functions from the brain stem) who can remain in the same condition almost indefinitely. Disconnecting machines or mechanisms or discontinuing treatment (medication, intravenous feeding) does not constitute homicide in the eyes of the law, given that the subject is clinically and *actually* dead.

180. Disthanasia is another neologism with the opposite meaning to orthothanasia. It means (from the Greek *dys*, bad, anomalous and *thanatos*, death) 'bad death', that is to say prolonging the natural course of death – rather than life – by all available means despite the fact that death is inevitable in the circumstances. This is something that arises chiefly in hospitals as one of the negative consequences of the constant progress made in the biomedical sciences. At the same time as achieving spectacular results with patients who would have been considered beyond help in the not too distant past and thus improving considerably the life expectancy of the population as a whole, the biomedical sciences have made it possible to delay death, which can imply prolonging the pain and suffering of the patient. This is a clear instance of how the advantages and disadvantages of technical progress are not always under our control. Awareness of these situations, with the enormous economic burden they imply for the families concerned and for the community, and the unlikely prospect of a change in the patient's condition or prognosis, has led to justifiable anxiety at the risks of medicine becoming excessively technical and of *unnecessary therapeutic cruelty* to the patient. This awareness, in turn, has led to greater sensitivity towards what is often termed 'the right to die with dignity' or 'the dignity of death'.

284. G. Higuera, 'Eutanasia: precisiones terminológicas', in *Dilemas éticos de la Medicina actual* (Public. Univ. Comillas, Madrid 1986), p. 149.

Beginning or continuing treatment when it is no longer called for because there is no realistic hope of the patient's regaining consciousness, demonstrates at the very least a serious lack of respect for the dignity of the human being, since it amounts to simply delaying death. It is also, therefore, a serious violation of a basic legal principle and limitation of positive law[285] which is explicitly recognized in our Constitution Article 10.1.[286] For this reason it has been rightly contended that such actions constitute 'inhuman and degrading treatment', explicitly prohibited by the Spanish Constitution in Article 15.[287] Respect for human dignity is applicable also to the death of the individual, although it can often prove somewhat complex. It might be deemed indignant (subjectively speaking) to subject the patient to artificial means or machinery which serve an objectively therapeutic purpose, although such an approach, if adopted, would considerably lessen knowledge of the ways and means that medicine can combat disease and death. If there is something that identifies the science of medicine and sets it apart, it is precisely this capacity to alter the course of nature in our favour. On the other hand, dying with dignity can also be understood in the sense of an individual who withstands physical pain and moral suffering and is able to rely on others (the doctor, the family) to do everything possible to fight death, even in hopeless situations where the prognosis is grim. This positive view of life should also be respected. Nevertheless, prolonging the life of the person when it is not in his interests to do so or assisting him to die, would amount to an offence in cases where the decision is not based on ethical principles, but for the economic benefit of the family, the health care system or for political or other reasons.[288]

The primary purpose of medicine continues to be health care, which implies preserving and prolonging human life, but this does not mean that suffering should not be alleviated or eliminated, as we said above.[289] Nevertheless, the doctor's duty of care is limited to the obligations imposed by *lex artis; lex artis* in fact demands that all treatment and any artificial measures to prolong biological life that are unnecessarily cruel should be discontinued where there is no rational reason to believe that the patient might recover (excluded from this of course are palliative measures to alleviate pain that are appropriate in the circumstances). Meeting these demands would not, therefore, constitute a punishable omission. This is worth clarifying and underlining.

In accordance with this function, fulfilment of the duty of care for the doctor is limited (*limitations of the duty of care*), as are all legal duties to act, to circumstances in which effectively prolonging life – not death – is practicable from

285. J. Cerezo Mir, 'La regulación del estado de necesidad en el Código Penal español', in *Estudios Penales y Criminológicos*, X, 1987, pp. 87 and f.
286. Article 10.1 of the Spanish Constitution can be translated as follows: 'The dignity of the individual, the independent development of personality, respect for the law and the rights of others are fundamental to public order and peace in society.'
287. Bueno Arús, 'Límites del consentimiento en la disposición del propio cuerpo desde la perspectiva del Derecho Penal', p. 14.
288. A. Eser, 'Límites del deber del tratamiento médico desde el punto de vista jurídico', in *Nuevo Foro Penal*, 1985, p. 447.
289. A. Eser, 'Límites del deber de tratamiento médico', p. 446; Romeo-Casabona, *El Medico ante el Derecho*, pp. 4 and ff.

the outset. The treatment must imply objective and rational possibilities of recovery. This is not the case, for example, of individuals in irreversible comas who will not regain consciousness because the reactivation of cerebral function is not possible, even when the situation arises as a result of a substantial deterioration in the patient's condition. The same goes for new-born infants with incurable abnormalities that will inevitably result in death in the short term. It is even less the case if there is some other pathological condition that occurs jointly with the abnormality or illness in question. Once the situation has been recognized, it is irrelevant for the criminal law that the decision involves the cessation of treatment with drugs, non-performance of a surgical operation or the switching off of any machines that are maintaining vital functions.

B. Juridico-Penal Evaluation of Strictly Passive Euthanasia

181. What remains therefore of passive euthanasia in the strict sense of the term and what is its legal position in the eyes of our positive Law? It is from this point onwards that the wishes of the individual concerned become relevant (and the issue more disputed). If the patient himself refuses life-saving treatment, however, the law recognizes his right to do so, as we said above.

Withdrawing treatment from a seriously ill patient where the *possibility of survival* still exists, even though the quality of life will be worse than prior to the illness or accident that has led to the condition (e.g., hemiplegic patients, non-terminal cancers, non-terminal kidney failure) constitutes legally punishable passive euthanasia if the patient has not given his consent, even where death is foreseeable in the long term. In such cases it does not matter if the person's life is being maintained by means of machines (respirators, pace-makers, kidney machines, etc.). The criminal law's response is to consider such cases as unlawful homicide (or murder or parricide depending on the circumstances) committed by omission, since the physician is in a position to guarantee life in such cases, as we shall see below, and has not been relieved of this responsibility by the patient giving his consent. This position as guarantor is a necessary condition for homicide by omission to exist. However, accurate appraisal by the criminal law requires further consideration of the nature of the physician's duty of care in such cases. If the physician has breached his duty, liability may arise, but not otherwise.

The legal duty of care occurs (*source of duty of care*), in principle, when the person who treats the individual in need of treatment has a special relationship with this person, a relationship known literally as 'a position of guarantor'.[290] This is to be understood as the situation of vulnerability that arises in relation to the legally protected interest (in this case, the patient's life) as a result of the special relationship created between the physician and the legal interest. The vulnerability of the life or health of the patient is the result of his submitting to treatment, from the point when the patient or his representatives cease to avail themselves of the services of

290. *See* on this issue J.M. Silva Sánchez, 'La responsabilidad penal del médico por omisión', in *La Ley*, n. 1632, 1987, pp. 1 and f.

all other doctors apart from the one treating the patient. Once the position of guarantor has been established it follows that a duty of care exists. To establish the limits of this duty of care the wishes of the patient must be taken into account. If the doctor wishes to begin or continue a treatment but the patient is opposed to this, the doctor is not obliged to act in all cases, according to Law 41/2002, of 14 November, on the autonomy of patients and rights and obligations with regard to clinical information and documentation and the Oviedo Convention.

182. There are two objective criteria that may help those concerned decide how to act in such circumstances. The first of these is from the patient's point of view (as can be seen, it is in reality an objective-subjective criterion), the second is from the point of view of the doctor.

1. The appropriateness or lack of appropriateness of a treatment or operation depends primarily on whether or not it is necessary from a therapeutic perspective, that is to say, once the possible risks and advantages that the treatment involves have been weighed up. The more delicate the patient's health, the greater the risks entailed and the lack of certainty with regard to outcome. This means that its therapeutic indication is reduced accordingly, and the treatment becomes elective. The weighing up of the therapeutic indication of the treatment corresponds to the physician who shall base his decision on his scientific and technical knowledge; however, the actual taking on of the risk must always rest with the patient regardless of the seriousness of the illness (all the more so when the illness is serious and prognosis uncertain). The patient is entitled to refuse treatment, even vital treatment, if the risks are very high and there is no guarantee of improvement. The physician's decision is an objective evaluation, which should be arrived at without taking the patient's ulterior motives into account, since these may influence the objective considerations. For example, the patient may wish to die so as to put an end to the suffering caused by the illness or to refuse a blood transfusion for religious reasons (however, let us just suppose that there is good reason to believe that the blood is contaminated by some pathogen: the hepatitis virus or HIV. This would constitute an objective fact with regard to the indication, in this case, a contraindication), etc. In a wider context, and as has been recalled above, the doctor must not use professional regulations or superior knowledge (principle of paternalism) as grounds to decide what is best for the well-being of the patient. It is the patient who is best able to decide with respect to the risks he is willing to take (principle of autonomy or self-determination).[291]

183. Beginning, continuing and extending treatment is obligatory only when there is a possibility that the physician (or to be more accurate, medical science) can bring about a cure. In the light of the patient's condition, if this is not possible and it has been established thus in accordance with the criteria of *lex artis*, there is no duty to treat the patient (aside from palliative measure to counteract pain and suffering). This would be the case in the terminal phases of an illness for which, by medical standards, no effective treatment exists. If, on the other hand, there is some

291. A. Eser, 'Problemas de justificación y exculpación en la actividad médica', in *Avances de la Medicina y Derecho Penal* (ed. S. Mir Puig, PPU, Barcelona 1988), p. 46.

chance of improvement or of the patient's regaining consciousness (or of this occurring at a later stage of development in the case of new-born babies) the obligation to treat the patient holds good, and if it is not fulfilled the physician risks prosecution for homicide by omission, provided that the position of guarantor exists. All these considerations are particularly relevant in cases where the patient cannot express his wishes for whatever reason (comatose state, new-born, etc.), although similar criteria apply also when the family and legal representatives act on the patient's behalf, in accordance with the terms of Law 41/2002, of 14 November, on the autonomy of patients and rights and obligations with regard to clinical information and documentation (Article 9).

184. The living will. The living will was introduced into the Spanish Legal Framework by the Convention for the Protection of Human Rights and Dignity of the Human Being with regard to the Application of Biology and Medicine: Convention on Human Rights and Biomedicine, and came into effect in Spain on 1 January 2000, following its ratification by Parliament. As Article 9 stated, 'It is important to highlight that according to this law, the implementation of the living will is delegated to the different Health Services Directors, one in each region.' Accordingly, some of the Spanish regions passed their own legislation on this topic. In practise, this meant that some differences (for instance, regarding the possibility of minors gaining access to a living will) could occur in Spain. The registers of the living would also depend on the Regional Governments but, in order to ensure their coordination, a central register, depending on the Ministry of Health, was created (Central Living Will Register).

This task was addressed by Law 41/2002, of 14 November, on the autonomy of patients and rights and obligations with regard to clinical information and documentation, which dedicated its article to tackle the Living Will tool. According to it, all Spaniards who have reached the age of majority, that is, 18 years of age (in some Regions also emancipated minors), with sufficient legal capacity and freely,[292] communicates their instructions about actions that should be taken into account should they reach a situation in which they can no longer freely express their wishes. If the person maintains the ability to let their wishes be known, this will always prevail over the contents of the Living Will Document. Thus, as long as the patient keeps sufficient capacity to communicate his/her preferences, health care professionals will take into account what he/she decides at each moment, not what is written in his/her Living Will. In other words, it will only be implemented in those situations in which the patient is unable to make decisions regarding his/her own health care or treatments, for example, if he/she is unconscious, in a coma or just incapable of deciding.[293]

The contents of the Living Will will be private and thus only available to the doctor attending the patient during a time of crises. The Living Will can also be

292. People declared legally incapacitated, providing there is no impediment in the legal sentence itself, and who, when deciding to make one, are capable of formalizing their declaration, are also allowed to redact a valid Living Will.

293. See: M.I. Tamayo Velázquez, et al., *A Guide to Making an Advance Health Care Directive*, Junta de Andalucía, 2013, at: https://www.juntadeandalucia.es/salud/rv2/pdf/GuiaVVA_English.pdf.

revoked, changed or replaced at any time by the interested party. The Living Will Document, which must not include any dispositions contrary to law and/or 'lex artis' (Article 11.3), may include:

(a) An expression of life goals and personal values. This provides guidance for the interpretation of the remainder of the document and serves to help the medical team before they take decisions.
(b) Instructions about medical treatment. It can refer both to an illness or injury that is being suffered at the time of granting the document or to any future situation. With the only limitation being good clinical practice and respect for the law, the medical interventions that the person wishes to receive or not to receive may be indicated. This means that people can choose the treatment they want to receive, but certain treatments will only begin when medical professionals consider them to be clinically indicated.

Living Will can be formalized in different ways: (1) By Public Deed executed before a Notary. (2) By a declaration before three witnesses, adults with full capacity to act, two of which must not have any direct relationship with the grantor. (3) By a declaration made in the correspondent Register.

The registration of the Living Will Document is not compulsory. However, if it is not registered, the obligation of letting people know of its existence will fall on the patient who must deliver a copy to the Health care centre so that it is included in their Clinical Records or the patient must carry with them. Once the Living Will is redacted, access to it is incorporated into the medical history. This means that health professionals can consult it if necessary and guarantees that the patient's wishes and preferences are respected. The Law also allows people to choose a person we trust as our representative or Health Care Proxy for making decisions on their behalf if they are in such a situation. In some regions, a second representative can also be appointed as a Substitute if, for some reason, the first one is unable to make these decisions.

It is important to highlight that according to this Law, the implementation of the Living Will is delegated to the different Health Services Directorades, one in each Region. Accordingly, some of the Spanish Regions have passed their own legislation on this topic. In practice, this means that some differences (for instance, regarding the possibility of minors to gain access to Living Will) might be found in Spain. The Registers of the Living Will also depend on the Regional Governments but, in order to assure the coordination of them all, a Central Register depending on the Ministry of Health was created (Central Living Will Register).

C. Active Euthanasia

185. Direct active euthanasia is always punishable according to the Spanish Penal Code. Indeed, the Spanish Penal Code includes an explicit reference to active euthanasia in its article number 143.4, which states that:

> Whoever causes or actively co-operates in the necessary, direct acts causing the death of another, at the specific, serious, unequivocal request of that person, in the event of the victim suffering a serious disease that would unavoidably lead to death, or that causes permanent suffering that is hard to bear, shall be punished with a punishment lower by one or two degrees to those described in sections 2 and 3 of this Article.

If the patient performs suicide with the help of someone else (only a conclusive statement from the individual concerned to the effect that he wishes to die will make the person who performed the act a mere accessory), the individual who performed the act should be punished as an accessory to suicide,[294] even when this person is a member of the family.

186. If, on the other hand, the patient did not consent because he was unable to as a result of his condition (unconsciousness due to a somatic illness, mental illness or deficiency, age), or was opposed to the act (a situation in which it would be difficult to imagine anyone committing homicidal euthanasia) or simply 'allowed it to happen' (a completely passive attitude), the act falls within the bounds of wilful homicide or, most probably, murder, because it is considered that there is premeditation – one of the necessary conditions for murder – when one takes the life of a helpless and defenceless person. The Criminal law responds to such cases with uncompromising force, and the Penal Code imposes its maximum punishment for the crime of murder.

D. Premature or Neonatal Euthanasia

187. There should be no difference between paediatric medical practice and medicine applied to adults and, as a result, the legal responses (or lacunae) should not differ greatly. The life of a child is worth just as much as that of an adult. Nevertheless, when the patient is a child or new-born infant there are specific aspects of such complexity that they make it difficult for the law to provide a clear-cut response. One of these is that in some cases it is not possible to know the child's wishes or preferences, since the child simply lacks wishes or preferences, which develop with age.

What we must clarify first of all is what is meant by the expression 'premature euthanasia'. In fact the expression itself is inappropriate as it does not refer to euthanasia in the strict sense of the word, which is what we have been discussing up until now. It does not concern helping someone who is suffering to die, but the elimination, by action or omission, of new-born infants (hence the term 'premature') who are viable, but who are seen to have deformities or serious brain damage. Such actions are in all probability eugenic, involving the elimination of beings who are devoid of 'valuable life', against whom the law does not discriminate (it could not do so), as we shall see further on. Furthermore, the right to life most definitely comes into play here, but not (for obvious reasons) the right to do as one pleases

294. Bustos Ramírez, *Manual de Derecho Penal, Parte Especial*, p. 50.

with one's life – or death – given that at the end of the day third parties and not the new-born baby take the decisions.

188. Direct active euthanasia of a new-born infant attracts the same firm legal response as its adult counterpart, with the difference that consent is not an attenuating factor in the homicide, murder or parricide of the new-born infant.

189. When it comes to the failure to provide treatment to a new-born infant with serious abnormalities, the same situation arises and the same problem occurs as with adults, particularly those who are in a comatose state. Once again it is necessary to establish the limits of a duty of care or a duty not to treat. The abnormality itself must not constitute the main reason for making the decision as it is irrelevant as an excuse before the law. A duty of care is maintained in principal and what should influence the doctor's decision is the child's life expectancy. Clearly this is where disagreement may arise.

190. We can distinguish a body of proposals that emphasize the child's future capacity to relate to others. Those who hold this view ask whether we should demand that the child be kept alive when the abnormality is irreversible and so serious that there is no chance of him being able to perceive and communicate.[295] The German Society for Medical Law (DGMR) proposed some year ago a series of Recommendations (*Einbecker Empfehlung*) of which the following deserve mention: the following are cases in which the doctor should not continue treatment:

(1) when lasting life cannot be maintained and it is simply a question of delaying certain death;
(2) despite treatment any possibility of the new-born child ever communicating with its environment has been discounted; and
(3) when the child's vital bodily functions can only be maintained in intensive care facilities.[296]

Other experts focus only on the child's chances of improvement, while also considering the disproportionate nature of the relationship between the effort involved and the suffering caused. This perspective has the advantage of reducing to reasonable dimensions the question of evaluating quality of life and therefore seems more manageable. We have emphasized throughout that children and adults should be treated equally and in the case of children the risk of causing additional suffering should be weighed up against the possible results of the treatment. It is thus held that there should be no intervention when there are multiple injuries and where the treatment will only cause suffering without actually stabilising the health of the child. The Department of Health and Human Services in the United States (DHHS)

295. A. Kaufmann 'Relativización de la protección jurídica del la vida', in *Avances de la Medicina y Derecho Penal* (ed. S. Mir Puig, PPU, Barcelona 1988), p. 46.
296. For the full text of the Deutsche Gesellschaft für Medizinrecht recommendations *see* 'Einbecker Empfehlung', in *Grenzen der ärztlichen Behandlungspflicht bei schwerstgeschädigten Neugeborenen* (H.D. Hiersche, G. Hirsch, T. Graf-Baumann, eds.) (Springer, Berlin 1987), pp. 183 and ff.

set out the following circumstances as being situations in which feeding or medical or surgical treatment should not be provided:

(1) if the new-born infant is in a chronic or irreversible coma;
(2) when the treatment would only prolong the inevitable process of dying, would not be effective or would not overcome or correct the life threatening situation and plays no role in the survival of the foetus; and
(3) when, apart from the other two sets of circumstances, the treatment would be inhumane.[297]

E. *Attenuation of or Exemption from Criminal Liability in Punishable Euthanasia*

191. In the first place, we can conclude that the *consent* of the individual concerned is not sufficient basis on which to ground the lawfulness of direct active euthanasia, though it is enough for treatment refused by the patient, even vital treatment, to be discontinued. This is particularly so when discontinuing the treatment does not imply any immediate risk to the patient's life or when the treatment itself involves additional dangers that the patient is not willing to face.

Nevertheless, consent does have certain attenuating effects on the unlawfulness (or wrongfulness) of the act, given that without consent the act would in some cases (active euthanasia, for instance) constitute manslaughter or murder. Let's consider the case, for example, when euthanasia is practised by the mother of the new-born infant. In fact, in this case the courts would convict the mother of murder. On the basis of the altruistic motive of compassion – not, it should be said, merely the desire to dispense with the economic and emotional burden of having an abnormal or seriously ill child – this family relationship can be seen in this case as an attenuating circumstance as Article 23 Penal Code (On the mixed circumstance of kinship) states that 'a circumstance that may mitigate or aggravate accountability, according to the nature, motives and effects of the crime, is when the victim is or has been the spouse or person with whom the convict has had a stable emotional relationship, or being the ascendant, descendant or biological or adoptive sibling of the offender or spouse or cohabiting partner thereof'.

192. The *motive of pity or compassion*, which is an altruistic characteristic that generally holds true for the forms of euthanasia analysed here, makes the act criminally less deserving of reproach when the motive can be clearly demonstrated, regardless of whether or not the act was requested by the victim. The basis for this attenuating circumstance is the temporary reduction of the mental faculties of the

297. M. Bueno Sánchez, 'Bioética y Pediatría', in *Anales Esp. de Pediatría*, 1991; N. King, 'Federal and State Regulation of Neonatal Decision-Making', in *Euthanasia and the Newborn* (R.C. McMillan, H.T. Engelhardt, J.R., and S.P. Spicker, eds.) (Reidel Publ. Co., Boston 1987), pp. 90 and ff.

person who acts under the emotional strain and distress of watching the other person suffer[298] (circ. 3ª Article 21),[299] especially when the person is a family member, a friend or close acquaintance. The same applies also to altruistic motives even when no significant distress exists (e.g., a doctor or nurse), in which case the attenuating circumstance is applicable by analogy (circ. 7ª Article 21).[300] Both attenuating circumstances, according to the case, qualify the offence considerably and can lead to a substantially lighter sentence (one or two degrees); thus, for example, the penalty for being an accessory to suicide, which is twelve years and a day to twenty years imprisonment, may be cut to a sentence of up to six months and one day in the most favourable circumstances. In such cases the court may then opt for a suspended sentence or remission (a suspended sentence means that any period of imprisonment is suspended).

193. In extreme circumstances *incomplete exemption* from criminal liability may be considered, once more based on the diminished mental faculties of the accused, as is the case of incomplete temporary mental breakdown (circ. 1ª Article 21, in relation to No. 1 Article 20 of the Penal Code).[301] It has even been argued[302] that it is possible – though rarely and only where the relationship between the two individuals is particularly close – that the mental disturbance may be so complete at the moment of performing the act – or omission – of euthanasia, that the defendant is unable to comprehend the unlawful nature of his conduct or to act in accordance with his comprehension. In this case, the criminal law would not attach blame to the person for his unlawful act and would completely exonerate him from punishment (No. 1 Article 20 of the Penal Code).

298. Bustos Ramírez, *Manual de Derecho Penal. Parte Especial*, p. 50.
299. States as follows: 'The convict acting due to causes or stimuli so overpowering that they produced fury, obstinacy or another similar state of mind'.
300. It reads thus: 'These are attenuating circumstances: 7. Any other circumstances analogous to those previously mentioned.'
301. According to circ. 1ª of Art. 21 'Those circumstances enumerated in the previous chapter, when the necessary conditions for exemption from liability are not met in their respective cases'. The previous chapter referred to is composed of Art. 20, only the first clause of which states: 'The following are exempt from criminal liability: 1. individuals who suffer a temporary mental breakdown, so long as this has not been deliberately sought for criminal purposes'.
302. Ma. D. Fernández Rodríguez, 'Problemática médico-legal de la eutanasia', in *Estudios Penales, I* (Serv. Publ. Univ. Santiago de Compostela 1977), p. 200.

Chapter 3. Specific Activities

§1. Termination of Pregnancy (Abortion)

I. The Offence of Abortion in Spanish Law

194. A fuller understanding of the complex question of abortion in Spanish law can only be achieved through a discussion of the legal rules relating to abortion and the cases in which it is punishable.[303]

195. The legal interest protected by the abortion law. As a general rule it can be said that from a criminal law perspective abortion consists of causing the death of the embryo or human foetus either in the womb or through causing its premature expulsion from the womb.[304] In the case of the latter some argue in favour of a lack of viability and maturity in the expelled foetus.[305]

The legal interest protected by the offence of abortion is the life of the conceived (embryo or foetus). This conclusion is reinforced in so much as the life of the conceived is a legally protected interest under the terms of the Spanish Constitution (Article 150), as was upheld by the Constitutional Court on 11 April 1985, and the Penal Code granted this protection under the Criminal Law in view of the vital interests of the individual and the community. It is normally accepted that alongside this primordial and basic interest there are also other secondary interests, such as the freedom of the pregnant woman, as can be seen in the longer sentences applied if the freedom of the pregnant woman is also impinged upon. Accordingly, the *material object* of the aggressive conduct is the embryo or the live human foetus implanted in the woman's uterus. Therefore, the offence is deemed to have been committed regardless of whether at the moment of termination the conceived is viable or non-viable outside the uterus, whether the action is performed inside or outside the womb, whether it occurs after expulsion or in fact involves provoking expulsion with the aim of terminating the pregnancy; beyond the parameters of the law are spontaneous abortion of non-viable foetuses (the embryo is always deemed non-viable) as well as ectopic pregnancies, since these are non-viable inside the

303. For a more complete account *see* C.M. Romeo-Casabona, 'La reforma penal del aborto: límite mínimo, figuras delictivas y sistema de las indicaciones', in *Propuestas para la reforma penal* (Centro de Estudios Criminológicos, Universidad de La Laguna, Santa Cruz de Tenerife 1992), pp. 143 and ff.

304. See J. Bustos Ramírez, *Manual de Derecho Penal. Parte Especial*, p. 59; G. Landrove Díaz, *Política Criminal del aborto* (Bosch, Barcelona 1976), p. 15; F. Muñoz Conde, *Derecho Penal. Parte Especial* (20th ed. Tirant Lo Blanch, Valencia 2015), p. 73; A. Serrano Gómez & A. Serrano Maíllo, *Derecho Penal Español. Parte Especial* (15th ed. Dykinson, Madrid 2010), p. 79; L. Rodríguez Ramos (with M.A. Cobos Gomez de Linares and J. Lopez Barja de Quiroga), *Manual de Derecho Penal. Parte Especial, I* (Akal, Madrid 1990), pp. 140 and f.; Silvia Fernández Bautista en Mirentxu Corcoy Bidasolo (Dir.) / Juan Sebastián Vera Sánchez (Coord.) et al., *Manual de Derecho Penal. Parte Especial (Tomo I)* (Tirant lo Blanch, Valencia 2015), p. 73.

305. *See* references in E. Farre Trepat, 'Sobre el concepto de aborto y su delimitatión de los delitos contra la vida humana independiente', in *Anuario de Derecho Penal y Ciencias Penales*, 1990, pp. 337 and f.

uterus; neither is the destruction of an embryo that is the result of 'in vitro' fertilization deemed to constitute abortion, so long as the embryo has not been implanted and nested in the uterus. The offence may be committed at any time between the moment of nesting (although the Penal Code does not define this explicitly) and the moment of birth. Up to this latter point no interest exists to which effective protection may be give under the Penal Code, whereas after the birth there is an independent human life that deserves protection of a different type; deformed foetuses or monsters are also covered by the offence, provided that they are viable inside the uterus.

196. Abortions performed outside Spain on Spanish citizens. In accordance with the provisions of the 'Ley Orgánica del Poder Judicial' of 1985, which is concerned with, among other things, the territorial jurisdiction of Spanish criminal law, abortion is only punishable when committed in Spain (Article 23.1), except where, under the complementary principle of personality (Article 23.2), it is also punishable in the country where it was performed (principle of double incrimination), apart from other requirements. As a result, Spanish women who travel to neighbouring countries where voluntary abortion is legal may not be prosecuted in Spain, notwithstanding the fact that the Spanish Penal Code would consider this as an offence, since the Spanish courts do not have jurisdiction over an act which is not an offence in the other country. This interpretation has been confirmed both by the Supreme Court[306] and Constitutional Court.[307]

II. Voluntary Abortion

A. *System Adopted between 1985 and 2010*

197. Since the reform of the Penal Code under *Organic Law* 9/1985 of 5 July – once the hurdle posed by an appeal on the grounds of alleged unconstitutionality had been overcome and the Bill amended in line with the Constitutional Court ruling of 11 April 1985 – and until the approval of Organic Law 2/2010 of 3 March of sexual and reproductive health and of voluntary interruption of pregnancy, abortion was legally permitted under Spanish law in any of the circumstances established by Article 417 *bis* of the former Penal Code, which did not include indication for socio-economic reasons.[308] Clearly the Legislature followed the criterion of rule-exception in this regard. The rule was that wilful abortion was banned in all cases,

306. Supreme Court Ruling (2nd Chamber) of 5 Dec. 1986, in the opposite sense to earlier decisions: 20 Dec. 1980, 15 Oct. 1983.
307. See Constitutional Court 75/1984, 27 June.
308. Article 417*bis* could be translated thus: 'Abortion performed by a doctor, or under his/her supervision, in an accredited health care centre or institution, be it public or private, with the explicit consent of the pregnant woman is not punishable in the following circumstances: 1st When it is necessary to avoid grave danger to the life or physical or psychiatric health of the woman and that this is stated in a certificate issued prior to the operation by an appropriate specialist physician other than the doctor who is to perform the abortion or under whose supervision the abortion is to be performed. In emergency conditions where there is a life-threatening risk to the woman, the

and was punished accordingly under the criminal law, even when the pregnant woman herself agreed to the abortion. The exception was that under certain circumstances authorized by the Law abortion was lawful, when specific conflicts of interests occurred, in which case specific principles applied. The Spanish Legislature opted for a system of indications, as opposed to one of time limits (which also responds to an assumption of conflict) or to an across-the-board right to abortion. To sum up, the situation in Spain between 1985 and 2010 was as follows: if the life or physical or mental health of the mother were seriously endangered (therapeutic or medical indication) or if the woman had become pregnant following rape (ethical or criminological indication) or, finally, if through prenatal diagnosis or some other procedure, evidence emerged that the foetus was likely to be born with significant abnormalities (eugenic or embriopathic indication), an abortion may be performed.

The reform of the regulation in the field of abortion was demanded by many sectors of society who felt that under the Penal Code provisions in the version in force until 2010 no conditions apart from therapeutic considerations rendered abortion lawful.

B. *In Force Regulation: Time Limits System of Abortion (Organic Law 2/2010 of 3 March of Sexual and Reproductive Health and of Voluntary Interruption of Pregnancy)*

198. The current regulatory framework on abortion is established in the Organic Law 2/2010, as well as in two Royal Decrees which develop certain particular aspects of the previous one: Royal Decree 825/2010 of June 25 on partial development of Organic Law 2/2010 and Royal Decree 831/2010 of June 25 of guarantee of health care quality of the system of voluntary interruption of pregnancy. One of the key issues covered by the first of these Royal Decrees, is the information to be provided to pregnant women in advance in certain cases of abortion, while the second is aimed at guaranteeing access to abortion in conditions of equality throughout the national territory.

Organic Law 2/2010 includes in its title the key concepts in order to understand the problem of abortion: the importance of sexual and reproductive health that the Organic Law 2/2010 directly connects with abortion. An aspect that seems undeniable is that advances in sexual culture will give raise to greater control by women in the reproductive process, and therefore will cause the decrease of the rate of voluntary abortions.

---

requirements for explicit consent and a written certificate are waived. 2nd When the pregnancy is the result of an act that constitutes the crime of rape under Art. 429, so long as the abortion is performed in the first twelve weeks of pregnancy and the aforementioned act has been reported to the authorities. 3rd When it is assumed that the foetus will be born with grave physical or psychiatric abnormalities so long as the abortion is performed in the first twenty-two weeks of pregnancy and the written statement is issued by two specialists from a public or private accredited health care centre or establishment, neither of whom shall perform or supervise the abortion. 2. In the cases envisaged in the previous clause the pregnant woman's actions will not be punishable even if the abortion is not performed in a public or private accredited centre or health care establishment or if the medical certificates not been issued.

The special connection between women's rights and sexual and reproductive health is noted by many international instruments. Within the United Nations system, article 12 of the Convention on the Elimination of All Forms of Discrimination Against Women adopted by General Assembly Resolution 34/180 of 18 December 1979 establishes that 'States Parties shall take all appropriate measures to eliminate discrimination against women in the field of health care in order to ensure, on a basis of equality of men and women, access to health care services, including those related to family planning'. The Beijing Platform for Action adopted at the Fourth World Conference on Women held in 1995, recognizes that 'The human rights of women include their right to have control over and decide freely and responsibly on matters related to their sexuality, including sexual and reproductive health, free of coercion, discrimination and violence'. Within the European Union, European Parliament Resolution 2001/2128 (INI) on sexual and reproductive health and associated rights makes several recommendations to Member States on issues of contraception, unwanted pregnancy, and sex education. These recommendations were based, *inter alia*, on the huge inequalities experienced by European women in terms of access to reproductive health services, contraception and abortion according to their income or country of residence.

The Convention on the Rights of Persons with Disabilities of 13 December 2006, ratified by Spain, requires States Parties to ensure that 'The rights of persons with disabilities to decide freely and responsibly on the number and spacing of their children and to have access to age-appropriate information, reproductive and family planning education are recognized, and the means necessary to enable them to exercise these rights are provided' and to ensure that these persons 'retain their fertility on an equal basis with others'.

Organic Law 2/2010 takes especially careful account of the constitutional doctrine laid out in the decisions of the Constitutional Tribunal. In Decision 53/1985, the Tribunal, though often divided on substantive questions, did lay out certain principles that were subsequently validated by jurisprudence and which served as benchmarks for this law. One of these principles is that the competing rights and interests involved in regulating voluntary termination of pregnancy are not absolute. As such, the legislature must 'balance the protected legal interests and rights at hand and attempt to harmonize them if possible, or if not, spell out the conditions and requirements for one of them to prevail' (Constitutional Tribunal Decision 53/1985). Although 'the system of laws does not consider the unborn as citizens entitled to the fundamental right to life guaranteed under article 15 of the Constitution', this is not meant to deprive them of all constitutional protection (Constitutional Tribunal Decision 116/1999). Prenatal life is a legal interest deserving of protection. While it is the role of legislators to extend such protection, they must not overlook the fact that the manner in which protection is configured and implemented is always contingent on guaranteeing the fundamental rights of pregnant women.

Organic Law 2/2010 recognizes the right to freely decide whether and when to have children. This implies, *inter alia*, ensuring that women can make conscious, responsible decisions as to whether to carry a pregnancy to term, and that these decisions are respected. Based on expert opinion and comparative law, legislators considered it reasonable to allow a period of fourteen weeks in which to guarantee the right of women to make an informed decision about termination of pregnancy, free from interference. This concept, referred to in Constitutional Tribunal Decision 53/1985 as 'conscious selfdetermination', considers that decisive third-party intervention to shape a pregnant woman's will provides no significant guarantees to the foetus while needlessly restricting the right to personal growth and development protected under Article 10.1 of the Constitution.

According to the preamble of Organic Law 2/2020 experience shows that prenatal life is best protected by policies that actively support motherhood and pregnant women. In the early stages of pregnancy, protection of a legal right is best achieved by working with the pregnant woman rather than against her. She can make a decision after being apprised of the services, assistance and rights to which she is entitled should she wish to proceed with her pregnancy; of the medical, psychological and social consequences of continuing or terminating her pregnancy, and of the counselling services available to her both before and after the procedure. The Law provides for a waiting period of at least three days and requires that information be provided in a clear, objective, pressure-free manner in non-threatening surroundings.

As noted in Constitutional Tribunal Decision 53/1985, a crucial milestone of the pregnancy process 'is the moment when the nasciturus becomes viable outside the womb'. Foetal viability, in the general consensus of the scientific community based on neonatology research, begins at approximately the twenty-second week. Until then the Law allows termination of pregnancy, provided that the life or health of the pregnant woman is at serious risk or that the foetus is seriously malformed. These health grounds for voluntary termination of pregnancy are complemented by steps designed to ascertain with complete accuracy that this is indeed the case. On top of that, Organic Law 2/2010 imposes a clear time limit on application of the so-called therapeutic indication. If a woman's life or health is at risk beyond the twenty-second week of pregnancy, the appropriate course of action is to induce labour, which fully balances her right to life and physical integrity and protection of the life in formation.

Beyond the twenty-second week, the law contemplates two exceptions for termination of pregnancy. The first refers to cases of 'foetal anomalies incompatible with life', an exception to considering prenatal life a protected legal interest under Article 15 of the Constitution (Constitutional Tribunal Decision 212/1996). The second exception applies when 'the foetus has an extremely serious and incurable condition, as confirmed by a Medical Committee'. Confirmation defers to the expert opinion of medical practitioners, based on current scientific knowledge 4. From the point of view of the regulation of voluntary abortion, Organic Law 2/2010 establishes in its Article 14 that pregnancies may be terminated within the first fourteen weeks of gestation at the request of the pregnant woman, provided the following requirements are met:

(a) That the pregnant women is informed of her rights and of available counselling and support services and assistance, pursuant to Article 17(2) and Article 17(4) of Law 2/2010.
(b) That at least three days elapses between delivery of the above information and performance of the procedure.

At the light of Organic Law 2/2010 the time limit solution is adopted in Spain in the field of abortion. Women can take a free and informed choice on the termination of pregnancy without interference from third parties during the first fourteen weeks of gestation.

In the event that woman decides within that period of fourteen weeks to opt for abortion, she takes her decision after being informed of all benefits, aids and rights to which she can access if she wants to continue her pregnancy, as well as the medical, psychological and social consequences resulting from the continuation of the pregnancy or of its interruption, as well as the possibility to receive counselling before and after the intervention (Article 17 Organic Law 2/2010 and RD 825/2010, of 25 June, of partial development of the Organic Law 2/2010).

According to Article 17 Organic Law 2/2010:

> 1. women expressing their willingness to undergo voluntary termination of pregnancy will be apprised of the existing methods, the conditions for termination set out herein, the accredited public health facilities offering this service, the formalities to be completed, and the conditions for public health system coverage. 2. Women choosing to terminate a pregnancy pursuant to Article 14 Law 2/2010 will be given a sealed envelope containing information on: (a) Public assistance and counselling services available to pregnant women and health coverage during pregnancy and childbirth. (b) Labour-related rights accruing to pregnant women and new mothers, available childcare services and assistance, government benefits, and other relevant childbearing incentive and assistance information. (c) Centres providing adequate contraception and safe sex information. (d) Centres where counselling can be obtained both before and after pregnancy termination. Such information will be available at all public health care facilities, or in those accredited to perform voluntary termination of pregnancy. For the purposes of Article 14 above, pregnant women will be issued a certificate attesting to the date information was provided.
>
> The contents and format of the above information will be set out in the regulations to be enacted by the Government. 3. In the cases contemplated in Article 15(b) of this Law, pregnant women will be additionally provided with written information on the rights of persons with disabilities, available public services and assistance, and community groups assisting such persons. 4. Prior to providing consent, all pregnant women will be provided the information required by Article 4 and Article 10 of Law 41/2002, specifically on the medical, psychological, and social consequences of continuing or terminating their pregnancies. 5. The information to be provided pursuant to this article will be presented in a clear, objective, and understandable manner. Persons with disabilities will have this information provided in suitably accessible formats and media. Written materials will specify that all information will also be provided verbally upon request.

The Organic Law 2/2010 complete the time limit system with the inclusion of two indications-the second one with two submodalities (therapeutic indication – Article 15.a Organic Law 2/2010 – and embriopathic indication – Articles 15.b and c Organic Law 2/2010) that allow abortion beyond the time period referred of fourteen weeks. According to Article 15 LO 2/2010 (*termination on Health Grounds*) exceptionally, a pregnancy may be terminated for medical reasons in any one of the following circumstances:

(a) Prior to the twenty-second week of pregnancy, if the woman's life or health is in serious risk, as confirmed in advance by a medical specialist not performing or supervising the procedure. Confirmation will not be required in emergency cases of immediately life-threatening risk. Specific requisites of this indication:
   - *Certificate of opinion issued by a specialist.* It is essential that a specialist issues the relevant certificate of opinion vouching not only that the danger to the life or physical or mental health of the pregnant woman actually exists, but also that the abortion is necessary to prevent the danger. The responsibility which rests with the physician is obvious, and the law also demands that he has to be a specialist in the relevant field, that is to say, in the type of illness from which the woman is suffering or from which she is probably suffering. In order to ensure the independence of the certificate of opinion the specialist who issues it must not be the physician who is to perform or supervise the abortion. The requirement of the certificate may be waived in emergency cases of mortal danger to the life of the pregnant woman, that is, when her life is under threat.
   - *Woman's life or health is in serious risk.* It must be a 'serious risk'. This alludes to the concrete and specific risk that in the relatively near future the pregnant woman will die or her health will be seriously damaged. It is no easy matter to establish the required degree of probability that such an event might occur; nevertheless, the degree required should be reduced in inverse proportion to the gravity of the threat, particularly where, for example, the woman's life is in danger.[309] Serious risk excludes from the indication all the usual discomforts and risks entailed in a normal pregnancy and birth. Serious risk to life may be of both organic and psychological origin. Extreme depression with suicidal tendencies would be classified as the second of these types of serious risks.

(b) Prior to the twenty-second week of pregnancy, provided that there is a risk of serious foetal anomalies, as confirmed in advance by two medical specialists not performing or supervising the procedure.

(c) In case of foetal anomalies incompatible with life as confirmed in advance by a medical specialist not performing or supervising the procedure, or when the foetus is found to suffer from an extremely serious condition that is incurable at the time of diagnosis, as confirmed by a Medical Committee.

In any case, a number of mandatory common requirements have to be met in order to practice an abortion under the Spanish legal framework (assessed under Article 13 Organic Law 2/2010):

---

309. De Vicente Remesal, 'El grave peligro para la salud psíquica de la madre en la nueva ley del aborto', *La Ley*, 1985, p. 8.

– *The abortion must be performed by a physician or performed under his/her supervision.* The Legislature has deemed the participation of a qualified person necessary to safeguard the life and health of the pregnant woman, in view of the risks entailed in the performance of an abortion. Furthermore, the Legislature has rightly emphasized[310] that the participation of the physician provides an additional guarantee and professional supervision to ensure that the process of abortion is carried out in accordance with the law, firstly by ensuring that the legal time limit is respected or that the indication which the woman claims to be applicable does in fact exist, as it is the physician who will be the first to benefit from the exemption from liability established by the law (i.e., physician who is to carry out or supervise the abortion). He should simply verify that the case does conform to the law (and its requirements).

The physician's participation, whether direct or indirect, that is, an abortion under his/her supervision, must conform to *lex artis* in all cases. Clearly, the most appropriate physician is a specialist in Obstetrics and Gynaecology,[311] but the participation of any other properly qualified physician capable of performing the abortion is equally lawful.[312] Supervision by a qualified physician, which the law offers as an alternative procedure, refers to the sharing out of functions among members of a team working together,[313] which implies that when the physician acts as supervisor he is still subject to *lex artis* as are all those who are physically involved. However, for the physician in this case *lex artis* primarily implies the evaluation of the capacity of the individual who performs the abortion under his/her supervision. As is discussed below, the complementary regulations distinguish between high risk pregnancies and abortions and those that do not entail such risks. Therefore, the physician's analysis of this situation is one of the most crucial elements in any consideration of the possibility of delegating (supervising) to another health care professional (general practitioner or specialist, intern or resident, midwife). This decision to delegate also depends on the intensity of subsequent treatment which may be required and the extent to which functions are delegated. These reservations are not sustainable, however, when the physician directs the pregnant woman herself, by instructing her as to pharmaceutical preparations that she should then administer herself or any other action that she

310. Díez Ripollés, 'Análisis de los elementos de la causa de justificación del art. 417*bis* del Código Penal', p. 216.

311. R.D. 831/2010, of 25 June on guarantee of health care quality of the system of voluntary interruption of pregnancy. Its Annex states that the health care establishments in order to perform high risk abortions or in case of pregnancies of more than fourteen weeks must provide at least (among other conditions) a Unit of Obstetrics and Gynaecology as well as Unit of Nursery and a corresponding blood bank.

312. A. Cuerda Riezu, 'El delito de aborto ante la Propuesta de Anteproyecto del Nuevo Código Penal', *Documentación Jurídica. Monográfico dedicado a la propuesta de Anteproyecto del Nuevo Código Penal (vol. I)*, 37/40, 1983, pp. 376 and f; Díez Ripollés, 'Análisis de los elementos de la causa de justificación del art. 417*bis* del Código Penal', Comentarios a la legislación penal. Tomo IX (Edersa, Madrid 1989), pp. 219 and f; Luzón Peña, 'Indicaciones y causas de justificación en el aborto', *Poder Judicial*, 13, 1989, p. 644.

313. *See* the fuller account in Jorge Barreiro, *La imprudencia punible en la actividad médico-quirúrgica* (Tecnos, Madrid 1990), pp. 113 and ff (with some interesting decisions on medical negligence for unjustified delegation of responsibility to nurses in obstetrics cases, p. 154); Romeo-Casabona, *El Médico y el Derecho Penal, I*, pp. 247 and ff.

should take (including performing the abortion herself under the physician's supervision). The same applies to members of the woman's family or her representatives (in the broad sense of the term): in such circumstances, as lay persons, they would not be prosecuted for illegal practice of medicine.

- *Abortions may be performed only in approved public or private health centre or health care establishment.* This requirement stems also from the previous one, in that it seeks to lessen the risks which abortion entails for the woman.[314] At the same time it provides a means of controlling and monitoring the number of abortions performed in Spain (by preventing clandestine abortions). As regards requirements concerning approval of centres or establishments, reference should be made to the regulations of the Royal Decree 831/2010, which distinguishes between centres for the performance of abortions that do not imply high risk to the pregnant woman and performed within fourteen weeks of conception and those centres which carry out abortions involving high risk and or after completion of the aforementioned fourteen-week period (Annex Royal Decree 831/2010). The approval of public centres is automatic once they satisfy the established requirements. Accreditation of private centres is the responsibility of the Autonomous Communities (Article 4 of the Royal Decree 831/2010).
- *Abortion must be performed with the express written consent of the pregnant woman or her duly authorized representative*, as the case may be, pursuant to the provisions in Law 41/2002 on Patient Rights and Medical Records and Information. Express consent may be dispensed within the cases contemplated in Article 9.2.(b) of the said Law.

199. Finally, it should be recalled that the termination of a pregnancy must never be for the purposes of donation or subsequent use of embryos or foetuses or their biological structures. Moreover, the medical team that carries out the abortion may not be involved in any subsequent use made of the foetus or embryo.[315]

C. Criminal Law Regulation

200. The introduction of the Organic Law 2/2010 has also led to the corresponding reform of the Penal Code on punishment of abortion, adapting the criminal sphere (and, basically, the scope of the prohibitions that it embodies) in these areas to the legislative model introduced in 2010. Abortion is regulated in Spanish Penal Code in its Title II (*On Abortion*) Book II (Articles 144–146 CP). The following crimes do exist in Spain, related to abortion:

(1) *Intentional abortion without the consent of the pregnant.* According to Article 144 Spanish Penal Code whoever perpetrates an abortion on a woman without her consent shall be punished with a sentence of imprisonment from four to eight years and special barring from practising any health profession or from

314. As for the previous requirement, the ruling of the Constitutional Court of 11 Apr. 1985 was to this effect, which led to its inclusion in the definitive version of the text of the law.
315. According to Art. 28.2 of Law 14/2007, of 3 July, on Biomedical Research.

providing services of any kind at public or private gynaecological clinics, institutions or surgeries, for a term of three to ten years. The same penalties shall be applied to whoever perpetrates an abortion having obtained the consent by the woman through violence, intimidation or deceit.

Active subject of this figure can only be a third party (not, therefore, the pregnant herself) acting without the consent of the woman. In this case a double attack does occur: firstly, to the life of the unborn child but also to the freedom of the pregnant woman. The penalties apply not only in case of absence of consent but also when consent by the woman has been obtained through violence, intimidation or deceit.

In order to determine when a woman is competent to issue consent at the light of Article 144 Spanish Penal Code the reference standard is established by Law 41/2002 of 14 November, regulating patient autonomy and rights and obligations regarding clinical information and documentation.

(2) *Intentional abortion with consent of the pregnant.* According to Article 145 of Penal Code:

> *1. Whoever perpetrates an abortion on a woman, with her consent, outside the cases allowed by Law shall be punished with a sentence of imprisonment from one to three years and special barring from practising any health profession and from providing services of any kind at public or private gynaecological clinics, institutions or surgeries, for a term of one to six years. The Judge may hand down the sentence in its higher half when the acts described in this Section are perpetrated outside an authorised public or private centre or institution. 2. The woman who causes herself an abortion or allows another person to cause it, outside the cases allowed by Law, shall be punished with a fine from six to twenty-four months. 3. In all cases, the Judge or Court of Law shall impose the penalties respectively foreseen in this Article in the upper half when perpetrated after the twenty-second week of gestation.*

First, it must be pointed out that Article 145 Penal Code incriminates abortions perpetrated on a woman *with her consent*. The cases established in Articles 145.1 and 2 Penal Code imply that the abortion is perpetrated 'outside the cases permitted by law' which is a de facto referral to the Organic Law 2/2010, concretely to its Articles 14 (time limit system) and 15 (abortion for medical reasons).

Article 145.1 Penal Code foresees an optional aggravation for the acts described in this Section (*The Judge may hand down the sentence in its higher half when the acts described in this Section are perpetrated outside an authorized public or private centre or institution).* On the other hand, and related to both Article 145.1 and Article 145.2 the Penal Code provides for a mandatory aggravation ('*In all cases, the Judge or Court of Law shall impose the penalties respectively foreseen in this Article in the upper half when perpetrated after the twenty-second week of gestation*').

(3) *Abortion within the cases admitted by Organic Law 2/2010 but omitting certain requirements.* Article 145 bis CP: '1. Punishment with a fine from six to twelve

months and special barring from providing services of any kind at public or private gynaecological clinics, institutions or surgeries shall be applied, for a term of six months to two years, to whoever, within the cases admitted by the Law, perpetrates an abortion: a) Without having verified that the woman has received prior information on the rights, public subsidies and aid to support maternity; b) Without the waiting period established in the legislation having elapsed; c) Without having obtained the required prior reports; d) Outside an authorized public or private centre or institution. In this case, the judge may impose the punishment in its upper half. 2. In all cases, the Judge or Court of Law shall impose the penalties foreseen in this Article in the upper half, when the abortion is perpetrated as of the twenty-second week of gestation. 3. The pregnant woman shall not be penalized under this provision'.

Article 145 bis Penal Code punishes cases of intentional abortions with the woman's consent within the cases admitted by Organic Law 2/2010 but omitting any of the requirements set out in points (a) to (d) of Article 145 bis 1 Penal Code.

(4) *Abortion by serious negligence.* According to 146 Penal Code 'whoever causes an abortion due to serious negligence shall be punished with a sentence of imprisonment of three to five months, or a fine from six to ten months. When an abortion is perpetrated due to professional negligence, the punishment of special barring from practising the profession trade or holding office shall also be imposed for a term from one to three years. The pregnant woman shall not be penalized under this provision'.

Under Article 146 Penal Code abortion is exclusively punishable by gross negligence, being unpunished, therefore, the abortion caused by minor negligence.

§2. Sterilization

I. Concept and Penal Scope

201. Spanish legal literature[316] tend to define the sterilization as the permanent or lasting removal of the reproductive capacity of a fertile man or woman by whatever procedure, be it surgical (suture of the deferent ducts or tubal ligation), or by means of biochemical or hormonal substances (though contraceptive pharmaceutical products do not fall within this definition), or by exposure to so-called absorbable radiation. The crime of 'castration' exists from the moment in which extirpation, amputation or the rendering useless of the masculine or feminine genital organs is produced, and it is subsumable under the type of offence in Article

316. In fact the Spanish Penal Code does not actually define what sterilization consists of Art. 149.1 stipulates that whoever who case to another, by whatever means, the loss or the uselessness of a principal organ or member, or of an sense, the impotence, the sterility, a severe deformity, or a serious somatic or mental disease shall receive a sentence of prison of between six years to twelve years.

149.1 of the Penal Code, given that the expression 'sterilization' has been included within the list of sanctioned behaviours of the aforementioned Article 149.1.

Sterilization is distinguished from castration on the basis that the latter implies the violent removal of the genital organs and has as a consequence not only the permanent loss of the ability to reproduce, as in sterilization, but also of other hormonal and endocrinal functions that affect the general behaviour of the individual, such as, in the sexual domain, diminished or total lack of libido and in the specific case of the male the very high accompanying risk of *coeundi* impotence or the inability to perform the sexual act.

The offence of sterilization includes reversible sterilizations which require surgical operation or similar procedures to restore fertility to the person. It goes without saying that this would not be the case, for example, of the removal of a diaphragm or intrauterine device (IUD), even where a physician has had to intervene.

II. Therapeutic Sterilization

202. The offence of sterilization is not considered to exist when it is therapeutic (e.g., in the treatment of prostate gland complications) or when it is the unavoidable outcome of some medical treatment (e.g., radiation treatment for cancer in the genital zone) provided that the following necessary requirements are met: medical indication, *lex artis*, curative purpose,[317] as well as, for other reasons, the informed consent of the individual concerned. Prophylactic or preventive sterilization may also come under therapeutic sterilization from the juridico-criminal point of view provided that the intended purpose is the avoidance of danger of certain grave injury to health or life in the future (e.g., if a woman in extremely poor health were to become pregnant).

Castration is not deemed to be an offence if performed for therapeutic or preventive reasons, where the life or physical or mental health of the patient is in danger. Even so, given the serious and irreversible consequences that it implies, therapeutic castration for psychological reasons is only permissible under the following circumstances:[318]

(1) proof beyond reasonable doubt that the abnormality or illness is not treatable by means of any other psychotherapeutic procedure;
(2) gravity of the abnormality or illness from the social point of view, rendering living with normal human dignity impossible or implying serious risks for the person affected;
(3) the consent of the patient.

317. Romeo-Casabona. *El Médico y el derecho penal, I,* p. 177; E.J. Armaza Armaza & E. Atienza Macías, "El tratamiento jurídico de las intervenciones en el aparato reproductor humano: esterilización, castración química y cirugía de reasignación sexual", in *Tratado de Derecho Sanitario, Vol. II,* A. Palomar Olmeda, J. Cantero Martínez (Dirs.) (Thomson Reuters Aranzadi, Cizur Menor 2013), p. 740.

318. Bleuler, *Tratado de Psiquiatría* (Espasa Calpe, Madrid 1969), pp. 127 and f.

To these requirements we would add the age of the patient and also the need for sterilization to remain completely disassociated from any criminal process or sentence, so as not to influence or coerce the individual into making the decision (e.g., in order to procure a lighter sentence or a reduction in the time to be served) as well as the patient's age.

III. Limitations on the Lawfulness of Voluntary Sterilization in Spanish Law

203. Voluntary sterilization, that is to say sterilization to which the individual concerned has consented – whether the individual is single or not – has been lawful under Spanish Law, even when it is not therapeutic, since 1983, year in which the Penal Code was revised as regards the effectiveness of consent to bodily harm, which is acceptable in the exceptional circumstance of sterilization. The Penal Code states that 'notwithstanding the provisions of the previous paragraph, valid, free, conscious and explicit consent exonerates from criminal liability in the case of organ transplants effected in accordance with the Law, sterilizations and transsexual surgery carried out by qualified physicians, except where consent has been obtained by foul means, or through payment or reward, or if the consenting party is a minor or incompetent to give consent, in which case no consent given by him or his legal representatives shall be valid (Article 156 of the Penal Code). The previous paragraph (Article 155) states that in the offences of injuries, if the victim has given his valid, free, spontaneous and explicit consent a punishment lower by one or two degrees shall be imposed. At this moment the Article 156 of the Penal Code includes a second paragraph that states that sterilization is not punishable when agreed by a court in the case of persons that permanently are unable to give consent, in the case of exceptional circumstances where serious conflict of protected rights occurs, in order to safeguard the interest of the affected, all in accordance with the provisions of the civil law.

A. Scope of the Lawfulness of Voluntary Sterilization

204. With Article 156 of the Penal Code a position of clear liberalization is adopted in terms of the power to dispose of the legal interest, since it affords a wider implicit recognition of the individual right to non-reproduction than can be deduced in practice from the depenalization of the use of other contraceptive methods. For this reason the introduction of the legal provision discussed here was appropriate precisely in relation to non-therapeutic sterilization.

As a result, sterilization of the individual who has given consent is lawful under Spanish law, provided that the requirements stipulated in aforementioned Article of the Penal Code for non-therapeutic sterilization are met, when it is motivated by one of the eugenic indications, socio-economic considerations (family planning), but also when no indication of any kind exists and the interested party has freely consented. However, sterilization by imposition or coercion, that is, against the will of the individual concerned (e.g., for State demographic policy reasons), is not permitted since it is clearly unconstitutional.

B. Requirements

205. In the first place, sterilization must be performed *by a qualified physician* and not by any other kind of person; frequently this physician will be a surgeon (for the removal of the fallopian tubes in the woman), but any other medical doctor capable of performing minor surgery is also appropriate (vasectomy in the male). The physician acts in the legitimate exercise of his profession and is authorized for this specific circumstance by the Penal Code itself. Nevertheless, for the physician's performance of the operation to be lawful consent must be given by the individual who is to be operated on. It is important to remark that the sterilization is forbidden if it is carried out by any other person, even if such person has enough training (students of Medicine or unauthorized graduates to practice their health profession) and counts with the consent of the affected person. In such situation the provision of the Article 155 will be applicable and a punishment lower by one or two degrees shall be imposed.

206. All *other requirements* included in Article 156.1 for sterilization to be valid centre on the conditions that must be satisfied with regard to the interested party's consent. It must be freely given (without coercion and not obtained under threat) and explicit (verbal or written),[319] furnished without foul play (not obtained by means of deception or erroneous belief), without payment or reward and the consenting party must be an adult with full use of his mental faculties, i.e., must not be a minor or incompetent. In any case, where the sterilization of minors or legally incompetent individuals is concerned, in view of the therapeutic indication involved, the general rules governing consent to medical treatment apply rather than these specific rules.

In some family planning centres it is customary to ask (apart from the court decision) both husband and wife to sign a document of consent, since the person who is not undergoing the operation will nonetheless be equally affected in terms of being able to produce offspring with his/her partner (all the more so in cases of vicarious or substitute sterilization). Although consent is a preventive measure designed to get round the possible problem of potential claims by the person who is not operated on (who might allege lack of knowledge of the performance of the operation or that he/she did not agree to its being performed), it is not a legal requirement and cannot therefore be demanded by law for the operation to be carried out.

319. *See* Arts 4, 8 and 10 of the Law 41/2002 of 14 November, regulating the autonomy of patients and their rights and obligations with regard to clinical information and documentation.

C. Sterilization of Minors and Mentally Handicapped

207. As we have noted, the first paragraph of the Article 156 of the Penal code establishes that the valid, free, conscious and explicit consent exonerates from criminal liability in the case of sterilization carried out by qualified physician. However, same paragraph includes an exception for this general rule: when the person who is to be sterilized for whatever reason is a minor he may not give valid consent, nor can such consent be given by the legal representatives; in other words, the individual cannot undergo sterilization. Minors do not generally present specific circumstances in terms of sterilization such as socio-economic or eugenic indications, but the case of the couple who has married before attaining their majority is of practical interest.

The first issue that must be settled is the meaning and scope of the term 'minor' as used in Article 156 of the Penal Code. Under the repealed criminal system it was necessary to clarify from the outset whether the Law seeks through the use of this term to make a connection with the concepts of private and civil Law (a minor according to the Civil Law is a person under 18 years of age) or, alternatively, whether the opposite interpretation in keeping with similar figures in Criminal Law is intended: a minor in the Criminal Law (according to the repealed Penal Code) was a person under 16 years of age. At the present, said discussion is no longer problematic given that with the new Penal Code the age needed to obtain civil and penal competence is exactly the same.[320] As a result, only those of 18 years or more who are not legally incompetent can give valid consent, and from this age onwards no restrictions may be imposed.[321]

320. In effect, there was a discussion to determine which interpretation is the appropriate to face the dilemma. Literature used to reject the second interpretation (a minor in the Criminal Law is a person under sixteen years of age) if no other arguments supporting its validity can be added, since there is no reason why the word 'minor' should have a single meaning for the Penal Code alone. Immunity from prosecution under the Penal Code to which one might seek to link the scope of 'minor' refers to the exclusion from criminal liability for a wrongful act committed by persons such as those to whom it refers (minors), while the case that concerns us here is not one of the elimination of liability from the consenting party – the minor – but from a third party, who is the person who will act or perform the action which, in principle, is prohibited if the aforementioned consent has not been given – i.e., the medical doctor to whom consent is granted. Consequently, what is of interest is when such persons do not have the recognised capacity to give their consent in view of their status as minors. Furthermore, the reference to civil notions in the Art. 428.2 of the repealed Penal Code (corresponding to the Art. 156 currently in force) would appear to be unequivocal, as are the other requirements that must be satisfied for consent, and particularly the inclusion of explicit mention of the legal representatives, which is a figure that is completely alien to Criminal Law, but which has a precise description in Civil Law, being linked to the civil minor and the legally incompetent person. The intervention of the Criminal Law through the repealed Art. 428 is aimed precisely at modifying these general provisions of Civil Law, by denying the representatives in the circumstances addressed by the article a representation that the Law recognises in principal (although we shall see below that this is not wholly accurate), albeit with important limitations when rights of personality or highly personal interests are affected. In conclusion, the Legislature did forge a link with the civil concept (Art. 315 of the CC). As a result, the literature used to consider that only those of eighteen years or more who are not legally incompetent can give valid consent, and from this age onwards no restrictions may be imposed.

321. *See* Art. 19 of Penal Code and Art. 315 of Civil Code.

208. The *legal representatives* are not empowered to give their consent on behalf of the minor. The point of departure taken by the criminal Legislature (Article 156 of the Penal Code), which coincides with that of its civil counterpart,[322] is the principle that rights of personality are not transferable.[323] Neither may the *judicial authority* substitute for the will of the minor and authorize sterilization; through such intervention by the authorities is not prohibited by Article 156 of the Penal Code, civil legislation only foresees that the parents may, in exercising their paternal authority, seek the assistance of the authorities (Article 154). This assistance may be regarded only as referring to those rights and duties recognized as resting in the parents in performance of their parental authority functions. Consequently, since they do not have the authority to substitute the will of the minor, it will be difficult for the judge to assist them in enforcing authority they do not actually have. Furthermore, in Spanish legal order there is no explicit recognition of such powers of substitution or representation of the minor (Article 158 of the CC) by the Judge or Public Prosecutor. Therefore, we may not arrive at the lawful sterilization of the minor by this route

However, as we mentioned before, we can still consider that offence of sterilization is not considered to exist, even if the affected person is a minor, when it is therapeutic (e.g., in the treatment of prostate gland complications) or when it is the unavoidable outcome of some medical treatment (e.g., radiation treatment for cancer in the genital zone). In any case, it is not a problem of a comparable entity to that of the legally incapacitated person and thus the current legal position of not allowing the sterilization of minors under any circumstances, with no exceptions, until they reach the age of majority would seem to be correct.[324]

209. A great deal of interest and indeed conflict surrounds the sterilization of the mentally handicapped, in view of the risks of an unwanted pregnancy occurring in the female, particularly when living in a communal environment (e.g., in special education centres and residential care). It should not be forgotten, however, that popular opinion has been moving towards the idea that these individuals should not be denied access to a sex life. In such cases a twin problem or indication occurs: that the child will be born with abnormalities or illnesses of genetic origin (eugenic indication), and the practical impossibility of maintaining the child financially and of carrying out the functions of motherhood (or, where applicable, fatherhood). Note also that the mentally handicapped are normally deprived of their civil rights, such as parental authority (socio-economic indication).

322. Civil Code, Art. 162: 'Parents with rights of authority are the legal representatives of their non-emancipated minor children, save in relation to 1. Acts concerning the child's right of personality or other rights which, under the law and bearing in mind his level of maturity, he can perform for himself'. Art. 267: 'Guardians are the legal representatives of minor or incompetent children, save in relation to acts which they can perform for themselves, either as the result of an explicit legal ruling to that effect or a proviso contained in the court's declaration of the child's incompetence'.

323. *See* on this point L. Díez-Picazo & A. Gullón Ballesteros, *Sistema del Derecho Civil, IV* (5th ed. Tecnos, Madrid 1990), p. 362; J.M. Lete del-Rio, *Comentarios al Código Civil y Compilaciones forales* (M. Albadalejo, ed.), IV (2nd ed. Edersa, Madrid 1985), p. 368.

324. For arguments in favour of banning the sterilization of minors, *see* L. Arroyo Zapatero, 'Los menores de edad y los incapaces ante el aborto y la esterilización', p. 19.

210. The understanding of the expression 'lack of aptitude to consent' as used in Article 156 of the Penal Code has raised similar issues to 'minor': the issue of choice between the criminal sense (the mentally deranged or persons who have suffered perceptual disturbance from birth or from early childhood, for example the profoundly deaf and dumb; Articles 20.1 and 20.3 respectively), or the civil sense (persons who have been certified as being legally incompetent). For the same reasons as those expressed above we should defend the second alternative, although leaving room for reciprocal interference from the two perspectives (the civil and the criminal). In fact, from the Civil Code we can deduce that the expression 'lack of aptitude to consent' as used in Article 156 of the Penal Code is distinct from that included in this body of law. Article 199 of the Civil Code states that no-one can be declared incompetent, except by judicial decision in accordance with the causes established by Law.

What is relevant in terms of the criminal law for the reasoning behind Article 156 of the Penal Code to be applicable is that the subject can understand de facto (whether or not he/she has been certified as being incompetent by the judicial authority) the scope and consequences of the decision to undergo the sterilization operation, and that he/she is in possession of the natural capacity to judge and understand the act.[325] Here, however, we encounter a limitation originating from Civil Law, namely, that if the person has been declared judicially incompetent capacitated he/she lacks the capacity to operate in civil life, which affects the validity of any legal actions carried out by the subject (such as entering into a contractual relationship with a physician for the purposes of a surgical operation). Referral to the terms of the incompetence stipulated by the judge in his decision is obligatory, given that otherwise the Law does not authorize the individual to voluntarily undergo a sterilization (Article 267 of the CC). If as frequently happens through oversight the judge's decision does not explicitly contemplate the incompetent individual subsequently consenting to sterilization for eugenic and/or socio-economic or other reasons, neither the incompetent person – under CC Article 267 – nor his/her legal representatives (who are prohibited by Article 156 of the Penal Code) may validly consent to sterilization. If, despite this, the individual has the de facto capacity to understand the nature of the act of consent (and given that the Penal Code does not place any obstacles to this situation), representation shall have to be made to the judicial authorities to modify the scope of the previous ruling of incompetence, as Article 212 of the CC envisages, so that the individual may validly express the consent required by Article 156 of the Penal Code, or, where applicable, his/her opposition to the sterilization operation.

To sum up, in the eyes of the criminal law incompetence denotes those who do not in fact possess the capacity for judgment, even though they have not been declared legally incompetent. Where such a person has been certified as being incompetent, he/she shall not be able to consent to sterilization, even in the hypothetical case that the person has the natural capacity of judgment to understand the

325. On this *see*, Romeo-Casabona, *El Médico y el Derecho Penal, I*, p. 316; J. Silva Sánchez, *La esterilización de disminuidos psíquicos* (PPU, Barcelona 1988), p. 46; J. Boix Reig, *La reforma penal de 1989* (Tirant lo Blanch, Valencia 1989), p. 132.

nature of the procedure.[326] An exception to this would be where there is an explicit statement to the contrary in the judge's ruling on incompetence. This means that the civilly incapacitated individual for whom this competence is recognized may validly consent – or express opposition – to his/her own sterilization which is a plausible situation in the case of persons suffering only slight mental disorders and who are capable of understanding the scope of certain important decisions. This solution would not be satisfactory, however, in cases of profound psychiatric disturbance, in which case neither the individuals concerned not their legal representatives may consent to sterilization.

211. Under the Penal Code currently in force an exception for those who are most profoundly disabled has been envisaged, since it is these individuals who are most seriously lacking in the ability to prevent a pregnancy through their own actions and since there is no good reason to repress their natural capacity for sexual expression and affection. This legal tendency was initially developed in the reform of 1989, which clarified and resolved the issue by permitting sterilization of an incompetent person suffering serious intellectual disability. Art. 156 PC establishes that the requirement here is that sterilization shall be authorized by the judge in the case of exceptional circumstances in which a serious conflict of protected rights occur, in order to safeguard the interest of the affected person, all in accordance with the provisions of CC. Although this article refers to CC, the fact is that the First Additional Provision of LO 1/2015 that reformed PC, states that sterilization must be authorized at the request of the legal representative of the incompetent person, and such authorization shall be given only after hearing the opinion of two specialists, the Public Prosecutor and following an examination of the individual concerned.

The term 'lack of aptitude to consent' which the law uses again in this new clause of Article 156 maintains the same meaning as that attributed by us with regard to the first clause,[327] with one qualification: given that the law says that sterilization shall be requested by the legal representatives, the 'lack of aptitude to consent' now refers exclusively to the individual who has previously been certified as being so by the civil judge, and *not* to the de facto (or presumably) incompetent person who would not have legal representatives in the first place nor could they act on his/her behalf.[328] Disability should be understood to mean a (serious) mental handicap of perinatal origin, that is to say, limited to mental deficiencies; furthermore, if one of the circumstances that are cause for incompetence under the CC (Article 200), given that this article distinguishes between illnesses and deficiencies, the term should have a stricter and different meaning in the Penal Code also; finally, if the CC demands in the same clause that deficiencies should be 'persistent', it alludes at the

326. The Attorney General, in his Consulta of 3/1985, *sobre la capacidad de los oligofrénicos para prestar el consentimiento previsto en el art. 428.2 del Código Penal* (on the capacity of mental patients to grant the consent envisaged in Art. 428.2 of the Penal Code), arrived at a similar conclusion.

327. Guallart de Viala, *La nueva protección penal de la integridad corporal y la salud*, p. 131; J. Tamarit Sumalla, *La reforma de los delitos de lesiones* (PPU, Barcelona 1990), p. 191.

328. Along similar lines, Circular No. 2/1990 from the Attorney General's Office, *sobre la aplicación de la Reforma de la Ley Orgánica 3/1989, de 21 de junio, de actualización del Código Penal.*

very least to the lasting nature of such deficiencies, if not their de facto irreversibility; all this leads to the conclusion that the legal expression does not refer to psychiatric illnesses that are distinguishable from deficiencies. That they should be 'serious' alludes to a profound disability, of the kind that rules out any valid consent on the part of the sufferer, in the sense that consent is an expression of sufficient maturity and the natural capacity for judgment, that is, those cases that the reform of the Penal Code has covered. Finally, a minor who presents a serious mental deficiency that is reasonably likely to 'persist into adulthood' (Article 201 CC) may be sterilized under this legal procedure in so far as this situation is covered by the exception included in the current Penal Code,[329] although here also doubts may be raised.

Exclusive responsibility for initiating the procedure rests with the legal representatives so that undesirable interference from third parties and the State itself may be avoided, given that neither the judge nor the public prosecutor can do anything until the parents take the initiative. The judge and prosecutor, for their part, will satisfy themselves that the sterilization is being performed for the benefit of the mentally deficient person and not in the exclusive interests of the legal representatives. The certificates of opinion issued by the two specialists shall refer both to the psychiatric condition of the incompetent subject as well as to environmental circumstances that may make the operation advisable or otherwise. The judge's examination of the incompetent minor enables him to assess the situation better and weigh up the possible repercussions of sterilization.[330]

In conclusion, decision-making by third parties is designed to protect the interests of the incompetent person, by favouring him/her in the areas of personality which may develop without the individual become stigmatized, such as the affective and sexual domains; in all cases, however, the circumstances of each individual shall always be kept in mind and generalizations avoided completely.

§3. Medically Assisted Reproduction

I. Social Context and Legal Background

212. The Spanish socio-political debate on medically assisted reproduction started in the eighties. At that moment, a Parliamentary Select Committee on the study of human in vitro fertilization and artificial insemination carried out an extensive work that concluded with a Report (*Informe Palacios*) including a list of recommendations (155 in all), as well as a number of suggestions from parliamentary groups regarding points over which there was disagreement. Soon afterwards, the Spanish Parliament approved the first Spanish Law on this issue, Law 35/1988 of 22 November on Assisted Reproduction Techniques. This first document was

329. Of the same opinion and arguing along the same lines, Guallart de Viala, *La nueva protección penal de la integridad corporal y la salud*, p. 132; and Attorney General's Office, *Memoria elevada al Gobierno de S.M.* (comments by Prosecutor Compte), Madrid 1990, p. 276.

330. E.J. Armaza Armaza & E. Atienza Macías, 'El tratamiento jurídico de las intervenciones en el aparato reproductor humano: esterilización, castración química y cirugía de reasignación sexual', pp. 741–743.

immediately followed by the approval of Law 42/1988 of 28 December on the donation and use of human embryos and foetuses or their cells.

213. Law 35/1988 comprised seven chapters, preceded by an extensive and well-documented Preamble, which included a definition of the pre-embryo, an entity that played a fundamental role in the regulation. The Law was, in general, a very liberal document, which allowed most of the various assisted human reproduction techniques currently available, including: artificial insemination with the husband's semen (*ex* Articles 5.8 and 8), with that of the partner when the couple are not married (*ex* Article 9.3) with a donor's semen (*ex* Article 5), etc. The Law also allowed the reception of an egg by an infertile woman who will complete gestation, and also the reception of a pre-implanted embryo (also called a pre-embryo) whose gametes of origin are not those of the couple, or the woman's egg and her partner's semen or that of a third party donor (*ex* Article 5.1). The only exception to this liberal approach was related to sex selection, which was strictly forbidden, except for therapeutic purposes, and a general ban on surrogacy and pregnancy substitution, which were not permitted by the Act (Article 10).

This legal framework built on 1988 was also quite conservative in terms of use of embryos for research purposes, as far as it banned research on viable embryos unless for the purposes of diagnosing, treating or preventing disease in that embryo. However, in doing so it was anticipating the judgment of the Spanish Constitutional Court,[331] which affirmed that the regulation provided Law 42/1988 of 28 December on the donation and use of human embryos and foetuses or their cells was based on the fundamental precept that biomedical research can only be conducted on non-viable human embryos and foetuses, case law that was reiterated in Constitutional Court Judgment 116/1999 of June 17.[332]

214. Law 35/1988 was never a peacefully accepted act. Indeed, three vetoes were lodged against the bill in its entirety, one of which came from the main opposition party, Partido Popular. From other, mainly technical, juridico-civil and legislative perspectives, the law faced a great deal of criticism.[333] Therefore, it was not surprising that, when the Partido Popular won the election by an absolute majority in 2000, it decided to introduce a dramatic change in the Spanish regulation on medically assisted reproduction, by approving Law 45/2003 on 21 November and amending Law 35/1988 on 22 November on Assisted Reproduction Techniques.

The main characteristic of this new legislation was the radical change in the regulation of the spare embryos issue. Law 45/2003 introduced a general ban on the creation of surplus embryos by limiting the number of fertilized ova to the amount of three, i.e., the number of embryos that were transferred into a woman's uterus according to the in-vitro technique routine at that moment. The act foresaw some exceptions to this general limit according to the concrete physiological

331. Constitutional Court Judgment 212/1996 of December 19.

332. Antonio Cabanillas Sánchez y Jorge Zavala, 'Ethics And Legal Keys To Biomedical Research In Spain', *The Age of Human Rights Journal*, 2 (June 2014) pp. 51–67 (62–63).

333. See, for example, F. Pantaleón Prieto, 'Contra la Ley sobre Técnicas de Reproducción Asistida', *Jueces para la Democracia*, 1998, p. 5.

characteristics of the couple. For this purpose, Royal Decree 1720/2004, which followed the 2003 law, defined the exceptions in which it was not necessary to apply the limitation.

This new ruling also provided a solution for the problem of the spare embryos generated according to Law 35/1988 by determining that any use of pre-embryos in cryostorage prior to its enactment should be decided by the couple or woman involved. Those involved could choose between maintaining them in cryostorage until they were transferred, donating them for reproductive purposes, or consenting to the use of the biological structures obtained upon thawing for research purposes, within the limits set forth in the law's final provision.[334] However, this new act did not last long. In 2006, after the change in the Spanish government induced by the elections in 2004, which were won by the socialist party (PSOE), a new legal framework was produced, including two fundamental acts: Law 22/2006 on 27 May regarding assisted human reproduction techniques and the Biomedicine Law 14/2007 on 3 July 2007.

II. The Main Characteristics of the Spanish Legal Framework on Assisted Human Reproduction Techniques

215. Law 14/2006 on 26 May on assisted human reproduction techniques introduced a new legal framework on assisted human reproduction, which was extremely generous, as it provided every woman with the right to access assisted reproduction treatments, regardless of if she were married, part of an unmarried couple, or a single woman. Consequently, the law allowed most of the assisted human reproduction techniques currently available in all of their different modalities such as artificial insemination with the husband's semen (e.g., Article 9), with that of the partner when the couple were not married (e.g., Article 9.3), or with a donor's semen (e.g., Article 6). The law also allowed the reception of an egg by an infertile woman who completed gestation, and the reception of a pre-implanted embryo (also called a pre-embryo) whose gametes of origin were not those of the couple, or the woman's egg and her partner's semen or that of a third-party donor (e.g., Article 5). However, it continued the ban on surrogate motherhood and non-therapeutic sex selection.

216. The law removed the controversial limitation on fertilising only three oocytes (a restriction that was introduced by Law 45/2003 on 21 November, as previously stated), which was strongly criticized by the Spanish National Commission on Assisted Human Reproduction as it supposed a great hindrance for infertile couples because it substantially reduced their chances of success.[335] Law 14/2006

334. Antonio Cabanillas Sánchez y Jorge Zavala, 'Ethics and Legal Keys to Biomedical Research in Spain', pp. 51–67 (62–63).

335. 'It is scientifically proved that the cumulative probabilities of pregnancy for a couple that undergo an IVF cycle rise from 35-40% to 65-70% if frozen embryos are available. Although, most specialists in Assisted Reproduction were strongly in favour of removing the restriction and the new proposal under which the decision on the number of oocytes to be inseminated must be decided by agreement, taking into account the couple's wishes and the medical judgement according to the

also allowed the freezing of oocytes and ovarian tissue for reproductive purposes (Article 11). The maximum period for freezing oocytes and embryos was not fixed in the law, leaving this to medical judgment with no set limit. According to the act, it would be the couple or the woman alone who decided on the future of their frozen embryos, giving the same options to all equally, irrespective of the date on which they were frozen.

III. Subjects: General Requirements

217. The first requirements revolve around the medical indication and *lex artis*: reasonable chance of success; no serious risk to the health of the woman or the possible child (Article 3.1); in the case of in vitro fertilization involving the transfer of embryos, only the number of embryos sufficient to produce a pregnancy may be implanted (Article 3.2).

218. Other conditions refer to women recipients, include (Article 6):

(1) The recipient must have reached the age of majority, that is, 18 years of age. No discrimination based on sexual orientation or marital status is allowed by the Law.
(2) Informed consent. It is not sufficient for the woman to have simply given her consent. Clearly she must also have sought the treatment freely and consciously. Consent and acceptance require prior information and even legal advice. Information should be provided by the medical teams and those in positions of responsibility in the health centres or institutions where the treatment is to be carried out. The information (and the legal advice) should cover the various possible factors and implications arising from the techniques, as well as their outcomes and foreseeable risks entailed. Biological, legal, ethical or economic considerations arising from the techniques should be covered also. Consent is to be expressed in writing on an official consent form (Articles 3 and 6) and all information relevant to the use of the techniques is to be recorded in the clinical histories of both donors and recipients. Confidentiality shall be maintained (Article 3.6). The possibility of the woman recipient withdrawing her consent is recognized and the process must be interrupted immediately this occurs (Article 3.5).
(3) The woman needs the consent of her husband, although with non-married couples partner consent is not compulsory. Through this requirement it is intended that the husband takes on paternity of the child even when fertilization has been achieved with donor semen or a pre-embryo donated by third parties. Exceptions to this are couples who are legally separated or divorced or those who are in a de facto situation of separation and vouch to the effect. The Law makes no specific mention of annulled marriages (Articles 73 and ff of the Civil

special circumstances of each case' (M. Boada, A. Veiga & P.N. Barri, 'Spanish Regulations on Assisted Reproduction Techniques', *Journal of Assisted Reproduction and Genetics*, 2003; 20(7), pp. 271–275).

Code), but it is understood that the consent of the former husband is not necessary in these circumstances. Neither would it be necessary if the couple were divorced, although in this case the Law does make specific mention, unnecessarily given that if they are no longer married he is no longer the husband.

If the couple are not married, the male party may give his consent prior to the use of the techniques, in accordance with the same conditions, so as to achieve the same effects in terms of paternity discussed below (Article 8). Withdrawal of consent is only possible *before the techniques have been applied.* The real issue is where the time-limit lies. Is it the beginning of the whole process or after an attempt at fertilization (successful or otherwise)? In order to bring this into line with the woman's rights to interrupt the process, 'applied' would have to be understood to mean even after an attempt at fertilization. In this way the male partner might still withdraw consent even though the process has begun (e.g., he may have given his semen, ova may have been removed from the woman and fertilization attempted unsuccessfully) so long as fertilization had not been achieved.

IV. Subjects of Assisted Reproduction Techniques

219. Donors. Donors must have attained the age of majority (eighteen) and have full capacity to act (an indispensable condition for the formation of a contractual relationship, in this case as a donor). They must be in good psycho-physical health to the standard stipulated in the compulsory protocol for donor suitability assessment, which shall include information relating to the donor's phenotype characteristics (so as to ensure similarity with the recipient) and verification that the potential donor does not suffer any genetic, hereditary or infectious diseases (Article 5.6), a requirement that is obviously included in *lex artis.* Provision is also made for the taking of measures to prevent more than six children being produced from the same donor (Article 5.7). The husband who provides semen for the insemination of his wife is subject to the same requirements governing normal donors, as are donations of spare gametes that might be used in the fertilization of any other woman (Article 5.8). It is understood, though not explicitly stated, that donation must be voluntary.

220. Donation can consist of gametes (semen and ova) and of pre-embryos. The contractual relationship involves no exchange of money and is formal and confidential with the donor and the authorized centre as parties to the contract (Article 5.1):

(1) the reference to no exchange of money implies that donation may not be made for the purposes of financial gain (Article 5.3). The donor may not receive payment and the centre may not sell gametes or pre-embryos;
(2) 'formal' here means that the contract shall take the form of a written agreement between the two parties, the donor having previously been informed of the purposes and consequences of the donation;

(3) 'confidential' refers to the fact that the donation shall be anonymous.[336] The identity of the donor shall remain secret and the name kept in coded form only in the Banks and in the National Donor Register. This is one of the points that has provoked debate among specialists particularly over the hypothetical right of a child to know his genetic origin, i.e., to know the identity of the natural father. The donor's name can in fact be revealed (without there being any publicity) in two sets of circumstances: if the child's life is endangered or when disclosure is necessary in criminal proceedings. In both cases the name can be revealed only if it is absolutely indispensable to avoid the danger or to achieve the legal purpose (Article 5.5). Under no circumstances can disclosure of the donor's name lead to any kind of legal kinship relationship (Article 8.3). Lastly, donations are not revocable except in the case of subsequent infertility on the part of the donor, who may then need his own gametes, in which case he must refund to the Centre all costs ensuing from the donation (Article 5.2). This extreme measure would be discriminatory if it placed a greater financial burden on the donor than it did on any normal recipients.

In the regulations relating to donation it is not very clear exactly how donation of pre-embryos takes place or what the nature of the contractual relationship is from a formal perspective. Clearly this is a complex issue, given that the pre-embryo is the product of two gametes (sperm and ovum) from a man and a woman, which means that there are two donors who must give their consent.

221. The female user may not choose the donor (Article 6.5). This condition stems from the anonymous donor requirement: users may not choose from among the donors available at the centre or provide their own donor, except in the case of an unmarried couple and then the donor partner would have to take on the corresponding obligations arising from paternity. Nevertheless, it would appear that the Law does not foresee the possibility of an unmarried male providing his own semen since it makes no reference to this. In such a situation the man would be considered an ordinary donor. In any case, the Law does not refer either to insemination with the husband's semen, which is clearly lawful; moreover, since it allows *post mortem insemination* with either the husband or the unmarried partner's semen (Article 9) there is all the more reason for considering that the unmarried male partner can provide semen for fertilization while he is still alive.

As a result, the decision as to choice of donor is made by the medical team on the basis of strictly medical criteria, and others stipulated by law, which are designed to guarantee the greatest phenotype and immunological match of the donor as well as the maximum level of compatibility with the woman and her family environment (Article 6.5). In reality, the Legislature does not seem to have understood just how such a choice might combine genetic compatibility with compatibility with the woman's family environment, which is after all a social factor, once the other requirements (designed to prevent interracial pregnancy, which might well raise other problems for the woman – e.g., the single woman – who wants to produce

336. *See* J. Gil Rodríguez, 'La reproducción humana asistida como acto médico y el fundamento del anonimato', in *Boletín de Información del Ministerio de Justicia*, n. 1593, 1991, pp. 1600 and ff.

children of this kind) have been met. A practical solution has been provided by considering the partner of the woman not as a donor but as a user of the techniques, so as to make it possible to use his gametes in the fecundation process, even if the legal support of these practices is unclear.

222. *Parents and children.* What reference the Law makes to parents and children relates, in the first case, to the participation of parents in the techniques and the assumption of legal, though not genetic, paternity that this participation implies, and, in the case of the children, to relationships of affiliation.[337]

223. The Law provides special regulations (Article 7.1), choosing to leave overall considerations with regard to relationships of affiliation to the general regulations contained in the Civil Code. The special issues dealt with are the possibility of withdrawal of consent, mentioned above, the fact that registration of the birth in the civil register must make no reference to the use of assisted reproduction techniques (Article 7.2) so as to avoid any possible future discrimination against the child and, finally, the fact that disclosure of the donor's identity in the cases where this is permitted does not imply legal paternity, as has already been stated above.

The case of the married couple. If the semen donor is the husband, no specific problem relating to paternity and affiliation arises except in the situation where the husband does not consent or withdraws his consent before fertilization. If the semen donor is the husband but fertilization is achieved after his death (*post mortem* fertilization),[338] his consent is decisive from a civil law point of view, as is the moment it was given. The regulation states that no relationship of paternity exists and no legal consequences arise between the *post-humus* child and the deceased husband 'when his reproductive material is not found in the woman's uterus at the time of death' (Article 9.1). In other words, as we will see later, if he does not give his consent to the fertilization of his wife while still alive. If, on the other hand, he consented, in a public declaration or sworn testament to his reproductive material being used to fertilize his wife within twelve months of his death, the legal result is paternity within the marriage (Article 7.2). Leaving civil issues apart, the time-limit once more must be determined. It would seem from a literal reading that it is not necessary for successful fertilization to have been achieved within this twelve month period but rather it suffices for the process to merely have been started. For example, an initial unsuccessful attempt may have been made and some of the deceased husband's semen is still available and is used later or seminal or pre-embryo implantation has been performed and the results are still not known during the six-month period.

---

337. On these issues, which bring us into the area of Civil Law, the vast literature published in Spain may be consulted. *See* in particular (various authors), *La filiación a finales del siglo XX. Problemática planteada por los avances científicos en material de reproducción humana*, 'II Congreso Mundial Vasco' (Trivium, Madrid 1988), passim.

338. *See* E. Serrano Alonso, 'El depósito de esperma o de embriones congelados y los problemas de la fecundación "post mortem", in *La Filiación a finales del siglo XX. problemática planteada por los avances cientificos en material de reproducción humana*, pp. 365 and ff; H. Campuzano Tom, *Reflexión en torno a los derechos de la viuda para ser inseminada artificialmente*, from the same volume, pp. 433 and ff.

When the married couple needs a donor's biological material (consisting of either the ovum or the semen or of a pre-embryo) and both give their consent to this in the terms established by the Law, there exists an irrefutable assumption (*iuris et de iure*) of matrimonial affiliation with the child born out of the procedure. This affiliation may not be challenged (Article 8.1).

In the case of a same-sex marriage (both females) the one with child will be considered as the mother of the child, while the other member of the couple could ask for the affiliation (Article 8.3)

224. The case of the unmarried couple. If an unmarried male[339] gives his consent prior to fertilization of his partner in the manner described above, the document of consent will be considered to be a reliable document under Article 49 of the Civil Registry Law, which means that it will imply recognition of paternity, although this in itself does not rule out the possibility of a paternity claim being made at a later date (Article 8.2).

There is also the possibility of *post mortem* insemination using the semen of the unmarried man. The conditions described above with respect to the married man apply equally and with the same effects in relation to Article 49 of the Civil Registry Law (Article 9.3).

225. Surrogate or hired mothers. As was stated earlier, surrogate motherhood was not permitted under the terms of the 1988 Law. As a result any such contract was null and void, whether or not payment had been made and regardless of whether the agreement was between the couple seeking these 'services' or intermediaries and the woman concerned (Article 10.1). The affiliation of any children born out of surrogacy was determined by birth (Article 10.2), that is to say, maternity lied with the woman who gave birth to the child regardless of whether the ovum was hers or that of another woman or the semen that of the male partner of the couple concerned. If the male partner had provided the semen (or if it had been provided by a third party donor unconnected with an authorized centre or by a donor in collusion with the centre) the biological father could claim paternity (Article 10.3). This would also be the case under the general statutory provisions of the relevant part of the CC.

V. Issues Related to Surrogacy

226. As previously mentioned, the Act retained the previously existing ban on surrogate motherhood. Indeed, it declares null and void the contract by which a surrogate pregnancy is agreed, with or without financial compensation, where a woman would then formally renounce her right to maternal filiation in favour of the party who ordered the child or another third party. (Article 10.1). Indeed, the affiliation of any children born out of surrogacy is determined by birth (Article 10.2), that is to say, maternity lies with the woman who gave birth to the child regardless of whether

339. We have used the expression 'partner' here though the Spanish Law uses no such term nor does it make any reference to such a condition, be it stable or unstable. The Law uses only the terms male and unmarried male.

the ovum was hers or that of another woman or the semen that of the male partner of the couple concerned. If the male partner has provided the semen (or if it has been provided by a third party donor unconnected with an authorized centre or by a donor in collusion with the centre) the biological father can claim paternity (Article 10.3).

However, in recent years a lot of Spanish couples decided to overpass this ban by travelling abroad to make use of this technique in countries where it is not regulated or has been legally accepted, such as USA, India, Ukraine, and Russia among others. Therefore, a complicate legal issue arose when those couples intended to register the filiation of their children in Spain in their own name, as far as it involved an obvious contradiction with our legal framework. Indeed, some of these couple's claims were refused by the Spanish Registries and Provincial Courts.

Finally the conflictive surrogate pregnancy reaches the Supreme Court as a result of an appeal filed to the Provincial Court of Valencia 2011, by a couple whose registration was refused. The Supreme Court resolved this issue in its ruling dated February 6th, 2014. It considered that in order to recognize the foreign certificate where the filiation is stated, it is necessary to conduct a thorough check of said certificate of the Registry that wants to be accepted, verifying that it is ordinary and authentic, so as to make sure that it offers similar guarantees to those required for the registration of the same deed in Spain, complying with the Spanish Law. As a consequence, this statement supported the refutation, that is, the recognition of filiation asked by the couples paying for surrogate motherhood abroad. However, it provided the appellants with an alternative way to solve the problem, by highlighting the possibility of claiming the paternity regarding the biological father – if he actually provided the gamete remains available according to the general rules – (Article 10.3).

The rationality supporting this solution was challenged by a vote authorized by one of the Judges, to which other three joined, stating that:

> *what counts is the recognition of the filiation resulting from the American legislation in relation to the protection given to children of Spanish nationals, regardless of a contract, in whose creation the underage did not intervene, whereby the contractual instrument cannot be the reason for the refusal of this recognition. The solving of the issue should be focused on deciding whether this decision is contrary to the international public order or not and see whether it can introduced within the Spanish legal framework to fill the corresponding legal purposes.*

Besides, to these four magistrates, the international public order must guarantee the prevailing interest of the underage, which requires the recognition of the filiation.

Indeed, the appellants did not accept the ruling and the proposed alternative. Soon afterwards, they filed a motion for dismissal of proceedings of the tribunal, arguing that its ruling breached some fundamental rules of the appellants: the right to legal protection, the right to equality and the privacy of the family. The appeal was dealt with by the Chamber of Civil Cases of the Supreme Court in its Ruling of February the 2nd 2015, which reasoned that the Ruling did not breach the invoked rights of the appellants. Therefore, the Chamber considered that '*there are no grounds to dismiss the proceedings of the ruling num: 835/2013, from February the 6th, issued by the Plenary Board of this Chamber*'.

Therefore, it could be stated that the Spanish Court have somehow decided that it is in the interest of the children to integrate them in their family de facto, as far as children cannot find themselves unprotected in a juridical limbo, but avoiding any breach of Article 10 of the Law on Assisted Reproduction Techniques. On this purpose, they have suggested the couples an alternative way to obtain a satisfactory ending–that of the claim of paternity on the basis of the biological link with the child. However, it should be a matter of priority to undertake a change in legislation which regulates the practice of surrogate pregnancy in order to provide for legal certainty for all subjects involved.[340]

§4. Preimplantation Diagnosis and Human Genetics

I. Purpose and Lawfulness of Preimplantation Diagnosis

227. In 1988, preimplantation genetic diagnosis was yet an experimental technique, whose potentiality for the improvement of IVF techniques and for the prevention of genetic disease were still to be fully confirmed. Even in this case, the 1988 Act allowed pre-implantation genetic testing not only as a tool to help assisted reproduction techniques in case of infertility or sterility, but also as a diagnostic and therapeutic tool for the detection of hereditary diseases with a view of facilitating treatment, where possible, or advice against the transfer of the affected embryo into the womb. Given the experimental stage, the regulation of the technique was left to future legislative interventions but the general absence of a specific regulation characterized the Spanish IVF regime.[341]

228. Therefore, it must be stated that an exhaustive general framework on preimplantation diagnosis was only settled in 2006, when Law 14/2006 on 26 May on assisted human reproduction techniques was passed.

229. According to this Act, the authorization of Preimplantation Genetic Diagnosis (PGD) may be granted in two situations: (a) for the detection of serious hereditary diseases, of early onset and not capable of postnatal healing treatment in

340. Emaldi Cirión, Aitziber, 'A much-needed legal response to an urgent issue', *Perspectivas*, nº 25, 2015, at: http://www.catedraderechoygenomahumano.es/images/boletin/boletin_25_eng.pdf.

341. Indeed, '*The 1988 Act introduced a regulatory framework for the use of assisted reproduction techniques based on three measures: the licensing and the monitoring of authorized assisted reproduction centres; the setting-up of a consultative body to inform the government and to elaborate appropriate legislative measures on the advances of assisted reproduction techniques, and the creation of a National Registry, in which assisted reproduction activities and gametes and embryo donation could be recorded and stored. Although these three measures were all introduced to ensure both the safety and the transparency of assisted reproduction activities, their actual implementation and evolution followed very different trajectories*'. V. Pavone & F. Arias, *Pre-Implantation Genetic Testing in Spain: beyond the Geneticization Thesis* (Instituto de Políticas y Bienes Públicos (IPP), CCHS-CSIC, Working Paper, Number 12, Madrid 2010), pp. 9–10.

accordance with the current scientific knowledge, in order to undertake a selection of pre-embryos that are not affected for their transfer; (b) for the detection of other alteration that could compromise the viability of the embryos (Article 12.1). Therefore, according to Spanish regulation, the use of PGD to detect serious diseases of early onset, which seriously condition the future development of a person are legally authorized by law. In all the cases that met these criteria, In Vitro Fertilization (IVF) centres and hospitals were simply expected to inform, through their regional authority, the National Assisted Reproduction Committee (CNRHA), from which no further authorization was required.[342]

It is worth to mention that, apart from both those situations, Law 14/2006 also foresees the use of PGD for other purposes, such as the selection of embryos for histocompatibility anti-genes (HLA) matching. In this occasion, the clinical case consists in a petition for PGD to detect a hereditary disease, together with the determination of HLA, requested by a couple with a child with a disease- let's say, acute myeloblastic leukaemia- and who need a compatible donor, which would be his or her future sibling previously selected in the embryonic stage. This use of PGD is, thus, perfectly legal in Spain. However, Law 14/2006 allows this procedure only when there is an express authorization by the corresponding health authority, which shall study it on a case by case basis and always when there previously is a favourable report by the National Assisted Human Reproduction Commission, which must evaluate the clinical therapeutic and social characteristics of each case (Article 12.2) In these events, the role of the National Organisation on Transplantation must be taken into account as the coordinating and counselling organization to the Ministry of Health and Consumption in matters related to the donation and transplantation of organs and tissues (Additional Clause 3).[343]

II. Embryonic and Foetal Therapy and Research

230. The developments in terms of embryonic and foetal research and therapy open up new perspectives such as a reduction in the number of abortions performed for eugenic reasons because they will allow for certain foetal abnormalities to be corrected.[344] It is worth recalling, in this sense, that on the international level there is a document of relevance here, namely, the Declaration of the Rights of the Child of 1959 which, despite its limited jurisdiction, recognizes the right to treatment even before birth (Article 4).

Due to this scenario, doctors are confronted by the peculiar situation of treating a 'patient', the foetus, who differs from the ordinary patient in the sense that it is

342. V. Pavone & F. Arias, *Pre-Implantation Genetic Testing in Spain: beyond the Geneticization Thesis*, pp. 10–11.
343. Emaldi Cirión, Aitizber, 'Preimplantational Genetic Diagnosis (PGD)', *Perspectivas,* number 9. Jun. 2007, at: http://www.catedraderechoygenomahumano.es/images/boletin/boletin_9_eng.pdf.
344. Some authors consider that in future all the current indications for abortion will cease to exist because treatment will be possible outside the woman's body. This will even be the case when the pregnancy endangers the woman's life as the foetus would be removed and placed in an artificial placenta. Interrupting a pregnancy will not therefore involve terminating the life of the conceived child. V.L. Lombardi Vallauri, 'Bioetica, potere, diritto', in *Giustitia*, 1984, p. 21.

inside the body of another person – the mother. All foetal therapies must inevitably be carried out through the mother's body.[345] As a result, the application of the term 'patient' to the foetus has specific and peculiar legal characteristics. This is particularly so with regard to bodily harm inflicted on the mother (e.g., if a caesarean or some other surgical operation has to be performed on her to reach the foetus or when certain drugs are administered), any dangers which treatment entails for her life and health, and the fact that she gives her consent to a treatment that will not benefit her directly (although it is not unusual for the mother also to present symptoms of some kind), but the child she bears. It should not be forgotten either that foetal therapy can give rise to injuries in the foetus that become apparent only after birth. Foetal therapy may even cause the child to die before birth or soon after.

As we have already seen, in Spanish law the life of the child is a legally protected interest independent of the mother. For this reason the law punishes wilful abortion – (and in some cases negligent abortion, Article 146 of the Penal Code) while acknowledging legal exceptions that allow abortion and the destruction of the foetus (mainly, that it is played in the first trimester of pregnancy, as previously mentioned). Moreover, the Spanish Penal Code includes two articles protecting the foetus against unfair harm. According to Article 157:

> Whoever, by any means or procedure, were to cause a foetus an injury or disease that seriously damages the normal development thereof or causes such foetus a serious physical or mental handicap, shall be punished with a prison sentence of one to four years and special barring from practising any health profession, or providing services of all kinds at public or private gynaecological clinics, institutions or surgeries, for a term of two to eight years.

Article 158, on the other hand, states that:

> Whoever, due to serious negligence, was to commit the acts described in the preceding Article, shall be punished with a sentence of imprisonment of three to five months or a fine from six to ten months. When the acts described in the preceding Article are committed by professional negligence, the punishment of special barring from practice of the profession, trade or office for a term of six months to two years shall also be imposed. The pregnant woman shall not be penalised under this provision.

Therefore, it can be concluded that the Spanish legal framework includes a general prevision mainly directed to physicians, which obliges them to provide good care of the child, avoiding any practise that might cause harm to the offspring or the human being it might become in the future.

231. Biomedicine Law 14/2007, *of* 3 July 2007 increased the protection on the embryos and foetuses during the pregnancy. Its Article 19 states that:

345. *See* W. Kapp, 'Der Fötus als Patient?', in *Medizinrecht*, 1986, p. 276.

> Any research in which a pregnant woman participates, which does not produce a direct benefit to her, or the embryo, the foetus or the child after birth shall only be authorised if the following conditions are met: (a) That the aim of the research is to contribute to the production of results that are for the benefit of other women, embryos, foetuses or children. (b) That research of similar efficacy is not possible to be undertaken in nonpregnant women. (c) That the research entails minimum risk and damage for the woman and, in its case, for the embryo, foetus or child. d) That the pregnant woman, or the legal representatives of the child, in its case, provide their consent in the terms provided in this Law.

Therefore, it is clear that any kind of research practise that entails a risk for the embryo or the foetus, when no benefit for the offspring is involved at all is strictly forbidden according to the Spanish law.

Finally, it is necessary to mention that Biomedicine Law also states that 'human embryos that have lost their capacity for biological development, as well as dead human embryos or foetuses, may be donated for biomedical research or other diagnostic, therapeutic, pharmacological, clinical or surgical purposes' (Article 28.1). Though, before proceeding to any intervention on human embryos, which have lost their capacity to biologically develop, or on dead embryos or foetuses, a record shall be made by the corresponding medical personnel that such circumstances have taken place. However, the use of the deceased embryos and foetuses can only be accepted if the abortion has not been provoked on this purpose. Indeed, the Act includes a clause that prevents this result: The termination of a pregnancy can never be for the purpose of the donation and later use of embryos, foetuses or their biological structures. The procedure and manner of the practice of terminating the pregnancy shall be subject only to the legal demands and limitations and the surrounding characteristics and circumstances. The professionals, who are part of the medical team that undertakes the termination of the pregnancy, shall not intervene in the use of the aborted embryos, foetuses or their biological structures. To this effect, the members of the research team shall leave written record of this matter, as well as the absence of any conflict of interest with the medical team.

III. Human Genetics

A. Legal Framework

232. Spanish law, albeit in a partial and sectoral manner, contains regulations which apply directly or indirectly to genetic innovations and studies of the human genome. To take Civil Law first, the Spanish Constitution of 1978 empowers the law to permit investigation of paternity (Article 39.1). This constitutional authorization is included in the Civil Code, which enables paternity and maternity to be investigated in affiliation suits, using all kinds of proof, including biological proof (Article 127.1), – and genetic proof –, even though no absolute certainty is recognized.

Nonetheless, paternity research poses certain limitations derived from the presumptions of paternity as contained in the Civil Code: moreover, the Constitutional Court has ruled that these tests cannot be made obligatory or carried out against the wishes of the person concerned, although courts may take a refusal into account when determining paternity.[346]

233. As regards labour relations, the Constitution stipulates that discrimination on the grounds of race, sex, religion, or opinion is unlawful, and extends these grounds to 'any other personal or social condition or circumstance' (Article 14), which means that personal health may also be included as a factor of non-discrimination; the Constitution also recognizes the right of personal and family privacy (Article 18.1). This principle of non-discrimination and the right to privacy are also recognized in the LGS (Ley General de Sanidad) of 25 April 1986, having been included in the list of patients' rights (Article 10.1), although it should be noted that these are applicable in relation to public health administrations and private health services only. 265. However, the principle of non-discrimination was also included in other binding documents, such as the Convention for the Protection of Human Rights and Dignity of the Human Being with regard to the Application of Biology and Medicine: Convention on Human Rights and Biomedicine (commonly known as the Oviedo Convention), which came into effect in Spain on 1 January 2000, following its ratification by Parliament. As article number 11 stated, 'Any form of discrimination against a person on grounds of his or her genetic heritage is prohibited'. However, Article 12 declared, 'Tests which are predictive of genetic diseases or which serve either to identify the subject as a carrier of a gene responsible for a disease or to detect a genetic predisposition or susceptibility to a disease may be performed only for health purposes or for scientific research linked to health purposes, and subject to appropriate genetic counselling'. Protection against the misuse of genomic information was also incorporated by Organic Law 15/1999 on 13 December, Protection of Personal Data, of which Article 7 excluded any kind of access to genetic information without the consent of the concerned people (and, in some cases, even if these people consent).

Finally, it is worth mentioning that the Workers Statutes Law, as amended by Royal Decree 2/2015, of 23 October, states in Article 4.2 c), second paragraph, that workers may not be discriminated against on the grounds of physical, mental or sensory handicaps, providing that they are fit to perform the work or job in question'; the law goes on to recognize in part (e) of the same section the 'right of persons to have their privacy respected, together with due consideration of their dignity'. Hence, firms' attempts to carry out gene probes on their employees are prohibited to the extent that they represent an invasion of their privacy.

346. *See*, for example, the rulings of the Supreme Court (Civil Chamber) of 14 Jul. 1988 and 28 May 1990.

B. *The Use of Human Gametes, Embryos and Foetuses for Genetic Research or for Other Therapeutic and Non-therapeutic Purposes*

1. Introductory Considerations

234. Doctors, researchers and jurists are fully aware of the ethical and legal problems raised by scientific breakthroughs which have proven to be effective in certain types of treatment and which have contributed to a marked reduction in child mortality and morbidity (such as, pathologies linked to Rh and the respiratory system). They have served also to increase our understanding of aspects of nutrition, foetal endocrinology and pharmacology, prenatal diagnosis, improved delivery and abortion techniques, human fertility, etc.

In spite of the proven advantages of such practices, many people have stressed the need for control and regulation in order to prevent risks to and manipulations with live foetuses during pregnancy, which may give rise to malformations which in turn would manifest themselves after birth, and also to prevent the risk of deliberately provoking pregnancies and/or abortions for the purposes of undertaking research with the foetus or to make use of use its tissues, with the consent of the mother (perhaps in return for financial or other type of reward). Equally important is the question of how the law should appraise and treat experiments carried out with live human foetuses extracted surgically in the course of legal terminations of pregnancy. Lastly, embryos obtained in vitro, prior to implantation in a woman (or even those which are not intended to be implanted) are valuable research material which is relatively easy to obtain. Furthermore, all such human biological components are liable to be used, and indeed are used on occasions, in the making of pharmacological and cosmetic products.

Hence the differing positions which have been adopted with regard to the problem of foetal investigation. Along with the promotion of freedom to engage in research (which is recognized as a fundamental right in the Spanish Constitution, Article 20.1 b), and, through it, scientific progress which will benefit future (and present) generations, protection must be afforded to embryos and foetuses, irrespective of their state or ultimate destiny (alive or dead; viable or unviable; inside or outside the womb; conceived naturally or in vitro; whether from an abortion or otherwise; presenting serious or non-serious risks; for the benefit of the foetus or for that of science in general, etc.).

2. Embryos, Pre-embryos and Foetuses

235. It seems worth to mention that the Spanish legal framework on the first stages of human life is built on a criticable distinction between pre-embryos, embryos and fetuses. According to Biomedicine Law 14/2007, *of* 3 July 2007, a 'Pre-embryo' is an embryo constituted in vitro that is formed by the group of cells that are the result of the progressive division of the oocyte from the time it is fertilized until fourteen days after, while the 'Embryo' is defined as a phase of embryonic development from the moment in which the fertilized oocyte is found in the uterus of a woman until the beginning of organogenesis and which ends fifty-six days from the moment of fertilization, with the exception of the computation of those days in which the development could have been stopped. Finally, the 'Foetus' is defined as an embryo with human appearance and with its organs formed, which matures from the fifty-seventh day after the moment of fertilization until the moment of birth, taking out of the computation those days in which the development could have been stopped.

3. Donation of Human Oocytes, Pre-embryos, Embryos and Foetuses

236. The donation of human oocytes, pre-embryos, embryos and foetuses is ruled by Law 14/2006 of 26 May on Assisted Human Reproduction Techniques and the Biomedicine Law 14/2007, *of* 3 July 2007. Donation of oocytes and pre-embryos is authorized by Article 5 of by Law 14/2006, previously mentioned. According to it, donation of gametes and pre-embryos for the purposes authorized by the Act is nonremunerative, formal, confidential and with mutual agreement between the donor and the authorized centre. The donation must never be regarded a lucrative or commercial process and must never be promoted by compensation offers or economic benefit. However, there are regulations on the financial compensation that is usually given to donors as compensation for physical inconvenience and travel. From time to time the Ministry of Health and Consumer Affairs, sets the criteria and financial limits for compensation, ensuring that these are not the only incentive for the donation.

The Minister of Health, with authorization from the Comisión Nacional de Reproducción Humana Asistida (National Committee of Assisted Human Reproduction), will periodically set essential conditions to ensure that the respect for donation being a nonlucrative action is maintained. Donation has to be anonymous, and gamete banks must guarantee the confident donor's identity. Individuals born as a result of assisted reproduction have the right to obtain general information about donors, but not their identities, with the only exception of extraordinary circumstances that makes it essential due to health purposes. Finally, the Biomedicine Law 14/2007, of 3 July 2007 states that in the case of oocytes, the consent of the donors shall make express reference to the authorization for the use of a specific technique or techniques that are to be applied to the donated oocytes. For that purpose, the health professionals who are responsible for collecting these oocytes shall provide the donors with the appropriate information before consent is granted, leaving clear written records of it all (Article 32.2).

237. The donation of human embryos and foetuses is ruled by the Biomedicine Law 14/2007, *of* 3 July 2007. According to its Article 29, the donation of human embryos or foetuses or their biological structures for the purposes provided in this Law shall meet the following requirements:

(a) *That the donor or donors of the embryos or foetuses have previously granted their express and written consent. If any of such donors is a non-emancipated minor or is disabled, then the consent of their legal representatives shall also be necessary.*

(b) *That the donor or donors or, where appropriate, their legal representatives, have been provided written information before the granting of their consent in relation to the purposes that might be achieved with the donation, its consequences, as well as the interventions that may be undertaken to extract embryologic or foetal cells or structures, from the placenta or casings, and of the risks that may follow from these interventions.*

(c) *That the expulsion, spontaneous or induced, of these embryos or foetuses has been made in the gestating woman and that it has not been possible to maintain their vital autonomy as provided in Article 28.3 2.*

The Act also clarifies that in the event that the person from whom the embryos or foetuses derives is deceased, it is necessary that there is no record of their express opposition. If the deceased is a minor or disabled person, then the donation shall take place unless there is a record of express opposition by those that exercised, in the life of the person, legal representation.

4. Research with Gametes, Pre-embryos and Embryos Which Are the Result of Artificial Reproduction Techniques ('in vitro') A General Approach

238. Law 14/2006 of 26 May on Assisted Human Reproduction Techniques authorizes the use of gametes for basic or experimental research, although they cannot then be used for reproduction (Article 14.1 and 2). The Act also imposes limitations on diagnostic or therapeutic procedures involving pre-embryos (i.e., those which have not yet been implanted in the woman). Such actions are permitted for diagnostic or therapeutic purposes where a real benefit is involved: if for the purpose of diagnosis, it can only be for assessment of viability or non-viability, detection of hereditary diseases in order to treat them where possible, or to advise against transfer for procreation (Article 12.1); if for therapeutic reasons, it can only be used to treat a disease or prevent transmission thereof, as long as reasonable and proven guarantees exist (Article 13.1), informed consent by the couple or the woman providing the embryos is required and the non-pathological genetic heritage/patrimony must not be altered (Article 13.2). A preliminary authorization by the corresponding Health Care Division is mandatory (Article13.3).

Finally, it is worth to mention that the Biomedicine Law 14/2007, of 3 July, explicitly states that intervention on the live embryo or foetus in the uterus shall be authorized solely when the purpose of such intervention is diagnostic or therapeutic in its own right, notwithstanding what is legally established on the voluntary interruption of a pregnancy (Article 30). Moreover, it also forbids abortion on donation purposes, stating that the termination of a pregnancy can never be for the purpose of the donation and later use of embryos, foetuses or their biological structures (Article 28.2).

239. Where intervention serves a different purpose than the well being of the embryo, particularly investigation and experimentation, the Spanish regulation combines both Law 14/2006 of 26 May on Assisted Human Reproduction Techniques and the Biomedicine Law 14/2007, of 3 July. According to Law 14/2007, human embryos that have lost their capacity for biological development, as well as dead human embryos or foetuses, may be donated for biomedical research or other diagnostic, therapeutic, pharmacological, clinical or surgical purposes (Article 28). However, embryos and foetuses can only be used for research purposes under the following conditions (Article 31.1 Law 14/2007):

(1) That they must be dead or they must have lost their capacity for biological development.
(2) That they must have been donated according to the procedures imposed by Article 29 of Law 14/2007.
(3) That an application has been drafted on the expected use and that it has been approved by the Guarantees Commission for the Donation and use of Human Cells and Tissues.
(4) That the corresponding autonomous or State authority has provided authorization to its expected use The team responsible for the authorized project must communicate its result both to the entity that authorized the submitted project, as well as to the Guarantees Commission for the Donation and use of Human Cells and Tissues (Article 31.2 Law 14/2007).

5. Research with Gametes, Pre-embryos and Embryos Which Are the Result of Artificial Reproduction Techniques ('in vitro'). The Guarantees and Procedures

240. Biomedicine Law 14/2007, *of* 3 July 2007 includes a number of clauses related to research with human gametes, pre-embryos, embryos and foetuses (Article 34). According to them, research or experimentation involving surplus oocytes or pre-embryos from assisted reproduction techniques, or their biological structures, for purposes related to the obtaining, development and use of embryonic stem cell lines or for other purposes not associated with the development and application of assisted reproduction techniques shall comply with the following requirements:

(a) That the research abides by ethical principles and the applicable legal regime, especially the provisions in this Law and the regulation that develops it, and that it follows the principles of relevance, feasibility and suitability, with particular obligations on the main researcher, the research team and the installations of the centre in which the research takes place.
(b) That it is based on a research project that is authorized by the State or an autonomous authority, after having received approval by the corresponding Guarantees Commission for the Donation and Use of Human Cells and Tissues, in projects dealing with matters established in Article 35. 2.

The authorization of research projects shall be conditioned to the project including, as a minimum, the following elements:

(a) The authorization of the management of the centre in which the research is conducted, as well as the approval of the corresponding Research Ethics Committee.
(b) The disclosure of any common relations and interests that exist, of whatever nature, or the absence of such, between the team and the centre that has been involved in the processes of assisted reproduction that generated the pre-embryos or in obtaining the oocytes.
(c) The written agreement to provide the relevant public authority the data that enables it to identify and to know the conservation of the cell lines that could be obtained as a consequence of the development of the research.
(d) The agreement to gratuitously convey cell lines that could be obtained in the development of research for use by other researchers.
(e) Where oocytes or pre-embryos are used, the indication and justification of their number and origin and the document of the informed consent, signed by the donor, or progenitors, respectively

Moreover, most of the research involving human pre-embryos, embryos or foetuses requires a previous approval of the Guarantees Commission for the Donation and Use of Human Cells and Tissues, an association composed of several persons, assigned to the Institute of Health Carlos III, of a permanent and consultative nature, aimed at providing counsel and guidance on research and experimentation with human embryonic biological samples and to contribute to the updating and dissemination of scientific and technical knowledge in this matter. The most relevant examples are:

(a) Research with human pre-embryos for the derivation of cell lines, for embryologic research and for other research purposes, except for those related to the development and application of assisted reproduction techniques.
(b) Research with human embryonic stem cells.
(c) The activation of oocytes through nuclear transfer for therapeutic or research purposes.
(d) Any other technique that, using human biological samples in whole or in part, can lead to the obtaining of stem cells.
(e) Research with embryonic cells or tissues obtained through any of the procedures mentioned in Article 33.2 (somatic cell nuclear transfer).
(f) Any other line of research that includes cell material of human embryonic origin or other functionally similar material.
(g) Research involving embryonic stem cell lines that come from another country, whether within or outside the EU. The origin shall be specified in the project submitted for authorization.

6. Genetic Engineering and Human/Animal Chimeras and Hybrids

241. Gene therapy is regulated by Legislative Royal Decree 1/2015 of 24 July which approves the refunded text of the Law on guarantees and rational use of medicines and health products of 2006 and developed by Royal Decree 477/2014, of 13 June 2014, on the regulation of the authorization of advanced therapy medicinal products. Instead, the carrying on of any intervention aimed at the introduction of modification in the genome of descendants, that is, genetic engineering affecting the germ line, is considered as a 'very serious' breach by the Biomedicine Law 14/2007, of 3 July 2007 (Article 74). It also considers as such the production of interspecific hybrids that use human genetic material, except the provisions in the Law on Assisted Human Reproduction Techniques, mainly the Golden Hamster test. Both actions shall be sanctioned with a fine of EUR 10,001 to EUR 1,000,000 and shall entail revocation of the authorization granted for that research or activity, according to the Act.

242. The manipulation of human genes for purposes other than eliminating or decreasing serious flaws or diseases also constitutes an offence according to the Spanish Code of Criminal Law. Its Article 159 states that all those committing this offence 'shall be punished with a sentence of imprisonment from two to six years and special barring from public employment and office, profession or trade for seven to ten years'. Its number 2 specifies that 'Should alteration of the genome be perpetrated due to serious negligence, the punishment shall be a fine from six to fifteen months and special barring from public employment and office, profession or trade from one to three years'.

7. Cloning and Stem Cell Research

243. Reproductive cloning is totally forbidden by the Spanish Legal Framework. The Spanish Penal Code states that:

> Those who fertilise human ovules for any purpose other than human procreation shall be punished with a sentence of imprisonment from one to five years and special barring from public employment and office, profession or trade from six to ten years. (…) The same penalty shall apply to punish creation of identical human beings by cloning or other procedures aimed at racial selection.

Even if the redaction of this article made no clear sense, it can be concluded that cloning was banned by the Spanish regulation. However, the offence has only been committed when the cloned cell has been transferred into a woman's uterus.

The case of therapeutic cloning was much more complex. As previously mentioned, the Convention for the Protection of Human Rights and Dignity of the Human Being with regard to the Application of Biology and Medicine: Convention on Human Rights and Biomedicine came into effect in Spain on 1 January 2000 following its ratification by Parliament. As Article 18.2 stated, 'The creation of human embryos for research purposes is prohibited', which made it clear that therapeutic cloning should be considered forbidden in all signatory countries, including Spain.

However the Spanish Government was willing to avoid this result. On this purpose, the Spanish regulator explicitly stated that a nuclear transfer under no circumstances generates a human embryo. For this purpose, Law 14/2007, of 2 July, on

Biomedical Research defined an embryo (Article 3.1) as '*a phase of embryonic development from the moment in which the fertilised oöcyte is found in the uterus of a woman until the beginning of organogenesis and which ends 56 days from the moment of fertilization, with the exception of the computation of those days in which the development could have been stopped*'. In this way, the regulation designated as embryos only the cellular structures which come into being as the result of a process of fertilization. Given that in a nuclear transfer there is no fertilization whatsoever, it is obvious that in that case we cannot speak of a human embryo. In concordance with this approach, Article 33 of the Law indicates the following:

Article 33.Obtaining of embryonic cells.
1. The creation of human pre-embryos and embryos exclusively for experimentation purposes is prohibited.
2. The use of any technique for obtaining human stem cells for therapeutic or research purposes is allowed, but only when it does not entail the creation of a pre-embryo or an embryo exclusively for this purpose, in accordance with the terms provided in this Law, including the activation of oocytes through nuclear transfer.

Based on this terminological construction, Spanish legislators affirmed in the Preamble to the Law that '*In accordance with the gradualist perspective on the protection of human life set out by our Constitutional Court in rulings such as 53/1985, 212/1996 and 116/1999, this Law expressly prohibits the creation of human pre-embryos and embryos exclusively for the purpose of experimentation. However, the use of any technique for collecting embryonic stem cells for therapeutic or research purposes that does not entail the creation of a pre-embryo or of an embryo exclusively for this purpose, and in the terms provided by this Law, is allowable.*' Therefore, we must highlight that 'therapeutic cloning' is not to be considered as proper cloning according to Spanish Law and, thus, it is not banned at all.[347]

§5. Psychosurgical Interventions

244. The control of particularly aggressive treatments such as psychosurgery, electric shock therapy and the long term administration of psychotropic drugs[348] raise a number of complex legal issues, particularly when such treatments produce or lead to major irreversible or lasting changes in the behaviour and personality

347. See I. Alkorta, I. De Miguel & D. Rodriguez, 'Cloning and the Oviedo Convention: The Sociocultural Construction of Regulation', in A. Webster (Ed.), The Global Dynamics of Regenerative Medicine. A Social Science Critique. Palgrave MacMillan, 2013. pp. 150–168.

348. *See* a fuller account in B.A. Weiner, 'Treatment rights', in *The Mentally Disabled and the Law* (Samuel J. Brakel/John Parry/Barbara A. Weiner, eds.) (3rd ed. American Bar Foundation. Chicago 1985), pp. 327 and ff. Weiner recognises the current importance of the use of drug therapy (because people can be treated as outpatients) but notes that most people have doubts about electric shock therapy and are still apprehensive given its negative image in the past (it was not used selectively and muscle relaxants were not given to prevent fractures). The future of psychosurgery, she notes, is in some doubt despite new developments in Neurosurgery.

(even when this would be described as 'abnormal' or pathological in the first place) of the patient, even bearing in mind that psychiatric treatment always implies some degree of change in the behaviour with which the illness is associated. In these cases it is a question of reconciling occasionally opposing interests, including those of the patients themselves. The wishes of the psychiatric patient should be borne in mind whenever he is even minimally capable of comprehending the nature of the treatment or intervention, even where the patient has been certified as being incompetent. When the decision has to be taken by third parties (e.g., legal representatives, relatives or physicians) it is essential that control mechanisms be put in place to guarantee that the treatment is absolutely necessary. Recourse to the courts and the public prosecutor may be necessary. Notwithstanding what has been said, it is important to remark that non consented psychosurgical interventions cannot be compulsorily imposed to a criminal offender, as a medical treatment developed within the frame of the so-called 'security measures'.[349] Aside from this there is no specific reference to these matters in Spanish law.

§6. Removal and Transplant of Organs, cells and tissues

I. Relevant Legislation

245. Spain, like many other countries, has specific legislation with regard to human organ transplants. The key piece of legislation is the Law 30/1979 of 27 October governing 'Removal and Transplant of Organs'.[350] This legislation, which has a pyramid structure, has been complemented and enhanced by numerous provisions some of which are recent. The Act on Patient Autonomy of 2002 and some administrative provisions on health care in general are also relevant here. On the whole, the legislation is very complete and covers the regulation of the various relevant issues relating to transplants in general as well as those of specific organs and specific types of tissue. The legislation addresses not only the legal issues involved in obtaining organs and tissues but also the crucial question of protecting and respecting the rights and interests of the individuals concerned. It also deals with organization, coordination, accreditation and authorization, together with purely procedural matters.

When explaining the characteristics of the Spanish system related to transplants we will base our analysis in the specific provisions devoted to organs, thus making the necessary concretions at the light of the in force regulations in Spain applicable to cells and tissues.

---

349. E.J. Armaza Armaza, *El tratamiento penal del delincuente imputable peligroso* (Comares, Granada 2013), pp. 253–256; A. Urruela Mora, *Las medidas de seguridad y reinserción social en la actualidad. Especial consideración de las consecuencias jurídico-penales aplicables a sujetos afectos de anomalía o alteración psíquica* (Comares, Granada 2009), p. 154.

350. Law 30/1979 of 27 October. *See* C.M. Romeo-Casabona, 'La Ley de trasplantes y sus repercusiones sociales', in *La Ley*, 1982, pp. 1 and ff; C.M. Romeo-Casabona, 'El Derecho ante los trasplantes de órganos. La ordenación jurídica de los trasplantes de órganos en España: Principios rectores', *en Revista General de Derecho*, n° 582, 1993, pp. 1915 and ff.

246. As regards provisions which develop the law further, the following items are relevant: the RD 1825/2009 of 11 November 2009 which approves the Statute of the National Organisation of Transplants, the RD 1723/2012 of 28 December 2012 which regulates the activities of obtention, clinical use and territorial coordination of human organs for transplantation and which sets requirements of quality and security, the Order SSSI/2512/2013 of 18 December which regulates the procedure of authorization for the performance of activities of promotion and publicity of the donation of human cells and tissues, the Royal Decree Law 9/2014 which establishes the norms of quality and security for the donation, the obtention, the evaluation, the processing, the preservation, the storage and the distribution of human cells and tissues, and the Order SSI/2396/2014 of 17 December which establishes the basic program of quality and security for the obtention and transplantation of human organs and which establishes the procedures of exchange with other countries.

Although this brief review of the Spanish legislation on transplants gives an impression of complexity, it should be said that the legislation is structured in such a way as to make it open to amendment in response to scientific developments, without the need to change the basic lines along which the legislation was constructed. Nevertheless, certain possibilities that are opening up in terms of organ and tissue transplants (sexual organs, the brain or parts of the brain, nerve tissue and cells) or the implanting of artificial mechanisms or anatomical parts from animals raise specific legal issues to which the current legislation may not be able to provide clear and precise answers.

247. Objectives set out in the Law. From the above the importance of a carefully thought out body of law which balances all the interests that come into play in the long and complex process of a transplant is self-evident. The legislation addresses these important issues in line with current European and global trends and sets out three main objectives in an effort to clarify any potential technical and legal problems:

(1) To facilitate the obtaining of viable – usable – organs for subsequent transplant operations performed on persons in medical need of such organs.
(2) To adequately protect the rights and interests of the individuals concerned so as to balance any possible conflicting interests, chiefly those of the living donor, the deceased donor and the recipient.
(3) To provide a legal framework for medical professionals and health authorities within which they may carry out such operations, unhindered by difficulties, and in accordance with guidelines which are, at least in theory, clear and easy to follow.

II. The Living Donor

248. Although the giving of organs by living persons for subsequent transplant to a person suffering from an illness who requires the organ affects the integrity of the body, which is in principle punishable by law (Articles 147 and ff of the Penal

Code on bodily harm offences), it is explicitly permitted by the 1979 Law and by the Penal Code itself (Article 156). It is not enough for the operation to be performed by qualified personnel (a surgeon) for this exemption to come into effect. The donor must also give his/her consent and all other requirements of the Law (Article 4) and the 2012 RD (Articles 8) and Royal Decree Law 9/2014 (Article 7) must be strictly adhered to.

249. Age and legal capacity restrictions. The donor must have attained the age of legal majority (18 years), be in full possession of his/her mental faculties and in sufficiently good health for the removal to be performed [Art. 4 a) and b) of the Law]. This means that minors may not give their organs (e.g., for use by a brother or sister who is suffering from an illness and who is also a minor), even where consent is given through the parents, as this is considered to exceed the scope of the rights and duties inherent in parental authority (Articles 154 and ff and 162 and ff of the Civil Code). This is intended to safeguard the interests of the minor, who, without such protection from the Law, would find difficulty in not succumbing to the moral pressure brought to bear by the family or/and would be subject to the danger of the family consenting on his/her behalf (if he is unable to express his/her own consent) in the interests of the recipient and at his/her expense. The same principles underlie the exclusion of the intellectually disabled, those suffering psychiatric illness or persons who for any other reason are unable to give their explicit, free and conscious consent. However, the Royal Decree Law 9/2014 (Article 7.1) makes an exception in the case of surgical residues or hematopoietic stem cells or other tissues or cell groups reproducible (*except in the case of surgical residues or hematopoietic stem cells or other tissues or cell groups reproducible whose therapeutic indication is or may be vital to the recipient*) because of its capacity for regeneration and because donation and transplant usually concern siblings. For reasons similar to those given above, the donation of organs, tissues and cells by the intellectually handicapped or mentally ill is not allowed.

250. Limitations related to the organ. The organ must be one whose removal is compatible with the continuing life of the donor and whose function can be compensated adequately and in a sufficiently safe way by the donor organism (Article 8 Royal Decree 1723/2012). As a result, the law allows the donation of organs or tissue provided that removal does not permanently affect the health or endanger the life of the donor. The donor's physical or psychological capacities should not be diminished by the removal of the organ nor should it result in the loss of any important bodily function. For this reason single vital organs may not be removed nor may single remaining organs from pairs (in cases of the prior damage to or loss of the second organ as a result of illness or injury). Limbs are also excluded as are any parts of the body the removal of which would involve diminished bodily functions. The removal of paired or double organs is permissible when the remaining organ can act as a functional substitute. The same is true of regenerable tissue (blood, bone marrow, bones, cartilage, etc.). A full and thorough medical examination of the donor is therefore needed to determine whether or not his/her current health would result in him being seriously affected by the removal of the organ. In the case of obtention of organs if the donor's physical and mental health are good enough for the removal to go ahead, a physician other than the one(s) who will perform the operation must make a statement to that effect (Article 8.3 of the Royal Decree 1723/2012). This physician is also responsible for providing the donor with all necessary information. In the case of obtention of organs, it is compulsory to have a favourable report of the Ethics Committee concerned.

251. Donor information and consent. The donor must previously have been informed of all consequences stemming from his/her decision and must have freely, consciously and impartially given his/her express consent. This is the key to the donor consent requirement, which is fundamental. In the first place, for consent to be valid it is essential that the donor has previously been fully informed as to the foreseeable somatic, emotional and psychological consequences involved and the long-term implications that donation may have in terms of his/her personal, family and professional life. At the same time he should be provided with information about the benefits that the transplant might be expected to imply for the recipient (Article 8 of the RD 1723/2012 in the case of organs and Article 7 Royal Decree Law 9/2014 in the case of cells and tissues). The relevant information must be given in an appropriate format. In the case of obtention of organs, consent must also be given in the presence of the judge (during the hearing in the course of the voluntary jurisdiction process opened for the transplantation), the physicians who provided the information and the doctor who is to perform the removal of the organ as well as the responsible person to give his/her conformity to the transplant.

Clearly, valid consent can only be given for the donation of the organs and tissues referred to above, in view of the fact that in Law valid consent to endangering one's own life cannot be given (e.g., consent to donating a vital organ). Neither is consent valid if it has been obtained under pressure or through coercion (e.g., from members of the family of the would-be recipient of the organ) or where financial or material interests have influenced the decision to give the organ concerned, as we will see below. The possibility of the donor withdrawing consent is considered. Consent may be withdrawn at any time prior to the operation without any further formality being required (an exception arises in cases of collection of hematopoietic progenitor cells from peripheral blood or bone marrow where revocation can only occur before the start of the conditioning at the receiver). Withdrawal of consent cannot give rise to any kind of claim for compensation.

252. Restrictions governing the subsequent use made of the organ. The Law stipulates that the organ must be for transplant in a specific individual with the purpose of substantially improving the person's chances of survival or quality of life (Article 4 d, 1979 Law). This requirement, which may seem obvious, implies that the whole process of donation must revolve around a specific potential recipient, in most cases a member of the donor's family. The process, therefore, begins with histocompatibility studies of both parties along with all other tests deemed necessary to guarantee the viability and success of the transplant operation. As a result, the process of donation by a living person may not commence until a candidate recipient has been selected, nor can the organ subsequently be donated to someone else as this would mean beginning the process all over again in order to comply with all the requirements of the Law. The clearly therapeutic nature of the operation, as stipulated by the Law, rules out donations for primarily experimental or research purposes, although this does not mean that the operation may not involve a certain degree of uncertainty as regards a successful outcome.

253. Anonymity of the recipient. Finally, the law stipulates that the anonymity of the recipient must be guaranteed. Clearly, we are faced here with a *Tapsus Legislature is* if this is also to be understood to apply to the donor, which would run counter to the other (and particularly the last of the) requirements noted above. Donations by living donors are usually made for members of their own family as a sign of solidarity and affection. This requirement, which is not adhered to in practice, does make sense in the case of donations after death as it would thus prevent members of the donor's family later taking advantage of the situation by demanding some kind of material or financial compensation from the recipient (alleging, for example, that the donor was the sole source of financial support for the family). It is, however, possible to arrive at a more satisfactory interpretation that eliminates this apparent incoherence, as we shall see shortly.

254. Consequences of donation: the lawful removal of the organ, cells and tissues. Adherence to all the above-mentioned requirements means that the attack on the physical integrity of the donor that the donation implied is lawful, as is the operation performed by the surgeon. Failure to comply in any way with the regulations (regulations are understood to mean material and substantial requirements and not merely formal or procedural requirements which would only give rise to an administrative offence only) is equivalent to the offence of mutilation and is severely punished by the Penal Code (Articles 149 and 150).

These observations are endorsed by the Spanish Penal Code which explicitly recognizes the possibility of consenting to attacks on one's physical integrity if this takes place in accordance with the provisions of the Law governing Organ Transplants. This provision is laid down in Article 156 of the Penal Code, which sets out the various conditions that must be fulfilled. These are essentially the same as those contained in the 1979 Law on removal and transplant, which can thus be regarded as being unaltered by the reform of the Penal Code.[351] Furthermore, the fact that the Penal Code makes explicit reference to this Law means that the other requirements continue to be applicable where the provisions of the Penal Code are not sufficient.

351. Article 156 reads as follows: 'Notwithstanding the provisions of the previous article, valid, explicit, conscious and freely given consent removes criminal liability in the case of organ transplants carried out in accordance with the Law, sterilizations and transsexual surgery performed by a physician, unless consent has been obtained under false pretences or through pressure or the promise of financial gain or if the person giving consent is a minor or is legally incompetent, in which neither this consent nor that of the legal representatives shall be valid (...).

III. The Deceased Donor

255. The Law on transplants (Article 5 of the 1979 Law) and to an even greater extent the Penal Code[352] seek to guarantee effective medical assistance andprotection of the life of a potential *post mortem* donor while even the most minimal chance of recovery exists. Nevertheless, this very real protection is compatible with the possibility of obtaining organs for subsequent transplant in the case of the death of the potential donor. It is on this question that the Law has been particularly explicit as regards resolving potential legal problems. At the same time it is here that most disagreement exists. There are two conflictive issues which we will examine now.

256. Definition, diagnosis and verification of death. Within the biological process of destruction entailed in the death of living beings a precise moment at which the process is irreversible must be fixed. Once this point is reached there is no possibility of saving the life of the individual in question (precisely because death has occurred). The moment must also be established early enough to ensure that organs and tissues may be removed and that they have not been affected by the process of destruction and are therefore suitable for transplant. A balance must, therefore, be struck through an early but faithful diagnosis of the moment of death, from which point on it is possible to remove the organs in biological conditions consistent with transplant.[353] Any doubt as to determining the moment when death occurs must be resolved in favour of the potential *post mortem* donor to the exclusion of all other interests no matter how important and pressing they may seem.

In contrast to the previous legislation (of 1950) the current Law has rightly established the point of reference for determining death as not depending on the cessation of certain vital functions, such as circulation or breathing, which can now be maintained artificially almost indefinitely. The Law takes as an alternative point of departure permanent irreversible brain damage which is incompatible with life (Article 5.1). This starting point and the other guarantees that are required for the death certificate to be issued should be viewed as being highly positive, given that in current medical practice an irreversible comatose state is considered to be sufficient basis for certifying that death has occurred. The Royal Decree 1723/2012 stipulates the conditions that must be fulfilled before such a diagnosis can be made (Article 8 and Annex), namely, certain signs deemed to be incompatible with life.

257. The specific conditions that the diagnostic team must fulfil in transplant cases constitute additional guarantees for the potential donor: the team must comprise three physicians, at least one of whom should be a specialist in procedures for determining death.[354] All three physicians must agree to certify death and must not be involved in the removal and subsequent transplant of the organ.

---

352. *See* Arts 138, 139, 143, 195 and 196: the crimes of homicide, murder, assisting a suicide, failure to fulfil the duty to answer a call for help and refusal of giving medical health care, respectively.

353. *See* C.M. Romeo-Casabona, *Los trasplantes de órganos*, pp. 61 and ff.; VVAA, *El nuevo régimen jurídico de los trasplantes de órganos y tejidos*, Comares, Granada, 1995, pp. 1 ff.

354. The team shall comprise a Neurologist or Neurosurgeon and the Chief Medical Officer of the unit or his/her substitute (Art. 5 of the Law and Art. 10 of the RD of 2012). In cases of violent death

258. Deceased donors; relevance of wishes. Major conflicts arise where there is a legal assumption that anyone who dies is a donor unless during his/her lifetime he has explicitly stated that he does not wish to be a donor: 'The removal of organs or other anatomical parts from deceased persons may be performed for therapeutic or scientific purposes so long as he has not explicitly expressed opposition to this.' (Article 5.2 of the Law).

Despite the somewhat striking nature of this sentence it should be noted that it is not so striking as previous legislation, in which the notion of assumed willingness to act as a donor was included as a third subsidiary procedure in potential donor cases that were subject to legal intervention (instances of violent death, as is known, are usually the most suitable for organ donation from the medical point of view) and the lack of opposition referred not to the deceased but to his/her family. A criterion similar to that of the Spanish Law of 1979 was adopted by the Council of Europe and proposed to Member States in Resolution 78 (Article 29). The World Health Organization takes a similar approach in its Guiding Principles for the Transplant of Human Organs (1991).

Of the various alternative criteria which the Legislature could have opted for the following deserve mention:

(1) express wishes of the deceased made known during his/her lifetime authorising donation;
(2) the same criterion with the addition of the subsidiary criterion (in the absence of consent on the part of the deceased) of consent by the deceased person's family;
(3) absence of explicit opposition on the part of the deceased or his/her family;
(4) lack of opposition on the part of the deceased alone; and
(5) no consideration given to the wishes of the individual concerned.[355]

259. Independently of what has just been stated, it is necessary to analyse the drawbacks that the alternatives imply in an effort to better understand the Spanish Legislature's reasoning in rejecting them:

(1) Positive act of personal donation. In the first place, we have the criterion of voluntary personal donation, that is to say, a positive declaration of the desire of the individual citizen to freely donate his/her organs, to take effect after death. This solution causes a variety of problems, particularly with regard to the fact that there is a very high potential demand for the organs of deceased persons and the difficulties involved in finding a donor and recipient who are biologically compatible. Furthermore, the cadavers that fulfil the stringent medical conditions that provide minimum guarantees of transplant viability are rare. Only those killed in road accidents and a further small number from accidents in the workplace with very localized head injuries (haemorrhages, tumours, vascular

(for example accident), in which the legal authorities have to intervene, a forensic doctor may also be included, although this is not obligatory and is intended rather to facilitate and speed up the legal process.

355. *See* a fuller account in Romeo-Casabona, *Los trasplantes de órganos*, pp. 71 and ff.

accidents) or cardiac arrest are usually considered to be genuinely viable candidates for organ donation, with the additional provision that they die in a hospital equipped to remove organs. Public information campaigns designed to create a favourable attitude to organ donations are costly and are slow to produce what are not particularly satisfactory results in the long term. They must reach the entire population and be repeated over and over again to maintain the desired level of awareness among the population. As we shall see below the task of providing information is, nevertheless, extremely important and is dealt with in the Spanish regulations.

(2) Irrelevance of the wishes of the individual. Neither does it seem appropriate to disregard altogether the wishes of the deceased, as made known during his/her lifetime. A series of cultural norms – of social and religious origin – in our society seek to maintain respect for the dead through a kind of spiritual bond between society – particularly family and friends – and the deceased. The Law has weighed up these collective sentiments and has regarded them as worthy of protection. For this reason the Penal Code punishes profanation of cadavers when there is a lack of respect for the memory of the death (Article 526). Respect for the deceased's memory also implies observing whatever wishes he would have expressed in terms of his/her body during his/her lifetime (so long as these do not violate any other public order requirements), for example, as regards his/her willingness or opposition to having parts of the body removed and transplanted to another person suffering from an illness. Transplant legislation seeks to respond to this concept in requiring the restoration and preservation of the cadaver.

260. The irrelevance of the deceased's family's wishes in the Spanish legislation. The Spanish Law does not require the consent of the family of the deceased except where minors or mentally deficient persons are concerned.[356] The reasoning given above is also valid here. It is a question of respecting the wishes of the deceased, not those of his/her family – whose wishes may be in conflict with those of the deceased – although at the same time it is recognized that the family are most likely to know or be able to indicate the wishes of the deceased if they were made known during his/her lifetime. But this does not mean that they have property rights over the cadaver, because no such right exists. Furthermore, from the humanitarian point of view it would seem ill-advised to subject the family to a further emotional burden after being informed of the sudden tragic death of a loved one – husband, son or daughter, etc. To do otherwise would be tantamount of burdening them with moral responsibility for deciding if another person should continue to live or have a better life as a result of their consent. They should not have to take on this responsibility in the first place, nor are they in the best position to do so. Because of this the Law makes no mention of them but the Royal Decree 1273/2012 indicates that

356. In fact the Law does not establish exceptions for these last two circumstances. For organs, Royal Decree 1723/2012 states that 'where minors or mentally deficient patients are concerned, opposition may be expressed by their legal representatives according to the civil legislation' (Art. 9.1) while the same applies for cells and tissues according to Art. 8.1 Royal Decree Law 9/2014.

the Hospital's Transplant coordinator, or the person in which he/she delegates, shall carry out the necessary checks on the will of the deceased person:

(1) investigate whether the donor made clear its will to any of his/her relatives or to the professionals who have treated him at the hospital, through the notes that they have done in the clinical history, or by the means provided in the current legislation.[357] Nevertheless, it is customary for physicians (or transplant co-ordinators) to seek the agreement of the family of the deceased, which is a sensible precaution as long as it is done tactfully.

Finally, it should be noted that even though no real conflict of interests arises in practice, the intangibility of the cadaver and the respect for related wishes in this regard (such as society values) are played off against the life and health of other persons. If any conflict were to occur the criminal law would provide the appropriate answer and would normally come down in favour of the life and health of the recipient.

261. As a means of recording possible opposition to the removal of organs, procedures for the provision of information and a register of volunteers have been established in authorized hospitals. It is clear that recourse may be made to other means apart from those established by the Regulations (Article 9 Royal Decree 1723/2012) to ascertain any possible opposition on the part of a potential donor (written declarations, membership of religious or ideological groups that are clearly opposed to interference with the cadaver, information from the family of the deceased, etc.). Possession of a donor card – one which is compatible with legal requirements – such as those issued by Associations of Patients (Federación Nacional ALCER), some Autonomous Communities or by the National Transplant Organisation or other such regional organizations makes the task of determining the wishes of the deceased very much easier.

IV. The Recipient

262. In contrast to the legislation of other countries, which do not concern themselves with this question, Spanish legislation includes guarantees to protect the recipient of the organ, as it is the recipient who is in fact subject to the main risks. These guarantees are as follows: that the operation is for therapeutic purposes; that the necessary medical tests have been performed prior to the operation and that all appropriate specific preparation has been undertaken and that the patient has been fully informed and has given his/her consent or that the family or legal representatives have consented in the case of minors and the mentally disabled (Article 6 of the Law). The Law has been particularly meticulous and scrupulous in its efforts to protect the legal interests of the recipient of an organ transplant, and anticipated the

357. Article 9.1 of the Royal Decree 1723/2012.

rights established by Article 10 of the LGS (updated by Law 41/2002 of 14 November on Patient's Autonomy nowadays in force – see Articles 4 ff.-), which also apply here.

Given that decisions taken are always of the greatest importance to the recipient, it is essential that the information requirement is scrupulously fulfilled prior to the transplant. Information is normally provided on two occasions: when the need for the transplant becomes evident and the patient's name is put on the waiting list and again when an organ becomes available for the recipient. The 1979 Law (Articles 6.1 and 2) is unequivocal as regards this information requirement, as is the Law 41/2002 on Patient's Autonomy on a more general level.

A problem arises in the selection of recipients and the criteria used to establish priority of one recipient over another. Clearly, only strictly objective medical criteria agreed upon by professionals can be considered in decisions concerning selection and priority. First and foremost it must be established that the patient is not suffering from a serious illness the risks of which would be greatly increased by surgery and, secondly, that he is in urgent need of the transplant. Optimum histocompatibility between the organ and recipient (and therefore the optimum chances of success) is also a prime consideration. A secondary criterion would be the length of time the patient has been waiting. On no account should social considerations be brought to bear[358] or should a patient be rejected because he suffers from another (corrigible) illness (e.g., an alcoholic recipient of a liver transplant).

V. Other General Guarantees

263. The guarantees described above refer to the requirements for transplants and are designed to protect the interests of donors and recipients alike. There are, however, further requirements that also protect these individuals, albeit less directly, and that in one way or another contribute significantly to the achievement of the objectives enumerated at the beginning of this section. The successful putting in place and functioning of the legal mechanisms designed to serve these objectives depend on these requirements. It should be said that many of these go beyond the limits of the purely legal framework, as they depend on the existence of the appropriate structure, organization and planning of health services and on funding.

264. Prohibition on the use of organs for commercial ends. Organs may not be bought or sold nor may the donor or members of his/her family or third parties ('intermediaries', hospitals, pharmaceutical or research laboratories) receive money in exchange for organs. The costs of donation should not have to be met by the donor or his/her family (Article 2 of the Law). By this means injustices that might

358. *See* World Health Organisation, *Guiding Principles on Human Cell, Tissue and Organ Transplantation* (as endorsed by the 62 World Health Assembly in May 2010, Resolution WHA63.22), Guiding Principle 9: 'The allocation of organs, cells and tissues should be guided by clinical criteria and ethical norms, not financial and other considerations. Allocations rules, defined by appropriately constituted committees, should be equitable, eternally justified and transparent'.

easily occur both in the case of recipients and potential donors with limited financial resources or other limitations (e.g., prisoners seeking a reduction in their sentence) can be avoided. Even if in Spain no instances of the sale of organs of living persons have actually occurred, despite occasional attempts, the possible damage that can be done by simply offering such organs for sale in the media should not be underestimated. Such offers would cause great confusion among the general public and could even lead people to withdraw their names from donor lists.

This issue has acquired on great importance in recent years because of claims that a black market in organs in developing countries benefits patients in the developed world or in rich countries. In Spain the buying and selling of organs from living persons is not only prohibited, as we have just seen, but severely punished by the Penal Code (Article 156 bis Penal Code).

Article 156 bis:[359]

> *1. Those who promote, favour, facilitate or publicise the unlawful obtaining or trafficking in human organs or their transplantation shall be punished with a sentence of imprisonment from six to twelve years in the case of a main organ, and of prison from three to six years if not a main organ. 2. Should the receiver of the organ consent to the carrying out of the transplant while being aware of its unlawful origin, he shall punished with the same penalties as in the preceding Section, that may be lowered by one or two degrees in view of the circumstances of case and of the offender. 3. When, pursuant to the terms established in Article 31 bis, a legal person is responsible for the offences defined in this Article, it shall be sentenced to pay a fine of three to five times the profit obtained. Pursuant to the rules established in Article 66 bis, the Judges and Courts of Law may also impose the penalties described in Sub-Sections b) to g) of Section 7 of Article 33.*

The World Health Organization plans to adopt various measures in an effort to stamp out these practices elsewhere: the World Health Assembly adopted resolution WHA 42.5 on the prevention of the buying and selling of organs on 15 May 1989, while its *Guiding Principles on Human Cell, Tissue and Organ Transplantation* (as endorsed by the 62 World Health Assembly in May 2010, Resolution WHA63.22) devotes several principles to this prohibition: principle 5 ('Cells, tissues and organs should only be donated freely, without any monetary payment or other reward of monetary value. Purchasing, or offering to purchase, cells, tissues or organs for transplantation, or their sale by living persons or by the next of kin for deceased persons, should be banned. The prohibition on sale or purchase of cells, tissues and organs does not preclude reimbursing reasonable and verifiable expenses incurred by the donor, including loss of income, or paying the costs or recovering, processing, preserving and supplying human cells, tissues or organs for transplantation'),

359. See Romeo-Casabona, 'La prohibición del tráfico ilegal y la exclusión de la comercialización de los órganos y tejidos. Artículo 156 bis del Código Penal', in *Revista Aranzadi Doctrinal*, nr. 7, 2010, pp. 171 ff.

principle 6 ('promotion of altruistic donation of human cells, tissues or organs by means of advertisement or public appeal may be undertaken in accordance with domestic regulation. Advertising the need of or availability of cells, tissues or organs, with a view to offering or seeking payment to individuals for their cells, tissues or organs, or, to the next of kin, where the individual is deceased, should be prohibited. Brokering that involves payment to such individuals or to third parties should also be prohibited'), principle 7 ('physicians and other health professionals should not engage in transplantation procedures, and health insurers and other payers should not cover such procedures, if the cells, tissues or organs concerned have been obtained through exploitation or coercion of, or payment to, the donor or the next of kin of a deceased donor'), principle 8 ('all health care facilities and professionals involve in cell, tissue or organ procurement and transplantation procedures should be prohibited from receiving any payment that exceeds the justifiable fee for the services rendered') and principle 9 ('The allocation of organs, cells and tissues should be guided by clinical criteria and ethical norms, not financial and other considerations. Allocations rules, defined by appropriately constituted committees, should be equitable, eternally justified and transparent'). Article 14 of the Council of Europe's Resolution (78) 29 also prohibits profit making.

A significant preventive measure with regard to the trafficking of organs taken from cadavers is the use of all possible means to guarantee that the recipient should not know anything that would identify the donor or his/her family and, similarly, that the donor's family at the same time should have no information about the recipient and his/her family. Responsibility for maintaining this level of confidentiality lies with the staff of the health care centre, regardless of their professional status or the nature of their duties. This obligation is explicitly stated in the current regulations with regard to organ transplants.

265. Intervention by the legal authorities. The removal of organs from those who have died of unnatural causes (through accident or any other kind of violent death) requires prior authorization by the Judge responsible for the case (Articles 335 and 342 of the Criminal Procedures Code). He shall give this authorization where removal does not present any obstacle to the pre-trial investigation, the cause of death being apparently clear (Article 5.3 of the 1979 Law). Strictly speaking this is not a guarantee relevant to the transplant process but rather to the work of the Judge in that it prevents the removal of organs in situations where this would hinder the establishment of the causes of death in cases where death may give rise to liability (either civil or criminal) or an insurance claim, etc.

266. Recognition of hospitals and medical teams. Authorization is only granted to those hospitals and teams that meet the stringent material, technical and professional conditions established by the law and that can provide evidence of adequate training and experience in these techniques and in associated treatments.[360] The health authorities take responsibility for supervising the work of these hospitals and

360. *See* Art. 3 of the Law and Arts 10 and 11 of the Royal Decree 1723/2012.

teams and may even withdraw authorization if performance is unsatisfactory or falls below the standards for which authorization was initially granted.

267. *Organizations for the exchange of organs from cadavers. The National Transplant Organisation and Authonomic (Regional) coordinations.* In accordance with the Law (Article 7), these organizations enable maximum benefit to be obtained from organs made available for transplant by means, for example, of locating the most suitable recipient – or even the recipient in most urgent need. Organs can be made available through the system to other centres in the same city or elsewhere in Spain and abroad. The system also controls the preservation of parts of bodies in 'organ banks' when this is scientifically feasible.

In order to achieve qualitative and quantitative improvement in transplant services it is essential to strengthen the regional health organizations and the national co-ordination of organ exchanges so as to ensure that the maximum number of organs can be removed and transplanted, optimum compatibility between the organ and the recipient can be achieved and also that patients in urgent need (hyperimmunized patients, those who are terminally ill as the result of the failure of single vital organs or the remaining organ from a pair) can be given the fastest possible access to transplants. This will help redress regional imbalances and give fuller effect to the principle of equality of access to medical assistance (Article 3 of the Health General Law). Responsibility for these functions lies with the National Transplant Organisation and the Authonomic Coordinations, which must be co-ordinated and supervised by the National Organization.

The creation of the position of Transplant Co-ordinator is a further important step in terms of the co-ordination and optimum use of organs or potential donors. Co-ordinators in each hospital involved in the removal and/or transplant of organs, regional co-ordinators for the Authonomic Coordinations mentioned above and a National Co-ordinator (who is also the director of the National Transplant Organisation) have been appointed.

The National Transplant Organisation was established under the Resolution of 27 June 1980 (being regulated at present by RD 1825/2009), but is also subject to the provisions of the Spanish Constitution of 1978 concerning the competences of the Autonomous Communities in the area of health and to the health system structure. Another more recent procedure that has contributed to an increase in the number of transplants and to increased organ mobility is the removal of several organs from a single donor.

268. *Information and health education.* The Royal Decree of 2012 (Article 6) provide for the carrying out of frequent and extensive information and educational campaigns to increase awareness of the contents of the Law, particularly in relation to the obtaining of organs from cadavers, thereby reducing the difficulties entailed in informing the family of the deceased at the moment of death and eliminating the all too often need for medical staff to seek their approval in order to avoid complications.

§7. Research with Human Beings

I. Conflicting Interests

269. Research in Medicine and the Biological Sciences has gradually improved our well-being and indeed our life expectancy. In the final analysis, after the appropriate laboratory studies and experimentation on animals, research almost always requires the testing on human subjects of new techniques and substances to which beneficial or therapeutic effects are attributed. It is at this point that the question of certain individuals (healthy or otherwise) becoming subjects of experiments arises, with all the risks and dangers that experimentation entails, even though these risks need not necessarily affect the experimental subjects themselves. A potential conflict of interests or of crucial values arises: on the one hand there is the need to carry out research with the obvious benefits that this brings to society and, on occasions, to the individual who has acted as an experimental subject; on the other, there is the right of these individuals not to sustain any damage to their health or to expose their lives to grave dangers, not to mention the protection of other individual interests that may be affected, such as freedom. The need for research is fully recognized in our legal order, but when it comes to experimentation on human subjects a series of provisions directly or indirectly seek to prevent any injury or harm to the person, given that his/her most prized legal interests are at stake.[361]

270. Because of differing objectives, effects, limitations and possible legal consequences, it is usual to draw a distinction between therapeutic experimentation and pure experimentation. The former consists of the application to specific patients of treatments the efficacy of which has not yet been entirely established from the scientific point of view and which, therefore, have not been included among medically recognized treatments. Pure experimentation refers to research carried out on those suffering from diseases or on healthy individuals with a view to obtaining scientific results that do not imply any immediate benefit to the person who acted as an experimental subject. This second type of experimentation is, therefore, governed by more stringent conditions.

II. Relevant Legislation

271. The Spanish Constitution recognizes and protects the right to 'literary, artistic, scientific and technical production and invention' (Article 20.1 b), as one of the fundamental public rights. It is obvious that scientific and technical production and invention inevitably involve research. At the same time, given its social significance, our Constitution also stipulates in the chapter devoted to guiding principles of social and economic policy that 'the public authorities shall promote science and scientific and technical research in the interests of the community' (Article 44.2).

361. C.M. Romeo-Casabona, 'Aspectos jurídicos de la experimentación humana', in *Revista de la Facultad de Derecho de la Universidad Complutense de Madrid*, n. 11, 1986, pp. 569 and ff.

Having said that, the fundamental right to scientific and technical invention and production is limited by the Spanish Constitution itself when it alludes to *respect for the rights recognized under the same heading* as the one in which this right is set out, namely, fundamental rights and duties (Article 20.4).

In fact, the constitutional prohibition of inhuman or degrading treatment (Article 15) imposes limits on *research and experimentation on human beings*, and is confirmed here because Spain has ratified and officially published the International Covenant on Civil and Political Rights of 1966 (27 April 1977, Official State Journal of 30 April) and it thus forms part of the domestic law (Article 96.1 of the Spanish Constitution). The Covenant groups both aspects together when it states that 'no-one shall be subjected to torture nor to cruel and degrading punishment or treatment. *In particular*, no-one shall be subjected to medical or scientific experiments without their freely given consent' (Article 7). The LGS provides for the minimum precautions and guarantees necessary when it requires that the patient be informed and that he gives his/her consent prior to the experiment, that the doctor and the administration of the health care centre agree to the experiment and, above all, that 'under no circumstances should it involve additional dangers to health [that of the patient]' (Article 10.4 of the LGS). These requirements, together with the principles of preservation of dignity and privacy and the avoidance of discrimination, underpin more specific legislation, namely, the Legislative Royal Decree 1/2015 of 24 July which approves the refunded text of the Law on guarantees and rational use of medicines and health products of 2006, the Royal Decree 1090/2015, of 14 December, which regulates clinical trials with medicines, the Ethics Committees on clinical trials with medicines and the Spanish register of clinical trials and title II of the Law 7/2007, of 3 July, on Biomedical Research (biomedical research that implies invasive procedures in human beings – excluding pharmaceutical research which is regulated under Legislative Royal Decree 1/2015-).

272. In the field of clinical trials with medicines and clinical devices the Legislative Royal Decree 1/2015 of 24 July which approves the refunded text of the Law on guarantees and rational use of medicines and health products of 2006 establishes a number of basic principles regulating clinical trials (*Title III-On Research with medicines of human use and their guarantees*; Articles 58–62), which have been developed further and completed by the aforementioned Royal Decree 1090/2015. Aside from the relevant administrative controls governing the trials themselves, their funding and the publications that may result from the trials, the Law on guarantees and rational use of medicine and health products has created Clinical Research Ethics Committees –replaced by Law 14/2007 by the Research Ethics Committees (whose functions in the field of clinical trials with medicines will be assumed in the maximum term of two years after the entry into force of RD 1090/2015 by the Research Ethics Committees with medicines but during this two years' term those functions will continue being assumed by the Research Ethics Committees put in place by Law 14/2007) with important functions in terms of laying down guidelines for the methodology to be employed, ethical considerations and the risks and benefits that may be entailed in the trials. The Law (in the version according to Legislative Royal Decree 1/2015) also introduces measures to guarantee respect for ethical principles, with the specific requirement that trials 'must be undertaken in conditions which assure respect for the fundamental rights of the individual and the ethical considerations which apply to biomedical research involving human beings, in accordance with the Helsinki Declaration and subsequent declarations updating these ethical considerations' (Article 60.2); similar terms are used in Article 3.2 of the RD of 1090/2015.

273. Research with human beings excluding the one related with clinical trials with medical products and medical devices which are submitted to their specific set of legislation is regulated in Spain by Law 14/2007 of 3 July on Biomedical Research (LIB). In order to practice such research Title II LIB (*Researches that imply invasive procedures in Human Beings*-Arts. 13–27) requires, among other conditions, the previous evaluation of the Research Project by a Research Ethics Committee (Article 16). The mentioned Research Ethics Committees are regulated under Article 12 LIB according to which Research Ethics Committees of the centres that conduct biomedical research shall be duly accredited by the competent body of the Autonomous Community concerned or, in the case of centres run by the Central Administration, by the competent body of the same, to ensure their independence and impartiality. The functions of the Research Ethics Committees are the following ones:

(a) To assess the qualifications of the senior researcher and the research team and the feasibility of the project.
(b) To balance the methodological, ethical and legal aspects of the research project.
(c) To evaluate the balance of risks and anticipated benefits arising from the study.
(d) To ensure the implementation of procedures to ensure the traceability of samples of human origin, without prejudice to the legislation of protection of personal data.
(e) To issue a report, upon evaluation of the research project, on all biomedical research involving human intervention or use of biological samples of human origin, without prejudice to other reports to be issued. No Research Project may be authorized or develop without the previous and mandatory favourable report of the Research Ethics Committee.
(f) To develop codes of good practice in accordance with the principles established by the Spanish Research Ethics Committee and to manage conflicts and generate non-compliance records.
(g) To coordinate its activities with similar committees of other institutions.
(h) To ensure confidentiality and exercise all other functions assigned by the regulations implementing this Act.

III. The Experimental Subject: Guarantees

A. *Weighing up of Risks and Benefits*

274. The weighing up of risks and benefits is fundamental in medicine and, by extension, in pure experimentation. This process of evaluation is essential because of the need for the researcher to observe a duty of care so as to avoid possible liability for negligence or liability of another type. Nevertheless, it is generally agreed that the level of acceptable risk in healthy individuals is not the same as for those suffering from diseases. This holds true only when experimentation on patients is carried out for their benefit, that is to say, when experimentation is therapeutic.

Following the criteria set out in the Additional Protocol to the Convention of the Council of Europe on Human Rights and Biomedicine, on Biomedical Research (Strasbourg, 25.I.2005) the LIB establishes some rules related to this aspect:

(1) Research involving human subjects may only be conducted in the absence of an alternative of comparable effectiveness (Article 14.1 LIB).
(2) Research shall not involve risks and burdens to the human being disproportionate to its potential benefits (Article 14.2 LIB).
(3) In addition, where the research does not have the potential to produce results of direct benefit to the health of the research participant, such research may only be undertaken if the research entails no more than acceptable risk and acceptable burden for the research participant (Article 14.3 LIB).

Similar provisions are established in the field of pharmaceutical clinical trials by Legislative Royal Decree 1/2015 (Article 60.2) and Article 3 of the RD of 1090/2015.

275. Experimentation for scientific ends on persons suffering from illnesses is effected through the use of new substances or techniques that have no relation to the illness or that, although related to it, are not primarily for the treatment of the illness. In therapeutic experimentation these substances or techniques can take the place of proven and recognized medical treatments; this is the case of placebos, be they inert or active, or of drugs or surgical procedures whose properties, efficacy and secondary effects are still not fully understood. Clearly, then, excessive and, therefore, unacceptable risk would be involved if any measures were taken that would interfere unnecessarily with the course of the illness by prolonging or aggravating it or that would result in irreversible injury unrelated to the spontaneous pathological process.

276. Needless to say, with *healthy persons* there is no risk of interference with pre-existing illnesses. However, in view of the principles whereby, on the one hand, a person cannot do with his/her body exactly as he pleases and, on the other, the inviolability of the human body (which means that it shall not be violated by others), and given also that the health of such individuals will not be benefited in any way by the experimentation, the potential risks of physical injury should be weighed up very carefully; moreover, where the research does not have the potential to produce results of direct benefit to the health of the research participant, such research may only be undertaken if the research entails no more than acceptable risk and acceptable burden for the research participant. The regulations governing clinical trials with medical products and research with human beings establish special guarantees and precautions for particular groups who may incur additional risks to their health: children and incompetent persons, research on persons in emergency clinical situations, pregnant women or women who are breast-feeding (Articles 5, 6 and 7 of the RD 1090/2015 in the field of clinical trials with medical products and Articles 19, 20 and 21 LIB in the rest of researches that imply invasive procedures on human beings).

B. Consent

277. The experimental subject's informed consent (Article 13 LIB and Article 60.4 Legislative Royal Decree 1/2015 of 24 July which approves the refunded text of the Law on guarantees and rational use of medicines and health products of 2006) constitutes the most important element in guaranteeing that the person may freely exercise his/her will and accept any risks involved. The subject may withdraw his/her consent at any time and is not obliged to give reasons for withdrawal, which under no circumstances will give rise to liability or loss of any kind or to any form of discrimination against the person concerned, in particular regarding the right to medical care (Articles 4 and 13 LIB and Article 4.5 of RD 1090/2015 in the field of pharmaceutical clinical trials).

The scope and efficacy of consent are conditioned by various factors – particularly relating to legal capacity to give consent – and the potential dangers to the subject's health. For this reason it would seem appropriate to draw distinctions between the most significant groups of experimentation subjects.

278. Patients and healthy volunteers. While the consent of patients who are to undergo experimental therapies poses no major problems, or, to be more accurate, these problems are similar to those that arise in the course of normal treatment,[362] very complex issues are entailed in the case of purely scientific experimentation, especially the requirement that the subject be informed prior to the experiment (applicable to both patients and healthy adults).

In fact, the free and informed consent requirement is often difficult to fulfil as it is incompatible with the nature and methodology of research itself. At some stage of the experimental process (phase III), in a bid to avoid subjective influence the person is not told whether the new drug or a *placebo* is being administered. In some cases even the researcher is kept in the dark (simple blind, double blind, crossed double blind method).

It would appear that these factors were not taken into account in the current regulations on clinical trials, judging from the emphasis they place on the duty to inform. These regulations stipulate that for the freely given consent requirement to be satisfied (preferably written consent or, failing that, witnessed consent; it must always be written if the test has no particular therapeutic value for the experimental subject) the subject must have been informed as to 'the nature, importance, scope and risks of the trial', and that he must have understood this information (Article 60.4 Legislative Royal Decree 1/2015 of 24 July which approves the refunded text of the

---

362. J. Ataz Lopez, *Los médicos y la responsabilidad civil*, pp. 57–99; Romeo-Casabona, *El Médico y el Derecho Penal, I*, pp. 311–85.

Law on guarantees and rational use of medicines and health products of 2006); the RD 1090/2015 is more specific in this regard in that it requires that consent shall be given after having understood the information furnished with regard to (among other aspects) the nature, the objectives, benefits, implications, risks and inconveniences of the clinical trial (Article 4.1 which connects with Article 29 of EU Regulation nº 536/2015 of the European Parliament and of the Council of 16 April 2014 on clinical trials on medicinal products for human use, and repealing Directive 2001/20/EC); consequently, there is no mention that information should be given as to the methodology to be followed. In our view, it would be adequate to provide full information on the trial process, at least in cases where there is no therapeutic benefit to the subject, including the use of a *placebo*, but to keep the subject in ignorance as to the point at which it will be administered or whether indeed it has been administered at all.

279. Minors and incompetent persons. The problems in relation to these groups are even more complex both from the ethical[363] and legal points of view. The Law on guarantees and rational use of medicines and health products of 2006 (see Legislative Royal Decree 1/2015) merely indicates that the information must be provided and that consent is the responsibility of the legal representative in the case of persons who cannot freely give consent, although the latter must express their agreement if they are able to understand the nature, importance and risks entailed in the experiment (Article 60.4). Related to research with human beings different from the above mentioned clinical trials with medical products and medical devices, Article 20 Law 14/2007 on Biomedical Research (*Protection of persons not able to consent research*) establishes –following the criteria of Article 15 Additional Protocol to the Convention of the Council of Europe on Human Rights and Biomedicine, on Biomedical Research– that Research on a person without the capacity to consent to research may be undertaken only if all the following specific conditions are met: (a) the results of the research have the potential to produce real and direct benefit to his or her health; (b) research of comparable effectiveness cannot be carried out on individuals capable of giving consent; (c) the person undergoing research has been informed of his or her rights and the safeguards prescribed by law for his or her protection, unless this person is not in a state to receive the information; (d) the necessary authorization has been given specifically by the legal representative and after having received the information required by Article 15 LIB, taking into account the person's previously expressed wishes or objections.

Exceptionally and under the protective conditions prescribed by law, where the research has not the potential to produce results of direct benefit to the health of the person concerned, such research may be authorized subject to the conditions laid down in previous letters b, c, and d, and to the following additional conditions: (1) the research has the aim of contributing, through significant improvement in the scientific understanding of the individual's condition, disease or disorder, to the ultimate attainment of results capable of conferring benefit to the person concerned or

363. *See* J. Gafo Fernandez, 'Dilemas éticos de la experimentatión humana', in *Razón y Fe*, no. 1042, 1985, pp. 616 and f.

to other persons in the same age category or afflicted with the same disease or disorder or having the same condition in a reasonable timetable; (2) the research entails only minimal risk and minimal burden for the individual concerned; (3) authorization for carrying out research must be notified to the Public Prosecutor's Office prior to the carrying out of the test.

Persons in emergency clinical situations may take part in clinical trials in the field of medical products or in research that imply invasive procedures in human beings as far as existing specific legislation is respect. At this point regulation is set in Article 7 RD 1090/2015 (*Clinical Trials in emergency situations*) and Article 21 Law 14/2007 (*Research on persons not able to consent due to their clinical situation*).

280. Self-experimentation. It is contended that self-experimentation is acceptable since the researcher is in the best position to know and judge at each stage of the process the risks involved in the experiment. From the legal point of view there is in fact nothing to prevent it, even in the event of injury or damage being sustained, given that the Penal Code does not punish self-inflicted injury.[364]

IV. Payment

281. It is currently felt that all experimental subjects should have *insurance* cover for all the risks entailed. The Legislative Royal Decree 1/2015 of 24 July which approves the refunded text of the Law on guarantees and rational use of medicines and health products of 2006 (Article 61; developed further by Article 9 and Article 10 of the RD 1090/2015) establishes this as a prior condition in all cases and makes the instigator of the trial, the senior researcher and the hospital or centre where the trial is to be carried out jointly liable for any injury sustained that is not covered by insurance, even where they are not at fault (objective liability for risk);[365] the Law also establishes an assumption – although evidence to the contrary can be presented – that any injury to the health of the experimental subject occurring during the trial or up to a year later is the result of the trial.

Payment to *compensate* for expenses or loss of earnings incurred as a result of the experiment is also admissible, provided that this does not take the form of a truly financial reward and is not the only reason why the person has agreed to undergo the experimental treatment. The payment of an indemnity to cover possible injury or discomfort as a result of the experiment is a different matter that comes closer to the idea of remuneration. We will now turn to this issue.

282. The issue of *remuneration* in the strict sense of the word has been hotly debated in both bio-ethical[366] and legal circles. There is a tendency to see it as acceptable in countries with an Anglo-Saxon legal tradition but to reject it in

364. Serrano Gómez & Serrano Maíllo, *Derecho Penal Español. Parte Especial*, p. 120.
365. *See* Ataz Lopez, *Los Médicos y la responsabilidad civil*, pp. 257 and ff; Romeo-Casabona, *El Médico ante el Derecho*, pp. 117 and ff on objective liability in medical practice.
366. On this *see* Gafo Fernandez, 'Dilemas éticos de la experimentatión humana', p. 616.

continental Europe. In other legal texts where the possibility of a person making his/her body available is discussed there is an assumption that this is done without reward as an act of human solidarity.[367] Nevertheless, the RD 1090/2015 which regulates clinical trials with medicines, the Ethics Committees on clinical trials with medicines and the Spanish register of clinical trials, establishes that in special situations, Research Ethics Committees with medicines may report favourably compensation to trial subjects for the inconveniences resulting from their participation in it, as long as they ensure that such compensation does not influence the subject's decision to participate in the study (Article 3.1.h). Compensation, if agreed upon beforehand, can be demanded, though needless to say any such amount will diminish proportionally to the participation of the experimental subject if he opts out at some point.

V. Guarantees in Relation to Research

283. Research in which human subjects are used must adhere to the strictest precautions in order that the interests of the individuals involved can be safeguarded. Regulations governing clinical trials of pharmaceutical products also address this issue in great detail, so much that in fact they have even caused irritation among some researchers (Legislative Royal Decree 1/2015 of 24 July which approves the refunded text of the Law on guarantees and rational use of medicines and health products of 2006 and RD 1090/2015). Obviously specific regulations also apply to experimentation on human subjects with non-pharmaceutical products (Title II Law 14/2007).

284. Among the more important guidelines that might be mentioned are the following: the need for the research team to be in possession of professional and technical *qualifications*, the availability of appropriate staff and equipment in the centre and the fact that the scientific value of the experiment itself should be assessed (among others, see Articles 16 and 22.2 of the Law 14/2007).

285. There is also *control* on the part of the Health Administration (Spanish Agency on medicines and medical devices in the case of pharmaceutical clinical trials – Chapter V RD 1090/2015– and competent health authority in the rest of researches with human beings), whose prior authorization is required. Monitoring and inspections ensure that the entire clinical trial process is formalized and time periods and conditions are established for the carrying out of any such trials.

286. In certain cases the Spanish Agency on medicines and medical devices may interrupt a clinical trial or insist that modifications be made to the protocol (Article 59.2 Legislative Royal Decree 1/2015 of 24 July which approves the refunded text of the Law on guarantees and rational use of medicines and health products of

367. For example, the Law on the Removal and Transplant of Organs, Art. 2.

2006). This is possible in situations where the law has been broken, where the conditions under which authorization was granted are altered or where the abovementioned ethical principles are not adhered to. The aim of such intervention is to protect trial subjects and to protect public health (Article 59.2 of the Legislative Royal Decree 1/2015). Needless to say, criminal liability may arise in serious cases involving homicide or grievous bodily harm, in addition to any liability in relation to the Administration.

§8. Transsexual Interventions

I. Lawful Medico-Surgical Sex Change Operations: Reconciling Physical Sexuality with Psychological Sexuality

287. Spanish literature tend to state that the phenomenon of transsexuality is closely linked to the irreversible desire to belong to the opposite sex to the biologically established, and to assume the corresponding role and to resort, if necessary, to an hormonal and surgical treatment that aims to correct this mismatch between mind and body.[368] In this sense, transsexuality implies a lack of correspondence between physical sexuality and psychological sexuality, such that all aspects of the individual's behaviour are affected. For reasons of clarity we have limited our discussion to two sexual variables, but specialists in the field distinguish a greater number of such factors: the sexual chromosome pattern; gonadial and morphological sexuality; hormonal sexuality and related secondary sex characteristics; morphology of the external genitalia; internal reproductive organs; sex as assigned at birth and throughout childhood; psychological sex and gender role. It is, therefore, necessary to analyse the various dysfunctions that can occur in transsexuals in relation to biological identity from the psychological, social and legal point of view.

A mismatch between the sexual organic and the psychological components entails serious difficulties for transsexuals in the development of their sexual and social lives as well as causing serious disturbances in the development of personality. These individuals in fact play a role (in keeping with their psychological sexuality) that is vastly different to that expected or demanded of them by society (the role dictated by their physical and, therefore, legal gender). It should be borne in mind with regard to this that in these cases the gender that appears in the Civil Register, which determines whether the individual is legally assigned to the masculine or feminine sex (as no third possibility is allowed) is logically the organic sex of the individual at birth, as determined by external sexual characteristics (it is here that errors occur in registering the sex of individuals who are pseudohermaphrodites).

When such mismatches occur the treatment of the patient logically involves eliminating the source of the mismatch in an effort to produce a correspondence between the physical and the psychological. A possible option – which would

368. This definition was developed by H. Benjamin. See E.J. Armaza Armaza & E. Atienza Macías, 'El tratamiento jurídico de las intervenciones en el aratato reproductor humano: esterilización, castración química y cirugía de reasignación sexual', p. 754.

appear to be the less drastic of the two as it involves no surgery – is adjusting the sexual psychology and behaviour of the person to their physical sexuality through psychiatric treatment, together with high dosages of hormones to accentuate the anatomical and physiological characteristics of organic gender. Unfortunately, to date this method has not produced very satisfactory results, due mainly to the length of time needed (several years) and also because the desired results are not always achieved at the end of the day and the patient's situation often becomes even more intolerable. For this reason surgery has become a more and more popular solution in recent years. In these circumstances it is the organism that goes through the process of adjustment or being attuned (at least in terms of outer appearance) to the sexual psychology and behaviour of the patient (it should not be forgotten that this is usually the preferred solution of the individuals concerned, who usually do not wish to come to terms with the sex to which they have been assigned organically and legally and reject their own genital organs which they regard as a deformity). This surgical operation consists primarily in amputating and removing the original genital organs and 'modelling' new artificial external organs (by means of plastic surgery using the genital tissue of the patients themselves) as well as the secondary sex characteristics, which also involves high dosages of hormones. Despite the high level of aesthetic – and functional – success of these operations, once they have been carried out the individual concerned suffers irreversible loss of his/her capacity to reproduce. To sum up, the appropriate surgical treatment to correct the discrepancy between physical sexuality and psychological sexuality, is known as Sex Reassignment Surgery. Such surgery may be focused on the genitals (vaginoplasty, phalloplasty, metadoioplasty) or elsewhere in the body (mastectomy, facial surgery).

288. Thus, by seeing these operations as fundamentally therapeutic we can regard them in a positive light from the juridico-criminal point of view. Transsexuals run serious risks of suffering personality disorders because of this complete rejection of their somatic sexuality. They see their own sexuality as an 'anomaly' and if no solution is found the conflict can lead to extreme reactions, and even to suicide. If, as we have seen, psychiatric and even hormonal therapy are doomed to failure in most cases, other solutions must be sought. We know that human health is multidimensional, that any disturbance has social repercussions (the person becoming marginal, for example) and that mental health plays a particularly important role in the general health of an individual given that psychological and somatic factors are inextricably linked.

As a result, if the physician believes that the solution lies in a physical – external – sex change so as to achieve harmony with the patient's personality, nothing should stand in the way of such an operation being performed. Clearly the medical indication is necessary (in the first place, a statement from the psychiatrist to the effect that there is a mismatch between physical and psychological gender and that other non-surgical measures have proven to be inadequate or ineffective, and an evaluation of the relative advantages and disadvantages of the operation for that particular patient) and the requirements of *lex artis* must be met. In such cases the physician has to consider (it goes without saying that the individual's views and wishes are of paramount importance in this respect) whether the patient's capacity to reproduce or a balanced mental state is more important in terms of his/her general behaviour.

While the loss of the ability to reproduce clearly affects an important aspect of biology in general and human biology in particular – the potential to have children and the paternal/maternal instinct – being mentally disturbed has implications for the development of the personality of the individual and his/her relationships with others, which would lead one to contend that this psychological aspect is of greater importance.

289. While these arguments are valid in the case of sex change operations with clearly therapeutic purposes, they are not when the purpose of the operation is not so clear, when there are other circumstantial goals or benefits (such as better prospects of employment in the artistic sphere, immature persons' desire to 'follow fashion', benefits related to specific sports, etc.). Nevertheless, the Penal Code, in permitting these surgical operations, makes no distinction between those that are therapeutic and those that are not, which means that the quality of lawfulness must be extended to all such operations – unless there is some problem with the consent of the individual concerned – regardless of the underlying reason. This lawfulness rests on the principal of individual self-determination. Even so, despite the Legislature's intentions, it would seem to be going too far to allow operations with such serious risks and consequences for the integrity of the individual to be carried out without careful weighing up of the therapeutic value – that is to say, verification that a truly transsexual pathology is involved – and of the thought given to the decision and how far the person is determined that the operation should be carried out. This would avoid hasty decisions that are later deeply regretted once the irreversible operation with all its consequences has been performed.

II. Achieving Harmony between the Sex of the Person and his/her Legal Gender or Legal Identity

290. The first unveiled[369] surgery of its kind was carried out in Copenhagen to George (later Christine) Jorgensen on December 3 of 1952. This intensified the debate about the penalization, or the admissibility, of this kind of medical practice. In Spain, 1983 is the key year in which the lawmaker expressly decriminalizes this medical intervention (until then, this behaviour could lead to the configuration of the offence of injuries according to the abrogated Penal Code). Since then, this type of surgery is one of the cases in which the patient's consent exempts the physician from criminal liability for the offence of injuries. Nevertheless, for many years the Spanish judicial practice had the need to resolve conflicts related to this matter counting only with the reference to the Case Law developed in the field of transsexuality.[370]

291. Nowadays, this issue has been regulated through the Law 3/2007 of 15 March, governing the registry rectification of the mention regarding the sex of the

369. In the decade of the 30s had been carried out similar surgeries in the United States.
370. Among others, some of the most important Rulings of the Supreme Court in this field are: Ruling of 2 Jul. of1987, Ruling of 15 Jul. 1988, Ruling of 3 Mar. 1989 and Ruling of 19 Apr. 1991.

persons. This legal response to transsexuality has been developed taking into account the fundamental rights recognized in the Article 10 of the Spanish Constitution. In this sense, the Preamble of the Law 3/2007 states that transsexuality is a social reality that needs an answer from the lawmaker in order to guarantee the freedom in the development of personality and human dignity, through the implementation of a number of mechanisms that allows the modification of the previous sex assignment registration, as well as the original given name, when this information does not have correspondence with the gender identity of the applicant.

In this sense, the new law aims to regulate the requirements to access to the modification of the registration related to the sex of a person in the Civil Registry, where such registration has no correspondence with his/her real gender identity; this Law also provides mechanisms to ensure the change of the given name in order to avoid the discordance with sex claimed (the modification of the registry will take place according to the governmental regulation of civil registry records).

292. According with the provision of the Law 3/2007, there are two general requirements that must be completed in order to be able to proceed with the modification of the registry:

(1) Diagnosis of gender dysphoria: Such diagnosis must be based in one report prepared by a physician or clinical psychologist. This report must record the existence of the discrepancy between the morphological sex and gender identity felt by the applicant (psychosocial sex), as well as the stability and persistence of the discrepancy and the absence of mental illness that may influence, in a decisive way, in the existence of such disagreement. It is important to remark that the Law does not require that the diagnosis must be issued simultaneously or successively by two specialists (the report of a physician or a clinical psychologist is alternatively required).

(2) Medical treatment for, at least, two years: Such treatment should aim to accommodate the physical characteristics of the subject in question with the appropriate of the sex sought by the applicant. Compliance with this requirement must be accredited by a report prepared by the physician who conducted the treatment or, alternatively, by a specialized forensic physician. It is important to highlight that, in this context, the legal expression 'medical treatment' refers to the hormonal treatment, given that such kind of treatment provides a sort of temporal continuity that is not present in the surgical treatment. As we have mentioned, according with the provision of the Law 3/2007, the aforementioned treatment should last, at least, two years in order to accommodate the physical characteristics with the corresponding to the requested gender. It is quite important to note that the Article 4.2 of the Law 3/2007 establishes that to concede the rectification of sex in the corresponding registry, the application of a Sex Reassignment Surgery as part of the aforesaid medical treatment will not be needed. This fact constitutes one of the most important aspects of Spanish law (as well as a change of approach in relation to the criteria maintained by the Supreme Court in Case Law) and responds to one of the historical claims of the transsexual community. However, to legally perform a Sex Reassignment Surgery, it is necessary that the applicant: (a) that the applicant count with a

favourable diagnosis report, (b) that a reasonable time has passed from the beginning of the pharmacological treatment, (c) that the applicant is an adult (eighteen or more years of age) and d) that the applicant has extended an express and written request in order to be submitted to the surgery. In this context is particularly relevant the right to receive information and the need to extend a personal, express and written consent, according with the provisions of the Article 8 of Law 41/2002 of 14 November, regulating the autonomy of patients and their rights and obligations with regard to clinical information and documentation.

293. Regarding the procedure to modify, in the corresponding registry, the information related to the sex of the applicant, we must indicate that the rectification must be processed following the gubernatorial process already regulated in the Law of June of 1957 on Civil Registry (particularly Articles 93–97). In effect, Article 93.2 of this Law establishes that the registry entry regarding the sex of the persons in cases of gender dysphoria can be modified.

III. The Transsexual, Marriage and the Family

294. We must emphasize that Law 3/2007 recognizes important legal effects to the rectification in the civil order. Second paragraph of its Article 5 establishes that the registry rectification will allow the person to exercise all the rights attached to its new status. Thus, the Law, despite maintaining the subject of transsexuality in the area of Civil Registry, concedes full civil effects to rectification, establishing therefore equal rights in the new situation.

295. In this sense, no legal obstacle should stand in the way of a transsexual's marrying when his/her new gender is legally recognized: such a situation is not included among the restrictions on marriage in Article 46 and Article 47 of the Civil Code, in which it is stipulated that both man and woman are entitled to marry under the provisions of this Code and that marriage will have the same requirements and effects when both parties are of the same or different sex (Article 44). The principal requirement is that they have given their consent to the marriage (Article 45). For such consent to be valid it is necessary for the future spouse to know about his/her partner's situation beforehand. The individual concerned must inform the intended spouse about the legal change of sex and the other organic and personal repercussions of this change, including irreversible infertility and any change in the transsexual's personal qualities. Only in this way can the parties avoid the marriage being null and void *ab initio* because of irregularities with regard to consent, as stipulated by Article 73.4 of the Civil Code, which defines as null and void marriages entered into as a result of 'mistaken identity or error as to the personal qualities of the marriage partner, this identity or these qualities having been determining factors in the giving of consent'. It should be said that knowledge of such a circumstance can be obtained from the Civil Registry, which must reflect any rectifications with regard to name and sex.

296. In the situation where the person that has undergone the sex change operation was already married, the person to whom he/she was married may logically be granted a legal separation and/or the dissolution of the marriage (divorce), despite the fact that this circumstance is not explicitly dealt with in the law (Articles 81, 82 and 86 of the Civil Code). It is a different matter if the transsexual had children before the surgical and legal sex change, in which case it should be understood – in the absence of any legal indication to the contrary – that the legal relationships that existed prior to the change and the duties and rights arising from these relationships are maintained (such as those in relation to heirs and parental authority).

Part III. The Physician and Health Care System

Chapter 1. Relation with Other Health Care Providers

297. In the field of health care other professionals work alongside doctors and perform an important role in assisting and treating patients. Under the broad term 'other health care providers' are included nurses, a category known literally in Spanish as 'technical health care assistants' or ATS (a type of nurse), doctors' assistants, midwives and auxiliary nurses. Traditionally these professionals have assisted the physician, but as medicine has become increasingly reliant on technology and more and more specialized, largely because of the advent of new and complex diagnostic and surgical techniques, it is now essential for these individuals to be highly qualified and, in most cases, have university level training.[371] They perform a series of tasks which, although complementary to those of the physician, are sometimes absolutely vital and it is often the case that the doctor cannot or does not know how to perform them.[372] Because of the increasing importance of these health care providers, and the need for greater control over medical activity (applicable here also),[373] more rigorous regulation of these professions is crucial. However, this is an area that has been somewhat neglected in Spain, as we shall see shortly.

Other qualified personnel such as pharmacists, psychologists and opticians also participate in health care. When we say that health care teams are multi-disciplinary it is not only because they comprise participants from the various branches of medicine, but also because such persons perform important functions.

298. A number of different provisions make reference to the relations among the different categories of health care providers. In various Statutes governing the activities of medical personnel and paramedical health care workers, the maintenance of good relations and co-operation among these professionals is demanded. In the particular case of physicians, Chapter 8 of the Code of Medical Deontology is devoted to the relationship between the physician and other health care providers:

371. *See* C. Segura & L. Martinez-Calcerrada, 'El médico ante el Derecho Civil', in L. Martinez-Calcerrada, *Derecho Médico I*, p. 54.
372. Llasmas Pombo, *La responsabilidad civil del médico*, p. 335.
373. *See above.*

Article 41.

1. Physicians must maintain good relations with other health care professionals and shall take into consideration their opinions with regard to the care of the patients.
2. The physician should not intrude upon the areas of competence of the staff that work with him and will ensure that each member of the group accomplishes correctly with its specific obligations.

§1. Pharmacists

299. Pharmacy as a profession forms part of the community health care system and contributes to the common cause of the other health care professions, namely, the preservation and recuperation of health.[374]

The specific know-how of pharmacists confer on them an important role which consists of the following functions:[375] control over the pharmaceutical products dispensed to the patient; in the case of minor ailments that do not require medical attention, dispensing medicaments for symptom relief; ensuring that medicines are used correctly and patients are warned as to any adverse effects; clinical pharmacy and vigilance in relation to pharmaceutical products in the community; the furnishing of information on medicines; the making up of prescribed medicines; the proper conservation of medicines in the pharmacy; the storage of substances that are subject to special restrictions on their use. As a health care professional, the pharmacist plays an active part in programmes for the promotion of health and health education in the community, and any other activities for which his university education has specially prepared him, particularly those relating to food and environmental health.

300. The pharmacist co-operates with the physician in the preparation of prescriptions and the dispensing of medicines, and undertakes clinical analyses which provide vital information on which diagnosis may be based.

§2. Dentists (See Part I, Chapter 1, §2)

§3. Nursing Profession

301. Traditionally included within the broad category of 'nursing' are a group of professionals who perform a wide range of functions that aid and complement

374. Martinez Cañizares, 'Farmacéutico y Sociedad', in *Revista ACOFAR*, 206 (1983), p. 13, quoted in F. Rico Pérez, *La responsabilidad del farmacéutico* (Trivium, Madrid 1984).
375. E. Lluch Martin, *Política Farmacéutica del Ministerio de Sanidad y Consumo* (Servicio de Publicaciones del Ministerio de Sanidad y Consumo, Madrid 1983), p. 21, quoted in Rico Pérez, *La responsabilidad civil del Farmacéutico*, p. 10.

medical practice. A number of such professions were recognized by Spanish health regulations as far back as 1860. In 1952 a distinction between ATS (a type of nurse) and midwife was established. In 1963 recognition was given to a further category, auxiliary nurses, the formal qualification for which is obtained in the vocational training system ('formación professional'). Auxiliary nurses assist hospital nursing staff with the care of the patient by performing tasks such as bathing, feeding, etc.

In 1977, with the establishment of Schools of Nursing, a new professional category requiring three years of university education was created.[376] The previous categories of ATS and midwife were given equal status to the new Diploma in Nursing and began to disappear as professions in their own right.

302. Since then, university education of nurses has allowed the profession to acquire functional independence, albeit as an integral part of the co-ordinated multidisciplinary health care teams (working alongside physicians, auxiliary nurses, psychologists, etc.) which are central to hospital care.[377] Nurses are responsible for the care of the patient (particularly in terms of treatment management), attending to the needs of the patient's family and, where relevant, assistance with community health care education (as delegated by physicians or psychologists) as teachers, researchers and administrators. It is important to draw a distinction between nurses and auxiliary nurses, who do not hold university qualifications and who work under the nurse in the primary care of the patient and his environment.

Holders of a nursing qualification may also practise privately in centres primarily concerned with the management of treatment prescribe by the physician, rehabilitation and primary care, in accordance with the entitlement to freely practise a profession which is recognized by Article 89 of the LGS and Article 35 and Article 36 of the Constitution.

303. Nevertheless, the lack of clear-cut regulatory guidelines to govern the role of nurses produces a good deal of uncertainty and is frequently a source of friction between nurses and physicians because of the confusion as to where the responsibilities of one end and those of the other begin.

304. There is a possibility that new regulations will be drawn up so as to conform to the requirements of the LGS, which stipulates in Article 84 that the government shall draw up a framework statute for, among others, qualified (auxiliary) health care personnel and auxiliary nurses employed by the Social Security system.

After the LGS was passed the Ministry of Health and Consumer Affairs produced a draft version in 1987 which attracted a great deal of criticism. This led to the preparation of another draft of a National Health Service Statute, which was made public in 1988 but did not go through Parliament. As a result, the Social Security Paramedical Health Care Personnel Statute (published by Order of the Ministry of

376. *See* Segura & Martinez-Calcerrada, *Derecho Médico I*, p. 54.

377. While they work in teams that are organized hierarchically, they are responsible for their own specific tasks; on this issue and for a fuller account of the hierarchical superior/subordinate division of labour, *see* A. Jorge Barreiro, *La imprudencia punible en la actividad médicoquirúrgica*, pp. 147–66.

Employment on 26 April 1973), which contains a statute for qualified (auxiliary) health care personnel and auxiliary nurses, should be understood to be still in force. Another piece of legislation are the Decree 2319/1960 of 17 November on the professional responsibilities of ATS, doctors' assistants, midwives and nurses, the still binding Royal Decree 1231/2001 of 8 November, by which the General Statutes of the College of Nursing Organization of Spain of the General Council and of Management of the Nursing Profession are approved (Article 54 of said document establishes that the mission of nursing services is to provide health care to individuals, families and communities in all stages of the life cycle and development processes), and the recently approved Royal Decree 954/2015 of 23 October, by which is regulated the indication, use and authorization of dispensing of drugs and medical products for human use by the nurses.

The profession itself has been pushing hard for a specific law to regulate nursing in a manner in keeping with the fact that these professionals are now university-qualified.

305. A consequence of the lack of political will to create the appropriate statutory provisions for the nursing profession is the decision by the European Court of Justice of 7 November 1991. The court condemned Spain's failure to implement within the prescribed time-limit the provisions of EC Council Directive 80/155 of 21 January 1980 on the co-ordination of legal, regulatory and administrative provisions regarding access to the professions of midwife and obstetric assistant and the exercise of these professions (which are now specialist fields included in the diploma in nursing).

306. A Code of Nursing Ethics was drawn up by the Spain's General Council for Nursing and passed by Resolution 32/89. The Code lays down guidelines for nurses in the fulfilment of their obligations under three broad headings: nursing and the human being; nursing and the community; nursing and professional practice. As regards relations with other professionals, Chapter 10 of the Code stipulates the following:

> *Article 63.*
>
> In order to provide the best possible service to the patient, nurses shall do their utmost to co-operate with other members of the health care team. They should always respect the areas of responsibility of other professionals, but should not allow these professionals to encroach upon their own professional autonomy.

§4. Paramedical Professionals

307. Physiotherapists: This was originally a branch of the profession of ATS, although since 1980 and the setting up of Physiotherapy Schools training has been taken out of Nursing Schools. Physiotherapy is aimed primarily at the rehabilitation of patients.

308. Chiropodists: This profession was established as a specialization within the broader category of ATS and is primarily concerned with the non-surgical treatment of the feet.

309. Optometrists: Optometry Schools have offered university training since 1974. Optometrists' work involves chiefly the grading and production of lenses. This is a group which often suffers from illegal practice.

Chapter 2. Relation with Health Care Provisions

§1. HOSPITALS

310. Hospitals are the foundation of the system of specialized medical care. Historically they were not strictly speaking health care institutions, but charitable hostels for the elderly, the poor, and for pilgrims, etc. In the nineteenth century the functions that hospitals perform today were the province of charitable organizations.[378] A major expansion in hospital services took place at the end of the 1960s as a result of improved human and material resources, though this was still not sufficient to satisfy the demands of public health due to the lack of a true hospital network. This was in part because specialized medical care was provided by the Social Security system which still lacked the means available in other centres to attend to the needs of public patients.[379] Hospitals belonging to the Provincial Governments, 'Cabildos Insulares' (organs of government in the Balearic and Canary Islands), and city councils were able to offer such services. This meant that there was the danger of duplicating specialized health care services as a result of the 1944 Law establishing the bases of the National Health Service. Aside from other factors, this alone was good reason to claim that the way in which the hospitals functioned was not entirely satisfactory and the idea of a coherent network of hospitals began to emerge as a means of achieving greater efficiency in hospital care. This was attempted through a number of statutory provisions, the first of which was the Law 37/1962 of 21 July which still constitutes today the basic legislation governing hospitals.[380] This law defines hospitals as follows: 'establishments providing medical/clinical care, regardless of the names they bear, without prejudice to the fact that such establishments may provide preventive, convalescent and outpatients' treatment as appropriate'.[381] However, neither this law nor any of the subsequent legislation has succeeded in arriving at an efficient specialized health care organization: 'the situation of specialized care in 1982 is characterized by the disorganization resulting

378. *See* J. Ortíz Díaz, 'Hacia una reordenación de la Sanidad Pública española: el problema hospitalario', in *Revista de Administración Pública*, no. 51, 1986, pp. 153–60 on the historical origins of hospitals.

379. Because of this Social Security Service established agreements with other private and public hospitals. These hospitals catered for public patients or provided the Social Security system with the material and human means of providing such a service.

380. Article 4 of the law refers to the setting up of a National Hospital Network. To this end, it establishes a Central Co-ordinating Committee for Hospital Services which, among other things, is responsible for (Art. 7) maintaining information on hospital needs and for building, adding extensions to, modifying or closing hospitals (Art. 5).

381. Article 1 includes a second paragraph that states: 'hospitals are also centres for the training of technical and health care personnel, for scientific research so long as the appropriate conditions for such purposes are satisfied in accordance with the nature and aims of each Institution. At the same time there should be adequate co-ordination between teaching centres'. Art. 65.2 of the LGS states that 'the hospital is responsible for inpatient care as well as specialized and complementary care as required in its area'.

from the multiplicity of public administration hospital management bodies and the failure to set up a satisfactory instrument for hospital co-ordination'.[382]

311. The 1962 Law regulating hospitals was developed further by Decree 575/1966 of 3 March on the classification and regionalization of hospitals. This was followed by a number of other pieces of legislation on various aspects of the hospital service, including the still operative RD 521/1987 of 15 April on the structure, organization and functioning of hospitals managed by the National Institute of Health ('Instituto Nacional de la Salud', known by its acronym INSALUD) and the reform of our National Health System introduced by the LGS of 1986. Article 65.1 of the LGS states that every Health Area should have at least one General Hospital which should be involved in the promotion of health, disease prevention, research and teaching as well as attending to patients' needs. These hospitals should thus complement the primary care network.

The public hospital infrastructure is still not sufficient on its own to provide health care services of high quality to the total population. For this reason the LGS, while still seeking to establish a single hospital network, arrived at a system under which private hospitals participate in public health care in two ways, namely, through association agreements and the linking up of private hospitals to the public system.

With regard to *agreements* with private health care institutions, the Public Administration, having previously given approval to the institutions and evaluated the optimal use that can be made of their health care resources, establishes the requirements and minimum conditions that are applicable to all agreements. The conditions and requirements established must include the reciprocal rights and obligations of both parties, guarantees that the service provided will be of the same quality for all clients and a prohibition against the introduction of services that are complementary to those already provided by public health care centres. Under similar conditions of efficiency, quality and cost, priority shall be given to institutions belonging to non-profitmaking organizations.[383] The Public Administration is charged with the carrying out of inspections of these private centres as regards health care services, administration and financial matters concerning each patient referred to them for admission (Article 94.2 of the LGS).

The *linking up of* private hospitals to the national health system enables them to enjoy a closer relationship with the public system.[384]

382. Elola Somoza, *Crisis y Reforma de la asistencia sanitaria pública en España*, p. 155. The author adds 'the efforts – efforts that have not been put into practice – to rationalise hospital management can be seen in various areas: the appointment of professional managers who are not necessarily medical professionals, the widely expressed desire to make the budget the responsibility of management, the development of a system to assess the quality of care and efficiency, and finally the drawing up of a list of rights of hospital users'.

383. *See* Art. 90 of the LGS.

384. *See* Pemán Gavín, *Derecho a la salud y Administración sanitaria*, p. 213.

312. Access to hospitals, which is open to all those who are ill regardless of their financial or social position, including prison inmates,[385] is granted once all other avenues of diagnosis and treatment in primary services have been explored, save for emergency cases. Hospital care is provided on in inpatient basis, through admission to hospital, and via outpatient consultancies and Casualty Services. It is important to remark that Law 16/2003[386] states that foreigners not registered or authorized to reside in Spain will receive medical care in the following situations: (a) In case of emergency caused by serious illness or accident, regardless of its cause, until the situation of medical discharge. (b) Assistance in cases of pregnancy, birth and post-partum.

Outpatient consultancies enable specialized care to be provided without the need for the patient to be admitted to hospital. The physician completes a Referral for Outpatients' Consultation which the Health Care Area Authority sends to the hospital concerned and the patient is given an appointment through the Admissions Service. There is direct access, however, to the Casualty Service in very serious cases.

313. Royal Decree 521/1987 of 15 April passed the Regulations governing the structure, organization and functioning of hospitals managed by the National Institute of Health. These regulations are aimed at improving the management and quality of care provided by hospitals in accordance with the principles laid down in the LGS. In this way, hospital services and activities are grouped together under the following categories: Hospital Administrator's Division, Medical Division, Nursing Division, Management Services and General Services.

(1) The top level of hospital management is the Hospital Administrator ('Director-Gerente') who represents the hospital and is its highest authority, with responsibility for the hospital's human, physical and financial resources. This person plans, manages, controls and evaluates the performance of all the hospital divisions and takes measures to ensure the smooth running of the hospital, especially in times of crisis and emergency. The Administrator produces periodic reports on hospital activities and an annual report (Article 7). The areas of responsibility of the Administrator's Division are patient relations, management, computing services, legal affairs, admissions, reception and information, staffing policy, analysis and planning (Article 9).
(2) The Medical Division, which covers the areas of Medicine, Surgery, Obstetrics and Gynaecology, Paediatrics, Central Services, Documentation and Clinical Files, Day Hospitalization, Home Hospitalization and any other activity in which medical care is involved, is headed by the Medical Director, whose most important functions are the management, supervision, co-ordination and evaluation of medical and other health care services in the hospital.

385. See Arts 35, 207 and ff of the Royal Decree 190/1996 of 9 February, governing the Prison Regulations ('Reglamento Penitenciario').

386. The original text the Law 16/2003 of 28 May, of Cohesion and Quality of the National Health System, was amended by the new Royal Decree Law 16/2012 of 20 April, on urgent measures to ensure the sustainability of the National Health System and to improve the quality and safety of its services.

(3) The Nursing Division is concerned with co-ordination of the units and services under its responsibility (wards, operating theatres, special units, outpatient's department, casualty, etc.) while the Management Division and General Services Department provide the administrative support and technical assistance necessary for the running of all other hospital divisions (financial management and administration, supplies, catering and maintenance, etc.)

§2. Preventive Health Care

314. Originally, public health care in Spain was more preventive than treatment-oriented. During the nineteenth century and up until the middle of this century the Administration took responsibility for public health only within the parameters of disease prevention, particularly the prevention of epidemics, and other health hazards arising from poor hygiene and medical treatment provided by unqualified individuals.[387] The Administration took on this preventive role because epidemics affected a considerable sector of the population. What the Administration was in fact concerned with was protecting collective health rather than individual health, which was primarily treatment-oriented.[388] This preventive focus can be seen in the Law of 28 November 1885, the General Public Health Instructions of 12 January 1904 and the Law establishing the bases of the NHS (1944).[389] However, the social and political situation in Spain led to the development in the public arena, and not just in the area of health care, of a greater concern with individual needs and an appreciation of the fact that the person in need of medical treatment could not, in most cases, afford to pay for treatment. As a result, the public health care service was made available not only to the poor and destitute, but also to those with insufficient means of support. In this way, the original State practice of organising health care from a preventive perspective for the population as a whole was finally abandoned in favour of an approach that took account of the dangers to individual health caused by common and frequent diseases and illnesses. The final stage in this process of evolution was the constitutional recognition of the right to health protection for all citizens resident in Spain.[390] Article 43.2 of the Constitution, apart from recognising

387. *See* Luis Morell Ocaña, 'La evolución y configuración actual de la actividad administrativa sanitaria', in *Revista de Administración Pública*, no. 63, 1970, pp. 136–40.
388. *See* Pemán Gavín, *Derecho a la salud y administración sanitaria*, p. 104, who gives more emphasis to the idea of the protection of collective health than to prevention as the basis on which the traditional health care administration was founded. On the other hand, the protection of individual health lacked a preventive element, and was centred rather on care provided by the Welfare ('Beneficencia') that catered for the needs of the poor.
389. The Law of 1944 devotes its Fourth Foundation to the fight against infectious diseases, and to disinfection, and fumigation and established preventive measures such as an obligation for the physician to notify the existence of disease or isolation measures; in the Fifth Foundation all matters related to External Health are dealt with, such as inspection and control of health hazards; and in the Tenth Foundations specific measures to fight trachoma, sexually transmitted diseases and leprosy are stipulated. *See* Cobreros Mendazona, *Los tratamientos obligatorios y el derecho a la salud*, pp. 350–9.
390. This is expressed in Art. 1.2 of the LGS as follows: 'All Spaniards and foreign nationals resident in Spain have the right to health protection and health care'.

the right to health protection, states in its second paragraph that the organization of and responsibility for public health shall be achieved through preventive measures and the provision of the necessary services. Similarly, the LGS states explicitly that the actions of the Public Administration in the area of health care should involve the treatment as well as the prevention of disease and illness (Article 18.2).

315. The right to protection of health includes, therefore, not only treatment to restore good health in cases of illness, but also the right to protection from possible health hazards that might affect the individual. For this reason the LGS lists in Article 18 – in Chapter II, entitled 'public intervention in individual and collective health' – a large number of specific actions in Preventive Medicine, such as:

(1) The care of high risk groups in the population and the prevention of both congenital and acquired disabilities.
(2) The promotion and improvement of sanitation, water supply, removal of liquid and solid residues, air pollution control, health inspections and the improvement of environmental health in all contexts including the home.
(3) Family planning.
(4) The promotion of mental health and health in the workplace.
(5) The control and prevention of food and drug-related health hazards.
(6) Informing the public on epidemiology.

Intervention by the public administration can consist of requiring authorization to be sought for any activity that might imply a risk or danger to health, and may, in cases of imminent and exceptional risk, involve the seizure or impounding of products, the imposition of temporary bans on activities, or the closure of businesses or facilities (Article 23 of the LGS). In short, all this means that, in contrast with the nineteenth century approach to health care, the current view is that the individual, and not just the social group, should be afforded health protection (prevention and treatment), in accordance with his rights as laid down in constitutional principles governing social and economic policy which the authorities are duty-bound to observe.

This has led the Legislature to confer on health the protection which it deserves and which is demanded by the Constitution, by legally regulating the manner in which certain dangerous activities should be carried out and stipulating the administrative sanctions applicable to breaches of these regulations. Moreover, actions that endanger or damage public health are treated as criminal offences.[391]

316. In order to assure the effectiveness of preventive medicine, when the risk to public health is imminent, provision is made for the adoption of government measures, including the curtailment of rights and constitutional freedoms, under Organic Law 3/1986 of 18 March, on Special Preventive Health Measures. This law grants the health authorities the right to impose treatment aimed at protecting the

391. The Ch. III of the Title XVII of Volume II of the Penal Code lists offences against public health.

individual or aiding his recovery. These measures may range from a simple medical examination to hospitalization and may affect the individual or groups of people, or those engaged in a particular activity. In the area of epidemics, the Royal Decree 2210/1995 of 28 December, creating national epidemiological surveillance network, established special measures for the control of outbreaks of disease, such as the obligation of the public to inform the authorities if they have contracted certain diseases and the drawing up by the authorities of weekly statistical reports containing specific information on cases of epidemics treated.

317. In certain fields preventive medicine has achieved a greater degree of organization, specification and stability, thanks to the maintenance of a preventive medical service made up of permanent units and specific types of health care services in certain health care contexts. Specific programmes have been drawn up for primary health care, family planning, mental health and obstetric psycho-prophylaxis. We refer here to the Family Planning Centres and Units, staffed by specialists in various fields (gynaecologists, midwives, psychologists, etc.), in which advice is given on sexuality and contraception. Prenatal, genetic and legal abortion counselling is also provided in these centres, as is treatment for sexually transmitted diseases. For their part, Mental Health Units are responsible for more than just treatment and they are involved in promotion, education and prevention through specific programmes related to problems such as alcoholism, drug abuse, etc. Lastly, Obstetric Psycho-prophylaxis Units are intended to provide pregnant women with information and health education to prepare them for the birth, puerperium and care of the new-born infant.

With regard to health in the workplace the LGS one again considers various basic preventive measures aimed at reducing risks to workers' health to a minimum. Article 21 of the LGS establishes the measures that Health Areas must take in relation to the prevention of risks to workers. They are responsible for monitoring working conditions and the work environment, drawing up guides on dangers in the workplace (including an obligation for companies to inform the health authorities on all substances used in production) as well as the setting up of an epidemiological control system on disease and mortality rates in the workplace, promoting, as far as is possible, the education and training of workers and management in the area of health in the workplace.

§3. Health Insurance

318. Historically, health care services were provided by means of private health insurance. The State did not take on responsibility for health care in the same way as it did for other public services. It only catered for those in the terminal stages of an illness and for the destitute, and did not concern itself with the medical profession, which was conducted entirely through private practice. For these reasons it is hardly surprising that at the beginning of this century there was a plethora of private health insurance companies through which physicians offered their services to individuals and families in exchange for regular payment. But this lack of interest on the State's part in community health and the medical profession has gradually-become a thing of the past as a result of the fact that most citizens were not in a position to pay for their own medical treatment. This led to the State taking on the role of social protector, using its public resources in the service of community health, initially through obligatory health insurance and later with the establishment of the Social Security system. Today both types of health service (private health care and Social Security) co-exist.

319. The Spanish Constitution states in Article 41 that 'the public authorities shall maintain a public Social Security system for all citizens that shall ensure a minimum level of care and service in situations of need, especially in cases of unemployment. Care and complementary services shall be free of charge'. Although the system was created to cover health risks to a specific group of people, namely wage-earning workers, it has gradually widened its scope to include a larger number and range of beneficiaries and to offer more services.

320. Law 55/2003 of 16 December, of General Statute of Statutory Personnel of the Health Services establishes the different kind of legal administrative relationships between the physicians and the Social Security. The Medical Personnel Statutes alone are applicable to Social Security physicians and leaves room for the individual or collective autonomy of physicians when contracted by the Social Security.[392] The statutory relationship between physicians and the Social Security does not preclude private practice, as the aforementioned article indicates elsewhere.

321. The Social Security system currently covers all citizens resident in Spain, together with certain non-residents and foreigners with work and residence permits. It comprises a General Regime and various Special Regimes, which are reminiscent of the old private health insurance systems. There are also differences in terms of the services which one is entitled to according to whether one is registered under the General Regime or one of the Special ones. The latter are an open list and the Government may at any time include them within the General Regime, although it should be said that they are becoming quite similar to their general counterpart in terms of the cover provided.

I. The General Regime

322. The General Regime of the Social Security system includes wage earners who normally work in Spain and certain specific classes of non-resident Spanish workers (civil servants or employees of international organizations, non-civil servant Spaniards contracted by the Spanish Administration to work overseas), and

392. M. Alonso Olea & J.L Tortuero Plaza, *Instituciones de la Seguridad Social* (12th ed. Civitas, Madrid 1990), p. 280.

wage-earning foreigners with residence and work permits in Spain. The employer must register his business with the Social Security and must ensure that the company registers the employees also. As soon as the business activity commences, employer and employee Social Security contributions are payable and are compulsory. These are calculated on the basis of the total remuneration that the worker is entitled to receive. Agreements between the worker and the employer such as that the worker assumes the obligation to pay part or all of the employer's contribution are null and void.

Registration with the General Regime automatically gives rise to various entitlements: health care, financial assistance for the unemployed, retirement and widows' pensions, etc. Health care consists of medical and pharmaceutical services as well as rehabilitation and, in some cases, prostheses and orthopaedic appliances. The services are available not only to the registered worker but also to his/her spouse or the person with whom he/she has lived, as man and wife, for at least a year prior to registration. Natural and adopted children are also covered, be they the children of the worker or the spouse, regardless of age or the legal relationship. The parents and grandparents of the worker and his/her spouse are covered provided that they live with the worker and are maintained by him/her and are not gainfully employed, receive no benefits from property or a pension exceeding twice the minimum wage and have no other individual entitlement to Social Security health care services.

Health care service covers common illness, accidents occurring outside the workplace, illness produced as the result of work, accidents in the workplace and maternity. Care is provided in the area of residence of the registered worker and outside this area when he/she provides proof of registration with the Social Security. Outpatient services, hospital care and house calls are also available through the system. Medicaments are free of charge when they are dispensed by Social Security health care institutions, and for pensioners, for those in receipt of temporary invalidity benefits or benefits in respect of profession-related sicknesses or accidents in the workplace. Social Security beneficiaries pay 40% of the retail price of drugs and medicines used frequently to treat certain illnesses and other specialist pharmaceutical products.

Free health care services are also provided for those without sufficient means of support (an income lower or equal to the minimum wage).

Financial assistance is provided in situations where the worker is temporarily or permanently unfit to work as a result of common illness, illness brought about by work, or accident, whether in the workplace or elsewhere, and maternity. A worker who is temporarily unfit for work, although he is still obliged to pay his social security contributions, is entitled to receive benefit for a period of twelve months, renewable for another six, in cases of accident or illness, and sixteen weeks for maternity (extendable to eighteen weeks for multiple births). Temporary invalid status is granted on expiry of the period of being temporarily unfit for work and if the worker still requires health care assistance and is unable to return to work. This category is applicable for a maximum period of six years calculated from the date when the worker was certified as being temporarily unfit for work. It is not applicable to cases of permanent illness or incapacity. A worker is certified as being permanently incapacitated when, after having undergone the treatment prescribed, there are still serious anatomical and functional disabilities that can be objectively determined.

They should be permanent and should diminish the worker's capacity for work or should make work impossible. There are several levels of incapacitation: permanent partial incapacitation for the person's normal work, permanent total incapacitation for the person's normal work, absolute permanent incapacitation for all types of work and grave disability.

Other types of financial assistance are provided for people with children in their care. The children must be under 18 years of age or, if they are legally adults, must be totally incapacitated for all types of work. The amount of benefit paid monthly for each child is quite low, although it increases in the case of large families or persons with low income (pensioners).

In most cases working life comes to an end at the age of 65, at which time the person – if he stops work – becomes entitled to receive a retirement pension if he has made social security payments for at least fifteen years, two of which must have been in the last eight years. The possibility of early retirement at the age of 60 also exists.

The following benefits are available in cases of the death of the worker, pensioner, person receiving temporary invalidity benefits or benefits while recovering from illness:

(1) Funeral benefit to assist with the cost of the burial.
(2) Widow's/widower's pension for the widow or widower of the deceased worker, provided that there has been a marital relationship, legal separation or divorce (although in some cases co-habitation is sufficient grounds for entitlement).
(3) Orphan's pension for children under eighteen or incapacitated adult children or for the deceased's adopted children, provided that adoption was granted at least two years before the death.
(4) Family pension for the deceased's blood relations such as grandchildren, brothers and sisters, mother, grandmothers, father and grandfathers living with the deceased and financially dependent on him/her and who do not receive a pension and have no adequate means of support.

There is also universal Old Age and Invalid Insurance for those over 65 who have no right to a pension under the different Social Security regimes, as long as they paid contributions for 1,800 days between 1940 and 1966.

II. Special Regimes within the General System

323. By virtue of RD 2621/86 of 24 December, special systems for railway workers, professional football players, salesmen, bullfighters and artists are governed by the rules of the general regime, with minor variations in terms of contributions, incapacitation and retirement.

III. Special Regimes within the Social Security

A. Farmworkers

324. This regime is applicable to wage earners and self-employed persons in agriculture, forestry and fishing. They have the same cover as workers under the General Regime, with minor variations (they cannot take early retirement, and are not entitled to temporary invalidity benefit, etc.).

B. Self-employed Persons

325. The category comprises persons aged over eighteen who normally work for themselves and are gainfully occupied without being subject to employment contracts. It includes also the spouse and family up until the third generation, authors, self-employed persons who are members of professional colleges or associations, self-employed foreigners. Entitlement includes health care, temporary incapacity for work, permanent total and absolute invalidity pensions and grave disability, funeral benefits, benefits payable to surviving relatives and dependents, and retirement benefits.

C. Seamen

326. This includes both self-employed persons and wage-earners and offers the same entitlements as the General Regime, save for a number of special features.

D. Coal Miners

327. Wage-earners employed in the following fall into this category: underground coal mining, opencast mining, manufacture of coal products, research, detection and extraction of coal from slag heaps, extraction of carbon and residual carbon-bearing water and other complementary activities. There are some special features in comparison to the General Regime.

E. Domestic Staff

328. This includes workers over 16 who are exclusively engaged as domestic staff for one or several heads of a family, provided that the work is done in the habitual place of residence of said person and in return payment is made for his work. The category includes child-minding, gardening, driving and other similar activities. The head of the family's spouse, dependent children, dependent parents and dependent grandparents are excluded. Here again there are special features in relation to the General Regime.

F. Students

329. Student insurance includes Spaniards below the age of 28 who are enrolled as full-time students or otherwise in secondary education or vocational training, the University Orientation Course, undergraduate university studies and post-graduate university studies leading to a doctorate. Foreign students under 28 who are nationals of countries with tacit or explicit reciprocal agreements are also covered when pursuing the above-mentioned studies. Affiliation to the system is automatic on enrolment. Medical attention is obligatory in cases of tuberculosis, surgery, neuropsychiatry and tocology. Access is provided, depending on financial circumstances, to radiotherapy, physiotherapy and some other services, as well as the treatment of injuries sustained in the school or university environment.

330. The Social Security also protects those who are willing and able to work, but who lose their jobs temporarily or permanently or whose hours of work are reduced by at least a third, resulting in loss or reduction of earnings. The Social Security provides two levels of unemployment benefit: contributory and supplementary.

(1) Contributory unemployment benefit is paid to wage earners registered under the General Regime or any of the Special Regimes, to those who are released from prison on completion of their sentence or on parole, returned emigrant workers and armed forces reservists, national reserve, troop classes and professional seamen. In order to be eligible for this benefit it is necessary to be currently registered with a Social Security regime which includes unemployment cover. Furthermore, the worker must be unemployed and have been paying Social Security contributions for a six-month period within the four years prior to becoming unemployed. Benefit is paid by the National Employment Institute ('Instituto Nacional de Empleo'), an autonomous entity dependent on the Ministry for Employment and Social Security.
(2) Supplementary benefit comprises a financial benefit and payment of the appropriate Social Security contributions. The duration and amount of payment depends on the class of benefit to which one is entitled. The following have the right to supplementary benefit:
    (a) Workers who have exhausted their contributory unemployment benefit entitlement and who have family responsibilities.
    (b) Workers over 45 who have exhausted their unemployment benefit payable over at least the previous twelve months and who have no family responsibilities.
    (c) Returned emigrant workers.
    (d) Workers who on becoming unemployed have still not completed the minimum period of contribution that would entitle them to contributory unemployment benefit.
    (e) Those released from prison.
    (f) Workers who have been declared fit or partially fit as a result of a medical examination that shows up an improvement in a case of grave disability or permanent absolute or total incapacity for the person's usual work.

   (g) Non-permanent full-time workers who have exhausted their contributory benefit or were not eligible for unemployment benefit because they had not paid the minimum number of contributions.
   (h) Unemployed workers over 52.
   (i) Casual workers included in the special farmworkers' regime.

(3) Unemployment cover includes the provision of health care services for workers who are no longer entitled to unemployment benefit or supplementary benefit or to health care through some other avenue. Conditions are that the worker must not have an income higher than the minimum wage, must have been registered with the Employment Office since the termination of unemployment benefit or supplementary benefit, must not have refused an offer of work and must not have access to health care through another avenue.

(4) Under Law 26/1990 of 20 December, which modifies the Revised Text of the General Social Security Law (*Ley General de Seguridad Social*) passed by RD 2065/1974 of 30 May, which sought to achieve a more compassionate system, Social Security financial benefits were made available to all (current regulation about this issues is established in the Legislative Royal Decree 8/2015 of 30 October, approving the revised text of the General Law of the Social Security). The right to retirement and invalid pensions and child benefit holds good for all citizens even if they have never contributed or have not contributed for a long enough period of time to be eligible for contributory benefits. Beneficiaries receive not only periodic financial assistance but also medical, pharmaceutical and social services. Minimum requirements established are: residence in Spain, insufficient means of support, and a minimum age requirement of 65 in the case of retirement pensions, and 18 (with the necessary degree of disability) for invalidity pensions.

331. A part from the Social Security, there exist *Mutualidades de Prevision Social* (Mutual Pension Funds), which are governed by Law 30/1995 of 8 November, concerning the regulation and supervision of Private Insurance, and aim to protect their members in case of death, old age, disability, medical treatment and other situations where a benefit or pension might normally be paid.

Selected Bibliography

Abellán, F. *Selección genética de embriones. Entre la libertad reproductiva y la eugenesia.* 'Biblioteca de derecho y ciencias de la vida', Comares, Granada, 2007.

Arruego Rodríguez, G. & R. Chueca Rodríguez. *Tribunal Constitucional y nuevos escenarios de la biomedicina.* en 'Rev Der Gen H', nº 12, 2000.

Ataz Lopez, J. *Los médicos y la responsabilidad civil.* Madrid, Montecorvo, 1985.

Aznar López, M. *Internamientos civiles y derechos fundamentales de los usuarios de centros sanitarios, sociales y sociosanitarios.* Comares, Granada, 2000.

Bellver Capella, V. *El Tribunal Constitucional ante la Ley sobre Técnicas de Reproducción Asistida: una valoración crítica.* in RevDerGenH, Nr. 11, 1999.

Benítez Ortúzar, J.I. *Delitos relativos a la reproducción asistida*, en J. Vidal Martínez (Coord.), 'Derechos reproductivos y técnicas de reproducción asistida', Ed. Comares – Ministerio de Sanidad y Consumo, Granada, 1998.

Bercovitz Rodríguez Cano, R. 'La protección jurídica de la persona en relación con su internamiento involuntario en centros sanitarios o asistenciales por razones de salud'. *Anuario de Derecho Civil*, 1984.

Bueno Arús, F. 'El consentimiento del paciente en el tratamiento médico-quirúrigico y la Ley General de Sanidad'. in *Estudios de Derecho Penal y Criminología*, UNED, Madrid 1989.

Carrasco Gómez, J.J. *Responsabilidad médica y Psiquiatría,* 2nd. Ed., Colex, Madrid, 1998.

Cobreros Mendazona, E. *Los tratamientos sanitarios obligatorios y el Derecho a la salud.* Gasteiz, IVAP, 1988.

Comisión Nacional de Reproducción Humana Asistida. *Primer Informe.* Madrid, 1998.

Comisión Nacional de Reproducción Humana Asistida. *Segundo Informe. Investigación con embriones sobrantes.* Madrid, abril de 2000.

Comité Asesor de Ética en la Investigación Científica y Técnica. *Informe La investigación sobre células troncales.* FECYT, Madrid, 2003.

Comité de Expertos sobre Bioética y Clonación. *Informe sobre clonación. En las fronteras de la vida.* FCS, Madrid, 1999.

De Ángel Yagüez, R. *Responsabilidad civil por actos médicos. Problemas de prueba.* Civitas, Madrid, 1999.

De Ángel Yagüez, R. 'Problemas legales de la historia clínica en el marco hospitalario'. *La Ley*, 1987.

De Miguel Beriain, I. *El embrión y la biotecnología. Un análisis ético-jurídico.* 'Biblioteca de Derecho y ciencias de la vida', 20, Ed. Comares, Granada, 2004.

De Miguel Beriain, I. *La clonación, diez años después.* Cátedra Interuniversitaria Fundación BBVA – Diputación Foral de Bizkaia de Derecho y Genoma Humano,

Universidad de Deusto y Universidad del País Vasco y Ed. Comares, Bilbao-Granada, 2008.

Elola Somoza, F.J. *Crisis y reforma de la asistencia sanitaria pública en España (1983–1990)*. Madrid, FISSS, 1991.

Emaldi Cirión. *El Consejo Genético y sus implicaciones jurídicas*. Cátedra Interuniversitaria Fundación BBVA – Diputación Foral de Bizkaia, de Derecho y Genoma Humano, y Ed. Comares, Bilbao – Granada, 1999.

Farre Trepat, E. 'Sobre el concepto de aborto y su delimitación de los delitos contra la vida humana independiente'. *Anuario de Derecho Penal y Ciencias Penales*, 1990.

Fernández Costales, J. *El contrato de servicios médicos*. Madrid, Civitas, 1988.

Fernández Hierro, J.M. *Sistema de responsabilidad civil médico-sanitaria*. 5th ed., Granada, Comares, 2016.

García González, J. *Límites penales a los últimos avances de la ingeniería genética aplicada al ser humano*, Edersa, 2001.

Gascón Abellán, González Carrasco & Cantero Martínez (coords.). *Derecho sanitario y Bioética. Cuestiones actuales*. Tirant lo blanch, Valencia, 2011.

Gómez Rivero, C. La responsabilidad penal del médico. Doctrina y jurisprudencia, 2ª ed., Tirant lo Blanch, Valencia, 2008.

González Morán, L. *De la Bioética al Bioderecho. Libertad, vida y muerte*. Universidad de Comillas – Dykinson, Madrid, 2006.

González Morán, L. *La responsabilidad civil del médico*. Barcelona, Bosch, 1990.

Guerrero Zaplana, J. *Las reclamaciones por defectuosa asistencia sanitaria*. Valladolid, 5th ed., Lex Nova, 2006.

Lema Añón. *Los problemas pendientes de la regulación jurídica española sobre reproducción asistida: la sentencia del Tribunal Constitucional y el primer Informe de la Comisión Nacional de Reproducción Asistida (Parte I y II)*. en 'RevDerGenH', nº 12 y 13, 2000.

Llamas Pombo, E. *La responsabilidad civil del médico*. Madrid, Trivium, 1988.

Mansilla Izquierdo, P.P. *Reforma sanitaria. Fundamentos para un análisis*. Madrid, Ministerio de Sanidad y Consumo, 1986.

Martín Mateo, R. *Bioética y Derecho*. Barcelona, Ariel, 1987.

Martín-Retortillo Baquer, L. 'Derechos fundamentales en tensión (¿Puede el Juez ordenar una transfusión de sangre en peligro de muerte, aún en contra de la voluntad del paciente?)', *Poder Judicial*, 1984.

Ministerio de Sanidad y Consumo. *Ensayos clínicos en España (1982–1990)*. M. Sanidad y Consumo, Madrid, 1990.

Mir Puigpelat, O. *La responsabilidad patrimonial de la administración sanitaria: organización, imputación y causalidad*. Civitas, Madrid, 2000.

Nicolás Jiménez, P. *La protección jurídica de los datos genéticos de carácter personal*. Cátedra Interuniversitaria Fundación BBVA – Diputación Foral de Bizkaia de Derecho y Genoma Humano, Universidad de Deusto y Universidad del País Vasco y Ed. Comares, Bilbao-Granada, 2006.

Palomar Olmeda & Cantero Martínez (Dircección). *Tratado de Derecho Sanitario, Vol. I y II*. Cizur Menor, Aranzadi, 2013.

Pemán Gavín, J. *Derecho a la salud y Administración sanitaria*. Bolonia, Publ. Real Colegio de España, 1989.

Requejo, M.T. 'Legal Analysis of the Spanish Basic Law 41/2002 on the Autonomy of the Patient and the Rights and Obligations with Regard to Clinical Information and Documentation'. *European Journal of Health Law*, 2003.

Rodríguez Pastrana, J.M. *El servicio público de la sanidad: el marco constitucional*. Madrid, Civitas, 1984.

Romeo-Casabona, C.M. *Los trasplantes de órganos. Informe y documentación para la reforma de la legislación española sobre trasplantes de órganos*. Barcelona, Bosch, 1979.

Romeo-Casabona, C.M. *El Médico y el Derecho Penal, I, La actividad curativa (licitud y responsabilidad penal)*. Barcelona, Bosch, 1981.

Romeo-Casabona, C.M. 'Human Life as Jurisdictional Value Protected by Criminal Law'. in *XXth Colloquy on European Law*, Council of Europe, Glasgow, 1990.

Romeo-Casabona, C.M. 'El tratamiento jurídico del enfermo mental en el Consejo de Europa y sistema de garantías en el Derecho Español'. *Actualidad Penal*, 1991.

Romeo-Casabona, C.M. *Configuración sistemática de los derechos de los pacientes en el ámbito del Derecho español*. Madrid, Instituto Nacional de la Salud, 1992.

Romeo-Casabona, C.M. 'Some Implications of Human Genome Analysis and Research in Spanish Law'. *Genome Analyse* Coimbra, 1994.

Romeo-Casabona, C.M. *Delitos contra la vida y la integridad personal y los relativos a la manipulación genética*. Comares, Granada, 2004.

Romeo-Casabona, C.M. 'La prohibición del tráfico ilegal y la exclusión de la comercialización de los órganos y tejidos. Artículo 156 bis del Código Penal'. *Revista Aranzadi Doctrinal*, nr. 7, 2010.

Romeo-Casabona, C.M. *El médico y el Derecho Penal, vols. I & II, 1*. Rubinzal Culzoni, Santa Fe, 2011.

Romeo-Casabona, C.M. *El Derecho y la Bioética ante los límites de la vida humana*, Ed. CERA, Madrid, 1994.

Romeo-Casabona, C.M. (Coord.). *Derecho biomédico y bioética*. Comares & Ministerio de Sanidad y Consumo, Granada – Madrid, 1998.

Romeo-Casabona, C.M. *Biodroit*. en Hottois & Missa (Éds.), 'Nouvelle encyclopédie de bioéthique', De Boeck Université, Bruxelles, 2001.

Romeo-Casabona, CM. (Ed.). *El Convenio de Derechos Humanos y Biomedicina. Su entrada en vigor en el ordenamiento jurídico español*. Cátedra Interuniversitaria de Derecho y Genoma Humano, Universidad de Deusto y Universidad del País Vasco & Editorial Comares, Bilbao – Granada, 2002.

Romeo-Casabona, C.M. *Los genes y sus leyes. El Derecho ante el genoma humano*. Cátedra Interuniversitaria de Derecho y Genoma Humano, y Editorial Comares, Bilbao – Granada, 2002.

Romeo-Casabona, C.M. *Editorial. The European Constitution, establishing a core of human rights as applied to tthe fields of Medicine and Biology*. RevDerGenH, Nr. 21, 2004.

Romeo-Casabona, C.M. *Genética, Biotecnología y Ciencias Penales*. Ibáñez & PUC Javeriana, Bogotá, 2009.

Romeo-Casabona, C.M. (Director). *Enciclopedia de Bioderecho y Bioética, Tomos I y II*, Comares, Granada, 2011.

Romeo-Casabona, C.M. & A. Martínez-Berganza Asensio. 'Le Médecin et les Droits de l'Homme en Espagne'. *Manuel sur le Médecin et les Droits de l'Homme*, Conseil de l'Europe (ed.), CEDAM, Milano, 1990.

Romeo-Casabona, C.M. & A. Urruela Mora. El establecimiento de un sistema nacional de notificación y registro de eventos adversos en el sector sanitario: aspectos legales, Granada, Comares, 2010.

Romeo-Malanda, S. 'El valor jurídico del consentimiento prestado por los menores de edad en el ámbito sanitario', *La Ley*, 2000.

Romeo-Malanda, S. *Intervenciones genéticas sobre el ser humano y Derecho penal*. Cátedra Interuniversitaria Fundación BBVA – Diputación Foral de Bizkaia de Derecho y Genoma Humano, Universidad de Deusto y Universidad del País Vasco y Ed. Comares, Bilbao-Granada, 2006.

Ruiz Vadillo, E. 'La investigación científica y el Derecho. Especial consideración de la ingeniería genética'. *Revista General de Derecho*, 1986.

Sánchez Caro, J. & F. Abellán. *Imprudencia y negligencia en la profesión médica*, Granada, Comares, 2001.

Silveira Gorski, H. & V. Méndez Baigés (Eds.). *Bioética y Derecho*. UOC, Barcelona, 2004.

Sola Reche, E., Hernández Plasencia, J.U. & C.M. Romeo-Casabona. 'La responsabilidad profesional del médico en el Derecho español'. *Responsabilidad penal y responsabilidad civil de los profesonales. Presente y futuro de los conhceptos de negligencia y riesgo. XXII Coloquio de Derecho Europeo*, La Laguna, Centro de Estudios Criminológicos, 1993.

Torío López, A. 'Instigación y auxilio al suicidio, homicidio consentido y eutanasia como problemas legislativos'. *Estudios Penales y Criminológicos, IV* (A. Fernández Albor, ed.), Santiago de Compostela, 1981.

Urruela Mora, A. *La eximente de anomalía o alteración psíquica a la luz de los modernos avances en Psiquiatría y Genética*. Granada, Comares, 2004.

Urruela Mora, A. 'La clonación humana ante la reforma penal y administrativa en España'. *Revista Penal*, nº 21, 2008.

Urruela Mora, A. & S. Romeo Malanda. 'Tendencias actuales de la jurisprudencia española en materia de responsabilidad penal médica'. in *Revista de Derecho Penal*, 34, 2011.

Valle Muñiz, J.M. 'Relevancia Jurídico-penal de la eutanasia'. *Cuadernos de Política Criminal*, n. 37, 1989.

Vega Ruiz, J.A. de. *El tratamiento jurídico del sida*. Madrid, Colex, 1992.

Vidal Martínez. *Comentario a la Sentencia del Tribunal Constitucional de 17 de Junio de 1999 resolviendo el Recurso de inconstitucionalidad número 376/89 contra la Ley 35/1988, de 22 de Noviembre, sobre Técnicas de Reproducción Asistida*. en 'RevDerGenH', nº 12, 2000.

VV. AA. *Información y documentación clínica. Su tratamiento jurisprudencial (1990-1999)*. Ministerio de Sanidad y Consumo, Madrid, 2000.

VV. AA. *Genética y Derecho*. Consejo General del Poder Judicial, Madrid, 2001.

VV. AA. *La ética y el derecho ante la biomedicina del futuro*. Universidad de Deusto, Bilbao, 2006.

VV. AA. *Controles éticos de la actividad biomédica. Análisis de situación y recomendaciones*. Instituto Roche, Madrid, 2009.

Index

The numbers here refer to paragraph numbers.

Index

Index

www.ingramcontent.com/pod-product-compliance
Lightning Source LLC
Chambersburg PA
CBHW071435230926
51846CB00001B/241
9789041169297